The Debate over Jewish Achievement:
Exploring the Nature and Nurture of Human Accomplishment

ALSO BY STEVEN L. PEASE
The Golden Age of Jewish Achievement

The Debate over Jewish Achievement:

Exploring the Nature and Nurture of Human Accomplishment

Steven L. Pease

Deucalion
Sonoma, California

CREDITS:

David Brooks' July 31, 2014 article, "The Character Factory" is reproduced with permission of *The New York Times*

The exhibit "Correlating Religion, Education and Income," shown in Part 2's item 6 was created from data provided by the Pew Charitable Trust Forum on Religion and Public Life Web site

First Edition 2015

ISBN: 978-0-9825168-4-3 paperback
ISBN: 978-0-9825168-5-0 hardcover
ISBN: 978-0-9825168-6-7 kindle ebook

Design by Deborah Daly, Daly Design, deborahdaly.com
Cover art: Etz Jaim by Bernard Korzeniak, www.korzeniak.com

PRINTED IN THE UNITED STATES OF AMERICA

Contents

Preface

Jews are the world's most disproportionate high achievers of the last 200 years or more.

That observation, while factual, seemed preposterous when I began my explorations more than ten years ago. Yet after writing *The Golden Age of Jewish Achievement* in 2009, speaking on the subject, being interviewed on radio and television, and soliciting criticisms and arguments to disprove the statement, I have come to believe it is simply true.

In doing the early research for that book, a question by Rabbi Harold Kushner nudged me not only to write the book that compiled the astonishing record, but also to go further. He said, "Steve, if Jews are such high achievers, why do you think that is so?" The effort to answer that question led me to conclusions I did not expect. I concluded that while there is no single cause, Jewish culture (some would call it "cultural capital") has been the primary impetus behind the performance.

Only one chapter (of twenty-six in that earlier book) focused on my answer to "Why?" and I used it to describe the alternative theories and then explain why I concluded that "culture" is the vital force behind disproportionate Jewish achievement.

As I toured the United States speaking about the book, many were curious about who I was and why I had written it. Most were surprised to learn that a politically conservative Gentile and life-long Republican was the author. As the questions and answers unfolded, attendees came to understand my immense respect for the Jewish people, as well as my comfort in my own skin. They learned I was not aspiring to become Jewish and that I think anti-Semitism is simply nuts.

Asked why I wrote the book, I sometimes used an analogy. Had I found my way to fifteenth-century Renaissance Florence before its incredible art was widely known, few would have been surprised that as a non-Italian, I would have written about the art, the place, and the talent. The astonishing record of Jewish achievement is such a story.

There was a second reason I felt compelled to write that first book—and this book as well. Namely, in my view, encouraging human achievement is important. As a kid I could not swim in Spokane, Washington's public swimming pools for fear of polio. Two Jews, Salk and Sabin, solved that problem with their vaccines. It was an immense human accomplishment. The prospect of death or life in an iron lung vanished. Polio vaccine is a simple illustration of how human achievement improves the lives of millions.

The Golden Age told hundreds of stories of high achievers. Their contributions to our welfare are enormous. And the philanthropy of those who became wealthy from their achievements is equally noteworthy. We need to laud and encourage more of it. This is how we make life better for everyone.

After briefly summarizing the magnitude and scope of the Golden Age performance, this book expands on the "Why?" hypotheses. It elaborates on the major theories raised over the years to explain disproportionate Jewish achievement, reviews new data, lays out new arguments, and explains where I finally come down and why.

Wide recognition of the importance of culture, and the need to encourage solid and positive cultural values—such as those that engendered *The Golden Age of Jewish Achievement*—deserve to be emulated. Jewish culture is unique, but its elements are not. We can learn from them.

Introduction

The Golden Age of
Jewish Achievement:
A Summing Up

For those who have read *The Golden Age of Jewish Achievement*, this material is a "refresher" before moving on to the newer information. And for those who haven't read the book, what follows does not include all the biographical profiles that many readers found fascinating. Nor does it provide the wealth of data from the book, but it does summarize its essence in very compact form.

The Golden Age set out to be the most complete study of disproportionate Jewish achievement ever put together. It began with the question, "Are Jews disproportionate high achievers?" and then laid out the answer. What it reported was astonishing. I concluded this has to be the single most impressive record of disproportionate achievement by any group of people over at least the last 200 years—and probably longer than that.

What that first book did to document their immense achievements, this one does to explore why it happened.

Why Is It Called "The Golden Age?"

When speaking on the subject of my first book, I typically began with two quotes. The first is by Roman Catholic and British author of *A History of the Jews* (1987), Paul Johnson:

> "Quite suddenly, around the year 1800, this ancient and highly efficient social machine for the production of intellectuals began to shift its output. Instead of pouring all of its products into the closed circuit of rabbinical studies, where they remained completely isolated from general society, it unleashed a significant and ever growing pro-

portion of them into secular life. This was an event of shattering importance in world history."

The second was by Jewish academic Raphael Patai. His 1977 book, *The Jewish Mind,* became a vital source for many who read it. Patai said:

> "In the wake of the Enlightenment, the suddenness with which Jews began to appear and make a mark in numerous...areas...is nothing short of astounding. It seemed as if a huge reservoir of Jewish talent, hitherto dammed up behind the wall of Talmudic learning, were suddenly released to spill over into all fields of Gentile cultural activity."

These two quotes were followed by an explanation:

> Jews have long been recognized for their contributions to history. Stories of Abraham, Moses, David, Solomon, Isaiah, and the numerous other prophets created and shaped early Judaism and the Jewish people. The Jewish Tanakh became Christianity's Old Testament and Jesus, Saul/Paul, Peter and the Apostles (Jews all) are the core of The New Testament, and thus Christianity. Later Islam honored Jews as "the people of the Book." Muslims, Jews, and Christians share a common legacy originating with Abraham. Thus, the religious and philosophical underpinnings for half the world's people begin with Judaism.

After biblical times there were important, but less well-known, figures such as Philo Judaeus (20 BCE to 54 CE), ibn Solomon Gabirol, also called Avicebron (1021 to 1058 CE), and Maimonides (1135 to 1204 CE), the most prominent Jew between Biblical times and Emancipation. After Maimonides, but before Emancipation, Spinoza, Moses Mendelssohn, Felix Mendelssohn (and perhaps Cervantes), were all widely known and respected Jews.

But before Emancipation, nearly all of the important Jews were philosophers, religious figures, musicians, and writers. Of the fifteen important historical Jews that Charles Murray identified for the years 25 BCE to 1800 CE in his book, *Human Accomplishment,* seven were philosophers, four were authors, and three were musicians. Only one, Paul Guldin (1577 to 1643 CE) was a scientist. Great as these and other Jews may have been in science and math before Emancipation— and there were significant Jewish scientists, mathematicians, and physicians in Golden Ages of Moorish and Catholic Spain—only Guldin is counted among history's most important.

This is where Johnson and Patai's revealing quotes are helpful. The "ancient and highly efficient social machine for the production of intellectuals" had been "dammed up behind the wall of Talmudic learning." Rarely were Jews focused on secular matters.

Martin Luther's October 31, 1517 nailing of the Ninety-Five Theses to the doors of the All Saints Church in Wittenberg, Germany not only unleashed the Reformation, it sparked more than 100 years of religious wars across Europe. Those conflicts cost ten million German and seven million French lives alone The wars lasted until about 1650.

The Enlightenment arose from the ashes and exhaustion of those wars. The ensuing 150 years of Enlightenment progress focused on promoting knowledge, science and intellectual interchange. The era of religious intolerance and violence was over. Catholics could sit down with Protestants in a shared exploration of new endeavors.

With that change in mentality, Jews were soon invited to participate as well. The Inquisition and the demands to convert, emigrate, or be persecuted, ended (or were dramatically curtailed, at least for a time). Instead, Jews were invited to participate. This had never happened before. It was revolutionary.

In 1807, Napoleon convened The Grand Sanhedrin where he asked leading French Jews twelve questions; among them, if they were full citizens would they be loyal to France, defend it, and obey its laws? When they said, "Yes!" he became the patron to the Jewish Emancipation that spread through Europe from roughly 1810 to 1880. Jews could vote. They could own real property. They could hold public office. They could serve in the military. They could pursue previously foreclosed careers. A world beyond the ghetto and historic oppression was opened to them.

From that came the Jewish Enlightenment (*Haskalah*) and a new Jewish denomination (Reform). Enormous numbers of Western European Jews began to participate in secular life.[1] This is the event of "shattering importance" alluded to by Johnson.

Over the nineteenth century, the record of Jewish achievements in secular domains began to appear and become ever more widely understood. By 1899, Mark Twain, an international figure at the time, noted:

---

1. The small number of American Jews at the time needed no emancipation. Like those who came later, Jews in America—roughly 4,000 in 1820, growing to 250,000 by 1880—were already blessed. (Johnson p 365–371) Following a brief awkward period in 1654, before Peter Stuyvesant was "convinced" by his Dutch superiors to let twenty-three Jewish refugees from Recife, Brazil into New Amsterdam, Jews in America were accepted with all the rights of citizens. Later, the rights were legally confirmed by the Declaration of Independence, the Constitution, and the Bill of Rights. George Washington added his personal imprimatur in a famous letter to the Jews in Newport, Rhode Island confirming their rights and the separation of church and state.

"Properly, the Jew ought hardly to be heard of, but he is heard of, has always been heard of. He is as prominent on the planet as any other people, and his commercial importance is extravagantly out of proportion to the smallness of his bulk. His contributions to the world's list of great names in literature, science, art, music, finance, medicine, and abstruse learning are also away out of proportion to the weakness of his numbers...."

In short, the Enlightenment, the Jewish Emancipation, and the secularization of Jews had combined to unleash something phenomenal.

Summarizing the Disproportionate Achievements

A single table from *The Golden Age of Jewish Achievement* (included as a two-page exhibit at the end of this Introduction) presents much of the research done for that earlier book. It reflects data on awards made annually through 2007-08, as well as one-off compilations—for example "The Greats of History"—that are not updated on an annual basis. Selected statistics also appear on the next page as a highly condensed summary of the full table. While these statistics clearly illustrate the remarkable magnitude and scope of Jewish achievement, it is also safe to say that, five years following the publication of *The Golden Age*, the phenomenal rates of disproportionate Jewish achievements continue unabated between that book and this one. For example Jews have won 27 percent of Nobel Prizes between 2008 and 2013; this is 4 percent higher than the average for the years 1901 to 2007. The recent Nobel data, and other selected updates, are provided in the text that follows.

For some readers, though, their eyes will simply glaze over when they see these charts. Nonetheless, I encourage spending a few minutes to mull them over. You might get to the same place by reading all of the more than 450 biographies in *The Golden Age*, but failing that, understanding the tables is the only way to comprehend the richness and breadth of disproportionate Jewish achievement in all of its particularity. The tables contain a lot of data, but by digesting them, readers will better appreciate and understand the explanations of causes that come later.

When perusing the data, keep in mind that in a room of 1,000 people assembled to represent the Earth's population, only 2 would be Jews—two-tenths of 1 percent. That is twelve to fourteen million people in a world of roughly seven billion. The same technique applied to the U.S. population would yield twenty to twenty-two Jews among the

Disproportionate Jewish Achievements—A Thumbnail

DISTINCTION	SHOULD BE/ HAVE WON	DID WIN OR WERE/ARE	MULTIPLE OF EXPECTED	% OF ALL
Nobel Prizes (1901–2007)	1.8	181	101	23%
Encyclopedia Britannica's				
Great Inventors (6000 BCE – 2003	0.6	13.7	22	5%
Ivy League Students (2003)	2,330	24,000	10	21%
Ivy League Presidents (2009)	0.2	4	20	50%
John Bates Clarke Medal (1947–2008)	0.6	20	32	67%
Pulitzer Prize non-fiction (1918–2008)	1.0	25.5	25	51%
Kennedy Center Honors (1978–2007)	3.2	41	13	26%
Symphony Conductors (1842–2007)	4.2	66	16	33%
Academy Award Directors (1927–2007)	1.7	31	18	37%
CEOs of Major Corporations – (1997)	1.5	16	11	22%
Forbes 400 (2007)	8.3	126	15	31%
Business Week – Philanthropic 50				
(2003–2007)	1.0	19	19	38%
Ladies Home Journal's				
50 Most Important Women (1998)	2.1	20	10	20%

1000 people—roughly 2 percent—six to seven million Jews in a country of more than 315 million

The rows show the distinction (the accomplishment in question). For example, the first row covers the Nobel Prizes awarded from their 1901 inception until 2007. The second column indicates how many Nobel Prizes Jews should have won based solely on their numbers as a percent of the population. That answer is only 1.8 Prizes—fewer than two of the 781 Nobel Prizes awarded in those years should have been won by Jews. The third column indicates how many Prizes Jews actually won. That number is 181. The fourth column indicates the 181 Prizes won is 101 times what we would expect given the small number of Jews in the world. The last column shows the percent of all Nobel Prizes won by Jews. While only two-tenths of 1 percent of the world's population, Jews have won an astonishing 23 percent of all Nobel Prizes. In the years since 2007, (2008 to 2013) Jews have won 19 of the 70 Nobel prizes awarded to individuals (27 percent). Clearly, they have not lost their edge.

In browsing the tables, note both the breadth of the domains in which Jews have accomplished so much (science, music, philanthropy, writing, academics, etc.) as well as the impressive performance in each one. (e.g. 51 percent of all Pulitzer prizes for non-fiction). No other group has come close.

To add color when I made public presentations, I pointed out that:

— Every one of today's major Hollywood studios was started by, or shaped, in important ways by Jews—even Walt Disney Studios. Disney was not Jewish, but when the studio fell on hard times after his death, it was his nephew, Roy Disney, who picked Michael Eisner. Eisner transformed Disney and made it much larger and more successful. Eisner was followed by Robert Iger who remains Disney's CEO at this writing.

— The same is true for all three of America's "big three" broadcast television networks: NBC, ABC and CBS. More than any other individual, it was Jewish immigrant David Sarnoff who largely created these industries. A boy wonder, he recognized and acted on the opportunities for radio broadcasting. He was equally prescient and important to television. Leonard Goldenson acquired what had been one of Sarnoff's two NBC stations in 1951, and built the renamed (and remade) ABC over his thirty-five year reign. In 1929, two years after its founding, William Paley took control of the nearly bankrupt CBS and built it successfully over his remarkable fifty-seven years as CEO.

— Half or more of all American department stores and specialty stores have been the creations of Jewish entrepreneurs and/or merchants. R. H. Macy was not Jewish, but the Straus family leased space and began acquiring stock. On Macy's death, they bought the remaining shares. Five generations of the Straus family ran or helped run Macys over a period of 100 years. Similar stories can be told hundreds of times over in describing the role of Jewish merchants in American retailing.

— In high tech entrepreneurship, just a few of the important names include: Intel (Andy Grove and Les Vadasz), Google (Sergey Brin), Oracle (Larry Ellison), Microsoft (Steve Balmer), Dell (Michael Dell), Qualcom (Irwin Jacobs), Facebook (Mark Zuckerberg), and on and on.

— In finance, the names are legion: Goldman Sachs, Rothschild, Warburg, Kohlberg, Kravis & Roberts, Wells Fargo, Lehman Brothers, Bear Stearns, and many more.

— Jews have been at the forefront of many activist movements: Samuel Gompers in labor; Gloria Steinem in feminism; Saul Alinsky the political activist and author of *Rules for Radicals*; Jerry Rubin, one of the Chicago Seven; Noam Chomsky, the linguist cum anarchist cum America critic; Andy Stern, the former head of the Service Employees International Union and frequent Obama White House guest before his retirement.

— In Olympic athletics, Jews have won 401 medals (1901 through 2007) —seven times the number they should have won based solely on their numbers.

— As World Chess champions, Jews have held the title 54% of the time since 1866.

— In the 113th United States Congress (Jan. 3, 2013 to Jan. 3, 2015), Jews were elected to 11 percent of U.S. Senate seats and 5 percent of the seats in the House.

— They also account for three of the nine Supreme Court Justices.

— *Time Magazine's* "Man of the 20th Century" was Albert Einstein.

— And finally, Jews wrote or produced two-thirds of Broadway's longest running musicals, while other great talents such as George Gershwin and Irving Berlin wrote American Classics like "Rhapsody in Blue," and "God Bless America."

These bullet points, and the following table, are just a sample from *The Golden Age*. It is a simply stunning performance.

A Summing Up - Achievements of Jews   Table 1

Distinction	Relevant Geography	Total Recipients	Projected Jewish Recipients	Actual Jewish Recipients	Jews As A Multiple Of Projected	Jews As A Percent of all Recipients
The Greats of History						
Hart's Most Influential 100 in History	World[1]	100	0.2	8	35	8%
A&E's Millennium 100	World	100	0.2	8	35	8%
Time Magazine's 100 of the 20th Century	U.S.[2]	67	1.4	13	9	19%
Intelliquest's World's Greatest 100	World	100	0.2	8	35	8%
Science						
Nobel Prize in Physics	World	181	0.4	48	116	27%
Nobel Prize in Physiology & Medicine	World	189	0.4	59	136	31%
Nobel Prize in Chemistry	World	151	0.3	30	87	20%
Total Nobels for Science	World	521	1.2	137	115	26%
Fields Medal (for mathematics)	World	48	0.1	12	109	25%
A. M. Turing Award (for computer science)	World	54	0.1	13	105	24%
Invention						
Encyclopedia Britannica's Great Inventors	World	267	0.6	13.7	22	5%
Education						
Enrollment in Ivy League Schools	U.S	115,000	2,380	24,000	10	21%
Military and Aviation						
United States Astronauts	U.S.	268	5.5	9	2	3%
Economics						
Nobel Prize for Economics	World	61	0.1	22	157	36%
John Bates Clark Medal in Economics	U.S	30	0.6	20	32	67%
Federal Reserve Chairmen	U.S	14	0.3	4	14	29%
Politics and Law						
U.S. Senators (108th Congress)	U.S.	100	2.1	11	5	11%
U.S. Congressmen & Women (108th Congress)	U.S.	435	9.0	26	3	6%
Largest Political Donors (Mother Jones List)	U.S.	100	2.1	42	20	42%
United States Supreme Court Justices	U.S.	110	2.3	7	3	6%
Nobel Prize for Peace	World	95	0.2	9	41	9%
Sports and Games						
NFL Hall of Fame Inductees	U.S	247	5.1	6	1	2%
NFL Team Owners (excludes "community owned" Green Bay)	U.S	31	0.6	9	14	29%
MLB Prof. Baseball Team Owners (individually owned)	U.S	26	0.5	5.5	10	21%
NBA Top 10 Coaches of All Time	U.S	10	0.2	2	10	20%
NBA Basketball Team Owners	U.S	30	0.6	10	16	33%
Naismith Basketball Hall of Fame Inductees	U.S.	285	5.9	20	3	7%
Olympics Medalists 1896 to date	see 5 below	16,167	66.9	231.74	3	1%
World Chess Champions - Years as Champion	see 5 below	122 yrs.	0.5	66 yrs.	131	54%
The Written Word						
Nobel Prize for Literature	World	104	0.2	13	55	13%
Pulitzer Prize for Fiction	U.S	82	1.7	11	6	13%
Pulitzer Prize for Poetry	U.S	89	1.8	17	9	19%
Pulitzer Prize for Non Fiction	U.S	50	1.0	25.5	25	51%
Pulitzer Prize for Drama	U.S	77	1.6	22	14	29%
Performing Arts and Comedy						
Kennedy Center Honorees	U.S.	157	3.2	41	13	26%
Conductors Major U.S. Symphony Orchestras	U.S.	202	4.2	66	16	33%
Composers "World's 50 Greatest" CD Collection	see 3 below	50	0.6	6	10	12%
Longest Running Broadway Musicals	U.S.	38	0.8	24	31	63%
Rock & Roll Hall of Fame Inductees	U.S.	238	4.9	29	6	12%

NOTE: Table 1 is reproduced from pages 412-413 of the 2009 book, *The Golden Age of Jewish Achievement*.

A Summing Up - Achievements of Jews

Table 1

Distinction	Relevant Geography	Total Recipients	Projected Jewish Recipients	Actual Jewish Recipients	Jews As A Multiple Of Projected	Jews As A Percent of all Recipients
Performing Arts and Comedy (cont.)						
Jazz Grammy Awards	U.S.	216	4.5	22	5	10%
Grammy Lifetime Achievement Winners (Indiv.)	U.S.	125	2.6	18	7	14%
Rate It All Ranking of Stand Up Comedians	U.S.	82	1.7	25	15	30%
Visual Arts and Architecture						
Phaidon's 500 Artists	see 3 below	500	6.3	37	6	7%
Combined Lists (7) of Great Photographers	see 4 below	587	7.4	153	21	26%
Combined Lists (6) of Master Architects	World	309	0.7	32	45	10%
Hollywood						
Academy Award Winning Directors	U.S.	83	1.7	31	18	37%
Greatest Movie Directors - Reel.com	U.S	55	1.1	15	13	27%
Greatest Movie Directors - Filmsite.org	U.S	75	1.6	27	17	36%
Star Power 500 Top Actors & Actresses	U.S	500	10.3	75	7	15%
American Film Institute Lifetime Achievement Awards	U.S.	35	0.7	8	11	23%
American Film Institute Greatest American Screen Legends	U.S.	50	1.0	6	6	12%
Radio and Television						
Radio Hall of Fame Inductees	U.S.	108	2.2	19	8	18%
Television Hall of Fame Inductees	U.S.	108	2.2	39	17	36%
High Tech Entrepreneurs and CEOs						
Entreprenuers (Fortunes Richest 40 Under 40)	U.S	27	0.6	6	11	22%
Forbes' 400 (November 2007)	U.S	400	8.3	125	15	31%
Fortune 500 CEOs						
CEOs of Major 1917 U.S. Corporations[5]	U.S.	153	4.7	7	1	5%
CEOs of Major 1997 U.S. Corporations	U.S.	72	1.5	16	11	22%
Fortune 100 CEOs	U.S.	100	2.1	15	7	15%
Fortune's 25 Most Powerful People in Business	U.S	25	0.5	6	12	24%
Finance						
Private Equity Hall of Fame	U.S.	26	0.5	8	15	24%
Real Estate						
Forbes "25 Real Estate Fortunes Among Forbes 400"	U.S.	25	0.5	18	35	72%
Social Activists						
Ladies Home Journal's "100 Most Important Women"	U.S.	100	2.1	20	10	20%
Philanthropy						
Business Week's 50 Leading Philanthropists	U.S	50	1.0	19	19	38%
All Nobels						
Total - All Nobel Prizes	World	781	1.8	181	101	23%

1) As of 2002, there were an estimated 14.3 million Jews in a world of 6.23 billion people. Jews were .00207 percent of the World's population

2) As of 2002, the United States population was 280,562,489. Of that number and estimated 5,807,000 were Jews (2.07 percent)

3) U.S., Canada, Europe, Australia, New Zealand and Israel,

4) Western Hemisphere, Europe, Australia and New Zealand Jews were .0126% of population

5) Jewish percent of the world population has changed over the 112 years of the Olympics. For this exhibit, the current percent (00207) was doubled to approximate the average

Part 1
The Debate

CHAPTER 1

The Debate History and Recent Developments

As described in the prior section, disproportionate Jewish secular achievements are a relatively recent phenomenon, as is the recognition and discussion of them. Before Emancipation there was little reason to take note of Jews as high achievers except in matters of religion and philosophy. History had others whose accomplishments shaped the world: Pericles' Greece, the Romans, the Ming Dynasty, the Italian Renaissance, the Spanish and Dutch Golden Ages, Elizabethan England through the Industrial Revolution. They and others like them were counted as having achieved greatness.

Then, following the Jewish Emancipation, a small trickle of Jewish high achievers turned into a stream and later into a torrent covering many domains of secular achievement. The torrent continues.

In 1846 we began to hear mid-Emancipation mention of Jews with Lord Ashley speaking before Parliament of their "powerful intellect," their being accomplished in music, poetry, medicine and astronomy and, "in every field, (being) more than a match for their competitors." Later, in 1853, French Count de Gobineau found the "Northern Europeans and Jews to be the two most intelligent people."

It is Charles Darwin's cousin, Francis Galton, (see item 6 in Part 2 of this book) whose 1869 book *Hereditary Genius*, expressed not only recognition, but also inklings of a credible theory to explain what was going on. Galton was brilliant. He was an anthropologist, tropical explorer, geographer, inventor, meteorologist, proto-geneticist, psychometrician, statistician, and eugenicist (he coined the term "eugenics"). He wrote 340 books, created the statistical concept of correlation, promoted "regression to the mean," and originated the expression "nature versus nurture." He was also prescient in foreseeing that the study of twins, particularly identical twins raised apart, would yield valuable insights into the heritability of traits, including intelligence. He said Jews are "rich in intellectual endowments"—which he believed were inherited.

But Ashley, de Gobineau, and Galton were not nearly as prominent as Mark Twain who, in March 1899, wrote the accolade quoted in the discussion of the term "Golden Age" (item 7). Twain did so in response to a question about anti-Semitism. He made a couple of mildly critical comments about Jews in his essay, did not intend to address the question of "Why?" and never directly mentioned genes or intelligence. But he did say Jews had strong families, low crime rates, were seldom drunk or disorderly, worked hard, took care of their own, were benevolent and peaceable, rarely if ever begged, and were generally industrious, honest in business, and trustworthy.

A little more than a decade later, in 1910, Dr. Mendel Silber's book *Jewish Achievement* (item 10) directly made the case for culture as a driving force. Silber identified more than a thousand high achieving Jews, organizing his discussion into domains such as jurists, statesmen, painters, composers, actors, etc. For each domain, Silber explained how Jewish culture and history had led to success. Three thousand years of experience with Jewish Law shaped them into successful attorneys and judges. Literary knowledge arising from study of Torah, Tanakh, and Talmud contributed to their skills as authors. And their long history as physicians helped explain their contemporary importance in medicine. For Silber, it wasn't that Jews were "chosen," or gifted. They just knew their stuff and worked hard.

At that point advocates for both nature (genes, IQ, heritability, etc.) and nurture (cultural values, environment, etc.) had begun to publicly frame their preliminary positions in writing. There have been many other theories over the ensuing years, but ultimately they all have shortcomings. The heart of the debate remains focused on nature versus nurture, and in that regard, the facts have become ever more complex and the arguments more sophisticated.

In part this is because over the last 200 years or so, science and research have advanced enormously as the world has shrunk and the achievements of the great have become more widely known.

Much of the progress involving genetics, heritability, twin studies, studies of culture and its effects, the genetics of Jews, and theories about Jewish achievement and the achievements of others are laid out in Part 2 of this book. It covers the major twists and turns in chronological fashion, briefly describing each of the major books, papers, discoveries, and arguments made since Darwin—and a bit before. Most of it is germane to this section and the next, and because you may find it interesting or wish to explore further, we have included it all. The next few pages will hopefully give something of a feel for those unfolding events and the parallel circumstances of the Jewish people over this critical 200 years.

Darwin's *Origin of Species* (item 4), describing evolution and natural selection, was published in 1859 just a few years before Mendel's 1866 explanation of dominant and recessive genes (item 5) and their role in plant and human traits. Both were seminal documents focused on explaining how plants and animals became what they are.

Ten years later, in 1869, Darwin's cousin, Galton (item 6), wrote *Hereditary Genius* and in 1904, Alfred Benet invented modern IQ testing (item 9) as part of a project for the French Government. Over roughly those same years, international competitions of various kinds emerged including the International Chess Championship in 1856, the modern Olympics in 1896, the Nobel Prizes in 1901, the Pulitzer Prizes in 1917, and others. Jews did well in all of them.

In the 1880s, Tay Sachs disease became the first of the so-called Ashkenazi genetic ailments to be described; others followed. John Fraser, a British author and travel writer wrote *The Conquering Jew* in 1915 documenting Jewish achievements in countries all over the world. Joseph Jacobs wrote the same about Jews in Europe and Thorsten Veblen wrote of Jewish success, attributing it to the fact that Jews had no country of their own.

Not covered in Part 2 are the years 1850 to 1935: the culmination of Emancipation and Jewish secular advances in Western Europe. At this same time eugenics emerged, the Pogroms in Russia unleashed mass emigration from the Pale, *The Protocols of the Elders of Zion* appeared (item 8), and Dreyfus was convicted in 1894, leading to the emergence of modern Zionism, the Balfour Doctrine, and early immigration to Palestine.

Throughout this period, Jews made great strides in secular achievement, and until the 1930s they felt Germany was among the most welcoming countries for them. But Germany's loss of World War I portended the emergence of Hitler and Nazism and from that came World War II, the Holocaust and the destruction of one-third of the world's Jews.

Generally quite hospitable for Jews, the United States had its own moderate levels of anti-Semitism, particularly with the influx of two million or more Jews from the Pale of Russia, the emergence of Communism, the deportation of Emma Goldman and Alexander Berkman, and the large Jewish enrollments at Ivy League schools. Nonetheless, Jews in America continued to be high achievers and ever more prominent in science, entertainment, activism, and invention, while also proving to be very successful in creating or leading important companies in film, radio, television, retailing, mining, publishing, finance, real estate, and other industries.

Following World War II, and the creation of the Jewish homeland in Israel, Watson and Crick discovered the double helix in 1953. This was the critical event that unleashed an astonishing sixty years of genetic discovery.

Starting in 1962, a number of contemporary popular books were published describing Jewish achievement, Jewish history, culture, and in some cases, genetics. They include:

> 1962 – Max Dimont's *Jews, God and History*
> 1969 – Ernst Van Den Haag's *The Jewish Mystique*
> 1976 – Arthur Koestler's *The Thirteenth Tribe*
> 1977 – Raphael Patai's *The Jewish Mind*
> 1987 – Paul Johnson's *A History of the Jews*
> 1998 – Thomas Cahill's *The Gifts of the Jews*
> 2000 – Steven Silbiger's *The Jewish Phenomenon*
> 2003 – Charles Murray's *Human Accomplishment*
> 2004 – Yuri Slezkine's *The Jewish Century*
> 2009 – Dan Senor and Saul Singer's *Start-up Nation*
> 2009 – Steven Pease's *The Golden Age of Jewish Achievement*
> 2011 – Richard Lynn's *The Chosen People*
> 2012 – Maristella Botticini & Zvi Eckstein's *The Chosen Few*
> 2014 – Simon Schama's *The Story of the Jews*

Collectively, these books provide a wealth of data, varied perspectives on achievement and its causes, and an excellent recap of the relevant history.

Charles Murray's book *Human Accomplishment* (item 50) was not focused on Jews, but they were the one group he singled out for extensive discussion. He wrote of the Jewish Emancipation and their ensuing disproportionate presence on his lists of history's most accomplished people. Murray suggested that genetics (elevated intelligence), culture (the historical focus on learning), and the probable interaction of both were all causative, and added that he expected advances in genetic research would soon begin to unravel their respective contributions.

Arthur Koestler's 1976 book, *The Thirteenth Tribe* (item 14), became controversial for popularizing an old theory that said Ashkenazi Jews are not rooted in Palestine, but instead are descendants of the Central Asian Khazar tribe that converted to Judaism and later emigrated to central and eastern Europe. Some, including Koestler, thought the theory might improve Jewish relations with Arabs and others. Instead, it was quickly used to undermine historical Jewish claims to roots in Palestine. More recently, Shlomo Sand weighed in with his 2009 book, *The Invention of the Jewish People,* which takes essentially the same line—Jews are not genetically related, but are a mixed group of converts.

Slezkine's *The Jewish Century* (item 53) added a wealth of data on the very few Jews who lived in Czarist Russia (rather than the Pale) before the Revolution. He documented their remarkably disproportionate importance in St. Petersburg and Moscow, as well as in the Soviet Union, where the Jewish population swelled after Jews from the Pale immigrated into Russia following the Revolution. He also covered Jews in America and the other geographies where they relocated after leaving the Pale.

Lynn's *The Chosen People* (item 110) is an outspoken advocacy for genetics as the reason behind disproportionate Jewish achievements, and he adds a wealth of information on IQ tests of various populations, plus a good deal of additional research he has developed on the topic.

Some of the other books touch on intelligence, including Patai's *The Jewish Mind* (item 15), but most, including Patai, gave culture the bulk of the credit for the achievements.

Senor and Singer's *Start-up Nation* (item 92) was unique in also crediting the meritocracy of the Israeli military and the near-universal draft as being significant forces behind the many Israeli high tech start-up companies in recent years.

Botticini and Eckstein's *The Chosen People* (item 132) is the culmination of their many years of research. They were the first to document Rabbinic Judaism's mandate for universal Jewish literacy after the Roman Conquest and destruction of the Second Temple. The book lays out just how important mandatory education was in shaping the Jewish culture into one of disproportionate achievements. A second book to cover Jewish history following the Inquisition is due out soon.

Simon Schama's *The Story of the Jews* is an excellent, often personal rendition of Jewish history from 1000 BCE to 1492 CE. Schama has a wonderful sense for the telling stories that represent an era, mark a historical turning point, or sometimes shatter widely held views of how Jews lived in the 2,500 years covered in the first of the two-book series.

Schama's earlier book, *The Embarrassment of Riches* (1987) (item 17), Thomas Sowell's Trilogy, *Race and Culture* (1994), *Migrations and Culture* (1996), and *Conquests and Culture* (1998) (item 24), Arthur Herman's *How the Scots Invented the Modern World* (2001) (item 30), Lawrence Harrison's *Culture Matters* (with Samuel P. Huntington in 2000) (item 27), his *The Central Liberal Truth* (2006), and *Jews, Confucians, and Protestants* (2012) (item 88), as well as Amy Chua and Jed Rubenfeld's *The Triple Package* (2014) (item 176), cover parallel stories of other, typically small groups of high achievers. And not surprisingly, there are significant cultural similarities between these groups and Golden Age Jews.

Genetics (Nature) – Progress and Controversy

Since the 1953 discovery of the double helix, an immense amount of research, including the fifteen-year (1990 to 2005) $3 billion Human Genome mapping project, has dramatically expanded our knowledge of genes and their links to diseases and traits. It has also invoked a good deal of angst, including concerns over its accuracy, predictive credibility, privacy, and uses of such data. Some worry that insurance companies will draw on the data to deny coverage or raise premiums. Others fear that employers might use it in hiring and firing decisions. Still others simply do not want to know what the information might tell them about future diseases they or their loved ones might develop.

For Jews, there are further concerns involving race, anti-Semitism, eugenics, and Ashkenazi origins, to name just a few. And given Jewish history, some of this worry is understandable. At times the issues became highly contentious. Even political correctness has popped up, prompting advocacy, by some, that such research should simply be suppressed. There have been numerous news stories and disputes, some of which are covered later in this book. Arguments have challenged the notion of race, and some people allege that nearly all genetic diseases have essentially the same incidence amongst us (they don't). On college campuses and in some public television programming, advocates have argued, "there is no such thing as race." Even *The New England Journal of Medicine* weighed in with a 2002 opinion piece titled, "Race is Biologically Meaningless."

Leading geneticists, including Dr. Neil Risch, then of Stanford and now University of California, San Francisco (UCSF), have challenged these assertions (item 38). Risch said they were simply wrong and he proved it with clear data on the different incidences of various diseases in different races. A year later, the *New England Journal* relented, saying, "…it would be unwise to abandon the recording of race when we have barely begun to understand the human genome and its clues to the genetic basis of disease."

As time passed, the worries gradually abated as genetic data proved ever more valuable for diagnosis, prenatal testing, determination of genetic risks, screening of newborns so they can be treated early in life, forensics, tests to confirm or deny paternity or maternity, and in many other uses.

Most fears of misuse have proven largely unwarranted. And as specific benefits have been publicized, public acceptance has grown. One example is a 2012 case where whole genome scans (all three billion base pairs) of healthy cells and cancerous cells from a single cancer patient were compared. That analysis revealed clues suggesting the use of a drug approved for a completely different kind of cancer. When tried, it almost immediately brought the mystery cancer into remission. Before whole genome mapping, that would have been impossible and the patient would have died. You can read that story and others in Part 2 (item 131).

Frustrations and Breakthroughs in Genetic Science

Advocates for nature (genetic endowments) as the principal force behind disproportionate Jewish achievement had high expectations their arguments would be borne out following completion of the Human Genome Project in 2003–2005. We would quickly identify the genes behind intelligence and other relevant traits and begin to understand how they worked. Genetics (nature) would trump, or at least outweigh culture (nurture) and the debate would be over. Nature would be declared the winner. So far, however, that is not what has happened.

There was remarkable research progress on many fronts, but most early hopes for simple, reliable medical predictions of disease risk based on genetics and development of effective treatments were disappointing. For the first seven years or so after the human genome was mapped, results were mostly frustrating. We were learning a great deal and much of it was fascinating and important, but we were well behind where we had hoped to be in identifying genes causing diseases and formulating drugs to cure them.

And when it came to traits such as elevated intelligence (that might support the genetic argument for disproportionate achievement), the more we learned the more elusive the task became. Not only did we make little progress, we found much of what we thought earlier was naïve. Even simple traits like height, proved much more complex than expected.

There are cases where a single gene mutation (or variation) causes a disease (or trait), but more often this has proven not to be the case.

It is much more complex than that. Disease risk probabilities originally assigned to specific mutations or variations were reduced as early estimates proved too high based on subsequent experience. The declining risk percentages (and reduced confidence in them), led to the view that family history, rather than a genome test result, was the better risk indicator for many diseases.

Part of the disappointment also arose because we began to learn so much about genetic phenomena we did not know before.

There were major discoveries in the relatively new field of "epigenetics," which had found that environmental conditions (some of which we think of as nurture, including maternal behavior) can cause genes to be turned on and off, or up and down without changing the underlying DNA or genes themselves. Further, in some cases, these epigenetic changes can be passed along to future generations (see Part 2 for data on this topic). Previously this was thought impossible. All of the genetic switches were thought to be reset to their default positions at conception. We now know that is not necessarily true.

Another relatively new genetic phenomenon was nucleosome wrapping and unwrapping. It can keep a gene from being expressed because it is "wrapped" or be expressed because it has become "unwrapped." Copy number variations, where there are more or fewer copies of particular genes than normal occur have also become better understood. We have even seen differences in the numbers of gene copies between identical twins. These surpluses or deficiencies in the numbers of copies may affect susceptibility or resistance to diseases such as non-small cell lung cancer, HIV infection, lupus, autoimmune disorders, autism, schizophrenia and others.

"Genetic Imprinting" can cause certain genes to be expressed or not, depending on the parent from which they come. If a functional gene mutates, it can cause disease with no ability for the counterpart gene from the other parent to intervene and avert the ailment.

Recently we also learned that the 100 trillion bacteria in our bodies play a role in what we previously thought of as genetic phenomena. Heart disease, diabetes, and autism are among diseases now thought to perhaps be influenced for good or for ill by what is called the "microbiome."

In October 2012, the ENCODE project reported on nine years of research by 440 scientists at thirty-two institutions. That research completely discredited the long held notion of "junk DNA," namely, that roughly 97 percent of our DNA does not encode for proteins, is not functional, and is probably vestigial. Rather than "junk," we have now learned that 60 to 80 percent of this "junk" DNA is part of a highly complex regulatory system for turning genes on or off and up and down at various times and for coordinating activities with other genes.

Another recent discovery is that some DNA is "jumping DNA" that seemingly moves from one place to another along the genome.

The New York Times article "Capacity of Genome to Predict is Limited" (April 3, 2012), and its counterpart in *The Wall Street Journal*, "Study Warns on Gene Maps," said the same thing. Though prices for whole genome tests had dropped spectacularly, even at $1,000 per test or less, the tests might not be worth it.

That position, however, may have proven a mite premature in light of recent progress. The article's assertion is still true for traits, but not for medical genetics. Those plummeting costs and the ever faster sequencing of whole genome tests have made possible important medical genetics breakthroughs. Increasingly, the tests are saving many lives as we have begun to nail down the genetic causes of diseases, particularly cancer, and in some cases been able to prescribe the right treatments to bring the diseases into remission.

But there have been no reports and similar breakthroughs in the genetics of human traits. No single gene, for example, has yet been found to materially boost intelligence by more than 2 or 3 percent. We have identified single genes that cause great harm and that can retard IQ, but not single genes that significantly elevate IQ. There have been many blind alleys, candidate genes that did not pan out and for which early test results could not be replicated. There seems to be a growing recognition that any one gene plays only a very small part in determining IQ. Humans are thought to have 20,000 to 25,000 genes, and some say perhaps a third to two thirds of them are involved in brain development.

So the bottom line is recent incredible advances in some areas (medical genetics) but little meaningful progress in others (the genetics of traits).

Further, as described later, we are beginning to see growing evidence that nature and nurture are not so much dichotomous forces as complementary phenomena. Each can affect and reshape the other. We will return to that topic several times in the coming pages.

The Twin Studies and Heritability

On February 20, 1979, Thomas J. Bouchard, Jr., a University of Minnesota Professor, read a newspaper story about Jim Springer and Jim

Lewis, identical twins who were separated when they were four weeks old (item 16). The story became something of a public sensation. Reunited for the first time at age thirty-nine, the two Jims found that each had first married a woman named Linda, divorced and then married a woman named Betty, and both had named their dog, "Toy." Both hated spelling in school and liked math. Both had been in law enforcement and both liked carpentry. Both had tension headaches followed by migraines. One weighed 154.90 pounds and was 70.90 inches tall. The other weighed 154.59 pounds and was 71.40 inches tall. Everyone was intrigued.

We were back to Galton and his 1869 insight that data on identical twins would be highly useful in studying heritability.

And if the genetic research discussed previously is cloudy, twenty years of studies of identical and fraternal twins reared apart and together, ten years of follow-up analysis of the data, and a 2012 book by a major study participant make it clear the twins' record is quite telling. Bouchard's MISTRA study gathered extensive data on nearly 140 pairs of identical and fraternal twins raised apart, plus an equivalent number of twins raised together.

Bouchard's data is complimented with studies from other places (Germany, England, Denmark, Chicago, and smaller studies from Japan, Finland, and Sweden), some dating back to the 1920s. Today, there are also large numbers of twins included in registries and twin studies at major universities worldwide. The University of Minnesota, for example, has more than 8,000 twin pairs and family members registered. Virginia Commonwealth University has 15,000 twin pairs plus their siblings. Twin studies have become a major area of academic research over the last thirty years.

In discussing Dr. Nancy Segal's 2012 book, *Born Together—Reared Apart* (item 130), which describes MISTRA, *Wall Street Journal* science writer Matt Ridley said in a June 23, 2012 column:

> "Today a third of a century after the (MISTRA) study began and with other studies of reunited twins having reached the same conclusion, the numbers are striking. Monozygotic (identical) twins raised apart are more similar in IQ (74%) than Dizygotic (fraternal) twins raised together (60%) and much more than parent-children pairs (42%); half siblings (31%) adoptive siblings (29%-34%); virtual twins or similarly aged but unrelated children raised together (28%); adoptive parent-child pairs (19%); and cousins (15%). Nothing but genes can explain this hierarchy."

That we inherit some part of our intelligence (the "heritability of IQ")[2] is clear. Identical twin studies generally put heritability between .4 and .7, with the figure rising as we age. Not only do identical twins share similar IQ levels, their IQs tend to converge as they mature. Some researchers see this as strong evidence that intelligence is largely genetic. So, if the search for genes that account for intelligence has proven more difficult than expected, the twins' data stands as strong scientific evidence of a linkage.

The same twin studies that looked at IQ have also built the case that if offspring are to have a chance to reach their potential, there is a critical need for a healthy early environment and a nurturing, preferably two-parent family. But beyond these fundamental needs, the value of the early family environment appears to matter less than we thought. The twins' data suggest that correlations in intelligence, interests, and traits occur despite often-significant differences in other aspects in the early environments.

The MISTRA (and other) data also indicate numerous medical conditions and personality characteristics are genetically heritable. Twelve percent of siblings or children of those with schizophrenia will also develop it (twelve times the risk for the general population). If one identical twin has schizophrenia, the odds are 50 percent the other will too. If one identical twin develops manic-depressive bipolar disorder, the risk for the other is 79 percent. Yet melanoma has no such correlation, and while alcoholism is thought to be 50 to 60 percent heritable, in countries where alcohol is forbidden, alcoholism is rare among twins.

The data suggest 40 to 66 percent of personality is genetically influenced, but individual traits vary widely. Radicalism was found to be 65 percent heritable; "tough-mindedness" 54 percent; religiousness 30 to 45 percent; and inclination to panic disorders 30 to 40 percent. Nonetheless, leading researcher Dr. Robert Plomin says, "niceness," in terms of being trusting, sympathetic, and cooperative, is mostly determined by the early environment in which a child is raised. And the data show the spouses of identical twins are often very different. It is unusual for the spouse of one to appeal to his or her twin.

I am married to a mirror image identical twin. They consider each other their best friend, but they are very different. My sister-in-law has successfully battled chronic lymphocytic leukemia. My wife has never had it, but she had appendicitis, which her twin never developed.

---

2. The figure given for heritability is not the percent of IQ thought to be inherited, but the proportion of the variation in a trait such as IQ attributable to genes within the subject population.

My sister-in-law is politically very liberal. My wife is very conservative. One is something of a theist. The other is an atheist. I could go on, but would probably find myself in big trouble!

A further point deserves mention. We know that in various studies of identical twins, the average IQ difference ranges from 6 to 14 points. The range of those differences in MISTRA studies went from 0 points, where both identical twins had the same IQ score, to 29 points (a surprisingly large difference). Readers may recall that IQ tests are normalized so that a 15-point difference represents one standard deviation. Thus, about 65 percent of IQ scores fall between 85 and 115 points (plus or minus one standard deviation from the mean score of 100). The average difference in IQs between identical adult twins is roughly half of one standard deviation. This is surprisingly high and is a reminder that "similar" does not mean "same." Considerable differences exist, even when the genetic makeup of two people is supposedly identical.

Questions About the Malleability of Intelligence

Scientists now believe that IQ may be more malleable than originally thought, particularly among those in their teenage years. Tests have shown IQ changes (up and down) of as much as 21 points between the ages of fourteen and eighteen. This was a surprise when the results were published in 2011. Conventional wisdom held that intelligence was more stable than that, and yet one of the teens whose scores improved the most attributed it simply to having finally found subjects that really interested him.

Just months later, we learned of data on 1,940 Scots over age 65 whose IQs could be tracked from their youth. Using blood samples and DNA analysis, researchers concluded that genes accounted for just 24 percent of the IQ changes over a lifetime, and "environmental factors" were likely to "play a larger role."

In the last few years, controversial experiments are providing some evidence that one form of brain exercise may alter IQ in the same way physical exercise can alter physiology and health. And like physical exercise, if it works, it may require a continuing commitment over a long period to sustain its benefits (see item 124 "Building a Smarter Brain" in Part 2 .)

And while it is not so much an indicator of malleability of individual intelligence, there is the Flynn effect named for James R. Flynn, a professor at the University of Otago, Dunedin in New Zealand. He was the first to discover that in many countries, overall IQ test results have been on an upward trajectory for decades, at roughly eighteen points per generation. In America, we have gained the equivalent of twenty IQ points. That is a huge change. "Genes," said Flynn, "don't change fast enough to explain this, but which genes are 'turned on' might." Improved nutrition, better schooling and test taking skills, a more stimulating environment, and several other theories have arisen in efforts to understand why the IQ scores keep rising. But one thing we think we know is that it cannot be genetic change in the traditional sense.

———

We know genes matter. A genetic disease like cancer is real and can be devastating. My height and hair color have little to do with my cultural values or my environmental history. No matter how much I might have wished for it to be otherwise, and no matter how hard I trained, a seven-foot athlete was always more likely to be a success at basketball than I would be at five foot ten.

Yet we also now know that epigenetics can dramatically change genetic expression. Nature and nurture interact.

So what does all this have to do with The Golden Age and disproportionate Jewish achievement?

CHAPTER 2

The Genetic Heritage of the Jews

Because most of today's Jewish high achievers are Ashkenazis, it is important to know who they are. Are their roots in Central Asia, as claimed by the Khazar theory, from the Middle East as part of the 4,000 year Jewish heritage, or from somewhere else? Are they genetically linked to the Sephardim, the high achievers of the Moorish and Spanish Golden Age? Are they linked to the Mizrahim, Jews who have generally remained around the eastern Mediterranean region and North Africa for thousands of years?

And how does one account for the genetic diseases to which Ashkenazis are more prone than others? Are those ailments part of a natural selection process, with the same genes stimulating enhanced intelligence? And if so, did that mental equipment help Jews survive and thrive through the anti-Semitic harshness of the late Middle Ages?

Many of these questions are now answered, or nearly so because of recent progress in genetic research, particularly drawing on the tools and capabilities that came after 2003 from human genome mapping and the spectacular drop in the cost of such tests.

Those test results have told us that while some of the Khazar population may have assimilated into the Ashkenazi population, they are not the dominant part of it. Though there are holdouts who argue for the Khazar theory, most leading genetics experts who have studied the data say the holdouts are wrong and the data clearly shows it. The bulk of the Ashkenazim consist of Jews of Middle Eastern heritage. The Ashkenazis simply are not Khazars who converted and moved west.[3]

The Ashkenazim most likely trace back to Jews who left the Middle East during pre-Roman, or early Roman times—but perhaps even as

---

3. This controversial and important topic is covered in Part 2, items: 14, 28, 36, 49, 90 and 100

early as the Babylonian era. They migrated through what is now central Italy up into the northern Roman Empire, and then on to Northern and Central Europe. Ashkenazim first appear in recorded history sometime between the sixth and eighth centuries CE.

The genetic data also appear to show that the Ashkenazi and Sephardic populations are much closer genetically than was thought just a few years ago. Both of them appear to have migrated through present day Italy, with the Sephardim then moving west to Spain and Portugal, while the Ashkenazim moved north into Central and later Eastern Europe.

From the time of the Babylonian conquest roughly 2,600 years ago, Jews migrated to destinations east as far as India, west to the Maghreb and later to North and South America, south to south central Africa and north throughout most of Europe. The recent genetic research says that most Jews retain a high level of shared genetic inheritance across those years and distances (the full geographic spread of the Diaspora). The only significant Jewish groups that appear to lack ancient Middle Eastern genetic roots are the Ethiopian Jews and perhaps some groups of the Indian Jews. Their DNA suggests they converted. But the Ashkenazim, Sephardim, Mizrahim, Iraqi, Iranian, and others, all share varying amounts of common Middle Eastern genetic heritage.

Research studies of genetic profiles of the priestly Cohanim have allowed geneticists to trace their particular roots back to the time of Moses and Aaron, and perhaps as far back as Abraham. But the genetic ties for the even more ancient priestly class of Levites, said to date from Levi, the son of the Patriarch Jacob, are less clear at this point.

Recent genetic mitochondrial (maternal) evidence suggests that a significant part of the Ashkenazim heritage comes from "founder" Jewish mothers who presumably moved with their husbands from Palestine and perhaps Babylon. Others—apparently single Jewish men who were perhaps traders of Middle Eastern heritage—married local women who converted to Judaism. And a few, but not many, may have been Khazar tribesmen and women whose ancestors converted to Judaism, moved west from central Asia and assimilated into the Ashkenazim.

It is probably through the limited intermarriage with local non-Jewish women that some Ashkenazim inherited northern European physical traits such as blond, brown, and occasional red hair, as well as blue and green eyes.

The genetic data are also relevant to the wide historic swings in the numbers of Jews as a percent of the world's population. Though recorded Jewish deaths from the violence of war, the Holocaust, and the pogroms of the Middle Ages were high, large numbers of Jews probably also opted out. One such decline likely followed the Roman Conquest and Diaspora and the commencement of mandatory education. Others may have occurred during the pogroms.

For reasons not yet fully understood the Ashkenazim are thought to have experienced a dramatic drop to perhaps as few as 3,000 families by the early to mid-sixteen hundreds. Then that decline was reversed and Ashkenazi Jews rebounded from that tiny base. By 1940, they were more than 80 percent of the world's 16.5 million Jews. In that increase, Jews quadrupled to eight-tenths of 1 percent of the world's population. This is still well below the era of King David, when Jews were 2 percent of the world's population, but it is substantially more than today's two-tenths of 1 percent.

Apart from the single Jewish men who married local women after arriving as part of a Diaspora movement, the rate of Jews marrying non-Jews was always extremely low through nearly all of the first and second millennia. With so few converting to Judaism, the genetic record confirms what geneticists call a very low rate of "admixture" and thus reduced genetic diversity. As Dr. Robert Pollack said in his Spring 2002 paper, "Some Genetics For Jews" (see Part 2, item 31):

> "Given the great numbers of versions of each gene available in the human species at large, long runs of identical versions of genes in two unrelated people will never occur by coincidence. But because the surviving population of Ashkenazi was so terribly small in the mid-1600s, and because it grew in an uninterrupted way from such small numbers, a large fraction of Jews today share long stretches of genes with each other.... The utter sameness of the DNA...means that every Jew whose ancestors come from Ashkenaz—about nine of every ten Jews alive today—is the descendent of no more than 3,000 families who survived the pogroms of the mid-1600s."

This is the context for Ashkenazi genetic diseases and discussion of the Cochran, Hardy, and Harpending (Cochran, or Cochran et al) theory of natural selection. The theory attempts to link the ailments to elevated intelligence, and through that to disproportionate rates of achievement.

Genetic Linkage of Heritable Ashkenazi Diseases with IQ

We don't know for sure why Ashkenazi Jews have higher average IQs than European and American Whites. But we do know the theory Cochran et al laid out in their June 2005 paper, "Natural History of Ashkenazi Intelligence," (item 62) which quickly received wide international exposure and became the subject of heated debate.

We also know the paper was the exposition of a theory, and not a report on the results of experiments to prove or disprove the theory.

The theory said certain genetic mutations that cause devastating genetic diseases for Ashkenazis, such as Gaucher's, when inherited from both parents, could instead confer significant benefits in brain development and higher IQs if inherited only from one. The higher IQs were said to allow Jews to succeed in the demanding but limited careers open to them in Medieval times. That success, in turn, led to a process of "natural selection" wherein those with higher IQs and successful careers had larger families than those who did not. "Natural selection" thus built an expanding population of smart Ashkenazis.

Many prominent and not so prominent critics vigorously challenged the Cochran theory. The debate is described more fully later and in Part 1 and in Part 2 of this book. But, as an overview, some very prominent and widely acknowledged genetics experts argued the theory was disproved by the genetic data itself. They said it lacked any evidence of a historic natural selection process for the genes in question (item 43).

Others said that "Talmudic traditions," (culture) rather than genes associated with Ashkenazi ailments were the driving force behind the natural selection. Some critics disputed the limited data in the paper correlating genetic ailments with higher IQs. They said the numbers of subjects for which there were data were too few to be meaningful, the data were of questionable quality, and notable ailments such as Tay Sachs had no apparent corroborating data at all. Some even questioned whether there is any elevated IQ average for Ashkenazis, and if there is, they were skeptical it would have led to the commercial successes that spurred larger families.

To date, no further research or experiments have appeared that would prove or disprove the Cochran paper. More than seven years after its publication, it remains a theory rather than an established fact.

Reported Levels of Jewish IQ

Because some theories of disproportionate Jewish achievement have linked performance with elevated IQs, and sometimes further with genetics, it is useful to understand where current research stands.

As already noted, modern IQ testing began with Benet (item 9) about one hundred years ago.[4] It has been subject to great controversy, particularly when comparing results for groups of people. Nonetheless, the tests and their counterparts have become commonplace, and their ability to measure performance and make reasonably reliable predictions about likely academic and career success is well documented. The SAT (since 1926) and Law School Aptitude Test (since 1948) have been used for college and law school admissions and have good track records in predicting academic success. The U.S. Military has a minimum IQ enlistment standard of 85, and found that lowering that standard to 80 resulted in too many recruits incapable of mastering soldiering. College graduates average IQs of 112 and medical doctors, attorneys, and PhDs average 125 or more.

Though Jews are typically a small percent of the overall population tested, there have been enough tests over time to establish reasonable confidence in the results. Professor Richard Lynn cited thirty-two tests in the United States between 1920 and 2008 in his 2011 book, *The Chosen People* (item 132). They involved more than 17,000 Jews, and for the sixteen tests since 1950, the average test score has been 110.7. Because most American Jews are Ashkenazi, this can be taken to be the approximate average IQ for American Ashkenazim.

Counterpart tests have shown that Ashkenazi, Sephardic and Mizrahim populations have higher IQ averages than non-Jewish populations among which they have lived, as well as significant differences between their own respective IQ averages. The Ashkenazim average is ~110[5], the Sephardim ~98 and the Mizrahim ~91. Some of the differences between the groups have generally been well known to Israelis. And recently, some say the differences in Israel are narrowing.

In looking at the predominant populations among which Jews have lived:

— The Ashkenazi average IQ of ~110 compares with an average of ~100 for American and European Caucasians.

— The Sephardic average IQ of ~98, is lower than the Ashkenazi average and roughly the same as that of American and European Caucasians, but it is higher than most non-Jewish populations

---

4. It is thought that the Chinese imperial examination system may have been the first use of IQ tests. It began around 600 CE and continued with interruptions until 1905. The tests were used to select the best administrative officials for the state's bureaucracy.

5. The symbol "~" is used in this book to represent the word "approximately" and thus reduce repetition of that word and others like it. It also helps avoid "three decimal place accuracy in a zero decimal place world."

among which Sephardics have long lived (Balkan Gentiles ~92.5 and Arabs ~84).

— The Mizrahim IQ average, of ~91, is higher than the ~84 of surrounding Arab populations among whom they have lived for thousands of years.

The data raise the question why Jewish IQ averages differ from group to group, particularly given the shared Middle Eastern DNA heritage. Why, for example, would Sephardim be about two-thirds of a standard deviation below the Ashkenazim and half a standard deviation above the Mizrahim?

In comparing the three groups, some also point out the differences in their histories of achievement. Ashkenazis are the most disproportionate high achievers of the last 200 years.

— Sephardic high achievers include Maimonides, Abravanel, Spinoza, Disraeli, Montaigne (whose maternal grandmother was Jewish), Ricardo, Montefiore, Cardozo, and perhaps Cervantes, among others. And nine Sephardim have earned Nobel Prizes[6]. The record is impressive, but not as impressive as the 172 Nobel Prizes earned by Ashkenazis through 2007. The results are not proportional to their respective populations (172 Nobel's for roughly ten million Ashkenazim versus nine for two million Sephardim).

— The Mizrahim have not done nearly as well as either of the other two groups.

— Some observers believe the Sephardic populations that fled the Inquisition by moving to Central and Western Europe and the Americas have continued to have high levels of achievement akin to their Ashkenazi brethren (e.g. Spinoza, Disraeli, etc.). That contrasts with Sephardim who fled to the eastern Mediterranean, Balkans and Northern Africa. Except for Canetti, the Nobel Prize results appear to support that notion. Nonetheless, this is only informed conjecture. There are no data to confirm it. Sephardic data in the United States and elsewhere are hard to come by, perhaps because their

---

6. Tobias Asser (Dutch) for Peace in 1911; Emilio Gino Segre (Italian) for Physics in 1959; Rene Cassin (French) for Peace in 1968; Salvador Luria (Italian) for Medicine in 1969; Baruj Benacerraf (Venezuelan) for Medicine in 1980; Elias Canetti (Bulgarian) for Literature in 1981; Franco Modigliani (Italian) for Economics in 1985; Rita Levi-Montalcini (Italian) for Medicine in 1986; Claude Cohen-Tannoudji (French) for physics in 1997. Harold Pinter, who won a Nobel Prize for Literature in 2005 was thought to be Sephardic, but that had been found to be incorrect.

numbers are quite small compared with Ashkenazis and because of intermarriage among the American Ashkenazim and Sephardim.

— Recent reports from Israel indicate that ever more Sephardim and Mizrahim occupy prominent positions in that country. This may mark genuine progress proven by performance and success arising from education and environmental stimulation. It may also be the result of "affirmative action" styled programs or simply wishful thinking. We simply don't know.

— Most (80 percent) of Haredim (ultra-Orthodox) are of Ashkenazi origin, but they are not seen to be high achievers in secular domains. It goes against their beliefs. They have substantially curtailed secular interaction, experience, and interest. Most Haredim discourage science education and interaction with non-Haredim. For them, the Enlightenment, Reform movement, and a more secular lifestyle are inconsistent with their values.

Two further observations about IQ and disproportionate achievement are in order. First, it seems clear the smarter you are, the better your chances of being a high achiever in some fields. A Nobel Prize for physics, medicine, or chemistry no doubt requires a superior IQ. So too must an international championship for chess or Bridge. But not all domains of high achievement require high IQs. Olympic winners may be smart, but they need not be brilliant to earn a medal. Also, great comedians, novelists, actors, businessmen, philanthropists, (or even authors) are not necessarily brilliant in the sense of IQ. In many fields of endeavor, aspirations, motivation, training, and other talents make an enormous difference.

A final point on this topic: Jews have earned too many Nobel Prizes in science for the results to be explained simply by higher IQs.

A strong advocate for the critical importance of high IQs as the cause of disproportionate Jewish achievement is Professor Richard Lynn of the University of Ulster. In *The Chosen People: A Study of Jewish Intelligence and Achievement*, he notes that with an average IQ of 100—for "European and American Whites" – and 110 for Ashkenazi Jews:

— 32 percent of Ashkenazi Jews will have IQs of 115 or more (one standard deviation above the mean of 100 for Whites); but only 16 percent of Whites will be as smart;

— 9 percent of Ashkenazis will have an IQ of 130 or more (two standard deviations above the mean of 100); only 2.3 percent of Whites will match them; and

— 1 percent of Ashkenazis (0.98 percent) will have an IQ of 145 or more (three standard deviations above the mean of 100); only 0.135 percent of Whites will do as well.

Given roughly ten million Ashkenazis in the world and 1.2 billion Whites, we end up with about 1.62 million Whites and 98,000 Jews whose IQs are 145 or more. Until quite recently, Jews and Whites have been the predominant winners of Nobel Prizes in physics, medicine and chemistry, so to simplify just a bit, if IQ is the main determinant for winning a Nobel Prize in science, and we only consider those Whites and Jews whose IQs are 145 or more as likely winners, then, about 6 percent of the Nobel Prizes for physics should go to Jews and 94 percent to Whites. In fact, through 2007, Jews won 27 percent of all the Nobel prizes for physics, 31 percent for medicine and 20 percent for chemistry.

We could do the same exercise for IQ levels of 130 instead of 145, and a similar exercise for chess championships or other domains. The math does not pencil. Something else is going on. If it is genetic, it appears not to be just the genetics of intelligence.

Others have pursued a line of thinking akin to that of Professor Lynn. One intriguing line of thought stems from a 1954 New York psychologist's report saying that of the 28 New York school students with IQs of 170 or more at the time of the report, 24 were Jews. In essence, the argument implicitly says there are a highly disproportionate number of Jewish "outliers" at the very top of the otherwise normal distribution of Jewish IQ scores. Perhaps that is the case, but it would seem that would be the only way for genetics alone to account for Jews winning 100 times the number of Nobel Prizes one would expect based on their population.

That single 1954 study is the only report I have ever seen suggesting such an idea. There are other reasons such a remarkable outcome might have happened or been reported, but, this is a very tiny data point. It encompasses only 28 student's scores. Most of the plausible explanations would not suggest this result is found in the large number of Jewish IQ tests administered over the years. Given how astonishing those results would obviously be to those who administer IQ test results, it seems almost impossible it would have gone unnoticed. Even Richard Lynn, who compiled one of the world's largest databases of IQ results, never mentioned a high incidence of high IQ Jewish outliers, and he was particularly focused on Jewish IQ levels as a major reason Jews are such high achievers.

In fact, unrecognized by many who advocate high IQ as the explanation for disproportionate Jewish achievement, Professor Lynn appears to have realized the anomaly pointed out above when he was writing *The Chosen People*. He resolved it by saying Jews must have a greater "motivation for achievement." He talked about them placing more importance on prestige, income, and education, while spending less time watching TV and more time doing homework. As such, Lynn appears to have undercut his own earlier position by effectively deferring to cultural values as a likely additional explanation. (For more, see the entries covering Professor Lynn's work in Part 2 (items 52, 83, and 110), including the December 2007 paper where he and a colleague then argued against Jewish cultural values as an explanation.)

CHAPTER 3

Culture Matters

In recent years, evidence has continued to mount showing that cultural values—what we treasure and believe in most deeply, what we revere and love, as well as what we hate and find most repulsive—can make an immense difference in who we are, what we do or don't do, and what we accomplish.

Consider these items, expanded on in Part 2:

— *Business Week* (June 2011) and *The Economist* (July 2012) reported on Mormons and their culture (see Part 2, item 108). The religion is less than 200 years old. It recruits converts largely from the middle and sometimes lower-middle classes. Converts come from no particular racial or ethnic community (and thus they share no common genetic heritage). But like Jews, Mormons are thought by many non-Mormons to be "different." And like Jews, they tend to have strong family values and stable marriages. Their children are encouraged to speak in public early, share leadership roles, and many later take on a two-year "mission" to a foreign country where they try to recruit converts and nearly always get "No!" for an answer—thus perhaps toughening them to keep carrying out their mission of conversion. They are only 1.4 percent of America's population, but they disproportionately occupy the corner offices of major American corporations. They fielded two of the nine candidates for the Republican nomination for U.S. President in 2012. Both the *Business Week* and *The Economist* articles suggest Mormon culture is the reason behind the performance.

— Dan Senor and Saul Singer's 2009 book *Start-up Nation* (item 90) told how in a world of seven billion people, Israel, a country smaller than New Jersey with a population of only 7.8 million, has

43

quickly become one of the world's top two countries in the high technology start-up arena. The other is the United States. Intelligence and education no doubt contribute to these start-ups, but the authors and their data suggest other factors as well. These include the cultural history of an always imperiled people, a military which operates largely as a meritocracy, delegation of immense responsibility to young soldiers of low rank, significant use of high technology by the Israeli Defense Force, the immigration of superb scientists from the former Soviet Union, the conversion from a socialist to capitalist economy, and a spirit of rugged entrepreneurship. Israel was not always a "start-up nation." The culture was changed, and its prominence as a "start-up nation" is a consequence of those changes.

— In 2012, Lawrence Harrison released his book *Jews, Confucians and Protestants* (item 88). It is a remarkable work explaining the values, beliefs, and attitudes of groups whose cultural capital has helped them realize their individual and collective potential. The book's focus is not only on Jews, Confucians and Protestants, but also Ismaili Muslims, Basque Catholics, Sikhs, Mormons, and others. Among common elements of their generally shared cultural capital are:

- A premium on rationality, achievement, pragmatism and material pursuits,

- Strong views that one can influence his or her own destiny,

- A future orientation in terms of planning, punctuality and deferred gratification,

- Belief that wealth arises from human creativity, can be expanded, and thus unlike Marxists, a belief that wealth and economic prosperity are not zero sum games,

- Belief that facts matter, and that those facts are verifiable and practical,

- General adherence to realistic but rigorous ethical codes,

- Appreciation for a job well done, tidiness, and courtesy,

- Belief that education is indispensable, promotes autonomy, creativity, and worthy dissent,

- Belief that we live to work and that hard work can lead to wealth,

- Appreciation of frugality as a source of investment and prosperity,

- Appreciation of entrepreneurship as a driver of investment and creativity,
- Promotion of reasonable risk taking,
- Belief that competition is good and leads to excellence,
- Openness to innovation and rapid adaptation, and
- Treasuring merit and meritocracy.

— Harrison, who is Jewish, then uses the framework to link such values to successful economies. Except for "rent seekers" who live off natural resources such as petroleum, it is difficult to think of successful world economies that do not live by most of the values framed above. Harrison also uses the framework to explain the success of the offshore Chinese, and how changes in Mainland Chinese cultural values since Deng Xiaoping help to explain China's recent success.

— Harrison's framework is consistent with Arthur Herman's 2001 book, *How the Scots Invented the Modern World* (item 30), and Simon Schama's 1987 book, *The Embarrassment of Riches* (see item 17), which covered two remarkable populations of earlier high achievers. The Scots, who demanded literacy in conjunction with the Reformation (so Scots could read the Bible), developed a highly educated society. Despite being only one-eighth of 1 percent of the world's population at the time, Michael Hart's book, *The 100*, says the Scotts managed to produce five of the fifty most influential people of all time. The five were: James Watt, James Clark Maxwell, Adam Smith, Alexander Graham Bell, and Alexander Fleming. The similarly tiny Golden Age Dutch population (see also item 167) was highly literate and tolerant, and it displaced the Spanish in international commerce. Holland was home to some of the world's greatest painters, such as Rembrandt, Vermeer, van Ruisdael, and Frans Hals. Among great Dutch scientists of their Golden Age were Christian Huygens and Anton van Leeuwenhoek and this was home to Spinoza before and after he was excommunicated as a Jew for his revolutionary rationalist approach to theology.

— Harrison's work complements other thinkers such as Dr. Thomas Sowell, whose fifteen year trilogy, *Race and Culture* (published in 1994), *Migrations and Culture*, (1996), and *Conquests and Culture* (1998) (item 24) explored how education, exposure to other peoples (rather than isolation), geography and its influence on exposure and commerce, and an urban, as opposed to a rural lifestyle are just a few of the influences that shaped cultural values, and with that, differences in achievement. His data were compelling:

– The offshore Chinese were 5 percent of Indonesia's population, but though immigrating poor, they ended up owning 80 percent of the country's capital.

– The Chinese minority in Malaysia earned more than 100 times as many engineering degrees as the native Malay majority.

– In the early 1920s, Jews were 6 percent of Hungary's population but half that country's physicians.

– Immigrants to the United States from Eastern and Southern Europe earned just 15 percent of the income of immigrants from Norway, Holland, Sweden and Britain.

– In the Austrian Empire of 1900, the illiteracy rate of adult Serbo-Croatians was 75 percent. For Poles it was 40 percent, and for Germans, 6 percent.

– In the 1960s, the majority of Nigeria's population lived in its northern provinces, yet they were only 9 percent of its university students and 2 percent of Nigerians studying abroad.

In short, all cultures may be interesting and worthwhile, but they certainly are not equal in terms of what their people achieve or don't achieve.

Among Sowell's other observations was his comment, "Over long spans of history, the racial reshuffling of relative technological ranking of different races and nations makes it hard to conclude that such standings are genetically determined."

— A May 15, 2011 *New York Times Sunday Magazine* story drew on Pew Charitable Trust data to plot a linear relationship between religion, education, and family income in the United States (item 106). Of the eighteen denominations illustrated, immigrant East Indian Hindus, Reform Jews, and Conservative Jews ranked highest in education and family income (75, 66, and 58 percent respectively for college graduation, and 68, 69, and 58 percent for families earning more than $75,000 per year). These percentages dwarfed the national averages of 27 percent for college graduates and 31 percent for U.S. families earning more than $75,000 per year. This fascinating chart is worth browsing. The linear relationship between education and income, and the differences between the various denominations, suggest shared cultural values among the different groups probably influence the outcomes. Also interesting is the fact that Catholics are now closing in on the national average for college graduates and slightly exceeding the average for income. This tends to corroborate the work of Lisa Keister at Duke who reported on recent gains in Catholic education and income levels arising from greater inclinations toward skepticism and autonomy among the younger Catholics. (See the May 25, 2007 David Brooks' column, item 81 in Part 2.)

— A March 18, 2012 *New York Times* story (item 120) by Yudhijit Bhattacharjee reported on the fact that learning multiple languages, which was once thought to risk confusing the brain of youngsters, instead enhances cognitive skill. Those who are bilingual have also been found to be more resistant to dementia than those who aren't. Perhaps no group has a longer history of multiple language skills than Diaspora Jews who often needed those skills to function in the communities to which they had moved, and to deal with those near and far with whom some communicated in conjunction with their careers in trading, finance, and other multi-national livelihoods.

— In November 2008, Malcolm Gladwell's book *Outliers* (item 86) highlighted David Greenberg, who appears to have single-handedly converted the culture of Korean Airlines cockpit crews for the better. He ended their dangerous deference to authority (the captain) that led to numerous fatal crashes, marking Korean as one the world's most dangerous airlines. Recruited from Delta Airlines, Greenberg made safety the paramount value. Cockpit colleagues now willingly challenge any captain who is doing something unsafe, and Korean Airlines has come to be recognized as a very safe choice.

— In May 2010, David Brooks' column in *The New York Times* (item 98) reported on General David Petraeus winning the Irving Kristol Award. Like Greenberg, Petraeus had shown, once more, that cultures are malleable and reshaping cultural values can positively affect behavior. Almost single handedly, Petraeus changed America's military culture in terms of how to best respond to an insurgency. The Bush "Surge" in Iraq was successful largely because of the attitude and behavioral changes Petraeus pioneered and championed.

— Thomas Kohut's book, *A German Generation* (item 117), released in February 2012, makes a powerful case for how the adversities of life for Germans born between 1900 and 1915, coupled with the values inculcated by Nazi ideology, created a culture that set these Germans up for a lifetime of blame (from their offspring and others) and their own chronic repression of the crimes, shame, and destruction they brought upon themselves and Germany.

— In reporting on two recent books, *The Talent Code* and *Talent is Overrated* (item 89), and the research behind them, David Brooks' April 30, 2009 *New York Times* column pointed out that one conclusion is that "IQ is generally a bad predictor of success." The data suggested only "slightly above average ability," coupled with perception of how far one might be able to go—and perhaps a modicum of insecurity—can trigger a remarkable performance. One of the authors is quoted saying, "It's not who you are, it's what you do."

— In December 2005, Dr. Angela Duckworth and Dr. M.E. Seligman of the University of Pennsylvania published "Self Discipline Outdoes IQ in Predicting Academic Performance" in the journal *Psychological Science* (item 69). It reported on a longitudinal study of 140 eighth grade students from an ethnically diverse magnet school. The work was later replicated in a study of another 164 students testing IQs and self-discipline using teacher reporting, self-reporting, monetary choice questionnaires, standardized achievement tests, and admission to competitive high school programs the following spring. Their work found self-discipline ("grit" as they termed it) was consistently a better predictor of academic performance than IQ.

— Culture also appears to shape Asian academic performance. For years, we have seen the ascendency of Asian SAT scores and academic results. In 1990, H.W. Stevenson and S.Y. Lee's paper "Context of Achievement" (item 19) compared 1,440 Minneapolis, Taipei, and Sendai, Japan students and observed that Asian mothers put much more emphasis on academic success, promote more effort, and are more realistic about their kids' performance than American moms. This is the "Asian family at the dinner table going over homework," the *Tiger Mom* whose daughters excel in academics and music, and the Asian mothers who think hard work is more important than raw ability.

— On May 14, 2006, Nicholas Kristof, who is married to an Asian-American, wrote a column in *The New York Times* (item 75) about a Vietnamese girl who arrived in the U.S. with no English skills and whose parents now work as manual laborers in Nebraska. She graduated valedictorian from her high school, went on to Nebraska Wesleyan and earned a Rhodes scholarship with a 3.99 grade point average. In describing her, Kristof noted that in 2005, the combined math-verbal SAT score for Asian Americans was 1090, versus 1068 for Whites, 982 for American Indians, 922 for Hispanics and 864 for Blacks. The young girl attributed her achievements to her need to respond to her parents' sacrifices. Kristof, in turn, attributed much of the success to the shared Confucian values held by Asians, from Japan through Korea and China to Vietnam.

— A June 10, 2005 column in *The Wall Street Journal* by Tunku Varadarajan (item 60) stated that Indian Americans had won five of the last seven National Spelling Bees and in 2005, despite being 0.66 percent of the U.S. population, took all three of the top places. Varadarajan, who is Indian American, attributed the success to an ethnic group that has "pushier parents than any other people, all of them very eager—no make that desperate—for their kids to succeed in school or anything that looks remotely like school." He said it was a cultural trait. "For millennia," he said, "India was the land where the poorest scholar was held in higher esteem than the richest businessman."

— A March 28, 2003 Science column in *The Wall Street Journal* by Sharon Begley (item 44) reported on different patterns of thinking by Asians and Westerners. Westerners, she said tend to focus on specific elements of an image, while Asians tend to see the bigger picture and the relationships between the elements. Interestingly, however, the patterns are highly malleable. Asians living in the West and Westerners living in Asia tend to "go native" and adopt local thinking patterns, while those in Hong Kong, with its combined Chinese and British history, have intermediate thinking patterns.

— On June 18, 2012, both *The New York Times* and *The Wall Street Journal* reported on a Pew Research Center Study, "The Rise of Asian Americans," (item 129) which said Asian Americans had surpassed Hispanics as the largest wave of immigrants to the United

States (430,000 in 2010). Though some dispute whether Hispanic numbers have declined that much, the demographics are nonetheless compelling. Asians, said the study, are more likely to hold a college degree (49 percent) than U.S. adults (29 percent) and they have higher household income, $66,000, versus $49,800 for Whites. Equally interesting were their values and strong emphasis on children, with 59 percent of Asians married versus 51 percent for American adults. Their children are much less likely to be born to a single mother (16 percent versus 41 percent) and more likely to be raised in a two-parent household (80 percent versus 63 percent). Of the Asians, 67 percent said being a good parent is one of the most important things in life versus 50 percent for American adults. With that, they are also more likely to be satisfied than the general public (82 percent versus 75 percent.)

— In a June 1, 2010 opinion piece, noted *Washington Post* columnist Richard Cohen (item 99) was straightforward in observing that his prior view of crime as an economic phenomenon has been disproved by the declines in crime through recent economic hard times. As he noted, "Whatever the reasons, it now seems fairly clear that something akin to culture and not economics is the root cause of crime."

— In March 2005 Alex Mindlin's story in *The New York Times* (item 59) described the persecution of twenty-nine-year-old Israeli Rabbi Nosson Slifkin's by twenty-three of his fellow Haredim (Ultra-Orthodox) rabbis for his heresies. His errors were in saying that some biblical creatures such as the unicorn and phoenix are mythical, that geese did not grow in trees, that lice do sexually reproduce, that distinctions between some kosher and non-kosher animals are inconsistent, that evolution did not disprove the existence of God, and that the Big Bang Theory might be consistent with Genesis. All of these contradicted the religious dictates of his fellow Haredim rabbis. Ironically, their attempts to curtail the sale of his books backfired. One interesting aspect of all this is that about 80 percent of Haredim are said to be Ashkenazi, with the balance Sephardic. Genetically, they are the same as their Golden Age brethren and presumably they share the same genetic predispositions for intelligence, disease and other traits. Nonetheless, while many of their cultural values are shared, some, such as those arising from the Enlightenment, and participation in secular society simply are not.

— Joseph Berger's June 12, 2012 story in *The New York Times* (item128) reported on the return to growth of Greater New York's Jewish population, which had rebounded to nearly 1.5 million. Part of this was the 220,000 Russian Jewish immigrants who have arrived since the 1970s. Nonetheless, the story behind the story was that the numbers of self-reported Reform and Conservative Jews were down by 42,000 and 38,000 respectively, while non-denominational (secular) Jews were up by 127,000, and the overall rate of intermarriage was 22 percent. The Haredim (Ultra-Orthodox) population was up by 115,000. Orthodox totals for Greater New York were 493,000 (or 32 percent of the 1.5 million Jewish population), and within New York City, their higher fertility rates have resulted in the children of the Orthodox (40 percent of the City's Jews) now constituting 74 percent of the City's Jewish youth.

— Maristella Botticini and Zvi Eckstein released *The Chosen Few: How Education Shaped Jewish History* in 2012 (item 132). The book culminates many years of research by these two noted scholars and a great deal of vetting by their academic colleagues. *The Chosen Few* documents the shift of Jews from a generally illiterate rural population of farmers in Palestine to a dispersed, highly educated people capable of mastering important and lucrative work others could not do. This all arose from the rabbinic mandate for literacy following the Roman Conquest and destruction of the Second Temple in 70 CE. It is a remarkable story of one of history's most consequential cultural transformations.

— In 2014, Amy Chua and Jed Rubenfeld's book, *The Triple Package* (item 176), was published. To the list of high achieving groups they and others have identified, such as Jews, Chinese, and Mormons, Chua and Rubenfeld added Nigerians, South Asian/Indian- Vietnamese- Cuban-, Iranian- and Lebanese-American immigrants, among others. At its core, *The Triple Package* is a powerful argument against race as a driving force behind success. Instead, of the authors attribute the remarkable achievements of the various groups to three shared cultural traits they believe drive performance: a qualified sense of superiority, some level of insecurity, and strong self-discipline, sometimes referred to as impulse control.

CHAPTER 4

Why? The Debate At This Point

So why have the Jews been such high achievers? *The Golden Age of Jewish Achievement* devoted a chapter to exploring alternative answers to this question. Since then, new research, the debut of additional theories, and my own further thinking have helped me refine my thoughts. So, at this point, how does the debate stack up? First, in this chapter, we survey the alternative theories.

The remainder of Chapter 4 describes my understanding of all of the significant theories and arguments that have been put forth to explain disproportionate Jewish achievement. In each case, I add my own analysis supporting some of the arguments and criticizing others. Some of these theories have been around for more than a century. Others are much newer and draw on more recent research. The point (and the reason for the word *Debate* in the book's title) is my intention to provide readers with the most complete summary and analysis of these arguments ever assembled in one place.

If *The Golden Age of Jewish Achievement* is the most complete analysis of disproportionate Jewish achievement ever compiled—and it is—this book intends to be the most complete review of all the significant theories and arguments about why it happened. There are critically important lessons to be learned here, with applications far beyond the Jewish community.

Ultimately, I explain where I come out and why, but first let's review the predominant theories.

Chance

The notion that Jewish achievements might simply be attributable to good fortune or a fluke can be dismissed out of hand. If Jews were disproportionately accomplished in only one or two fields, perhaps the argument might be valid. But across the range of achievements described in *The Golden Age*, it is statistically and logically impossible to conclude the disproportion arose from chance.

God's Chosen People

On this topic, like good fortune, nothing has changed since *The Golden Age* was published. Lightning may strike me, but this is not the cause.

Nonetheless, the concept of Jews as "God's chosen people" is still an explanation plausible to some (I received correspondence to that effect after my earlier book was published). Abraham entered into a Covenant with God, who promised to protect and revere his people if they obeyed his Commandments. "'Now Adonai (the Lord) said to Avram (Abraham), 'Get...out of your country, away from your kinsmen...and go to the land I will show you. I will make of you a great nation. I will bless you and...make your name great.'"

The Covenant was reaffirmed in B'resheet (Genesis) 17:2-7, and with Moses in Sh'mot (Exodus) 19:5. "Now if you will...keep my Covenant, then you will be my own treasure from among all peoples."

Being "chosen" might explain Jewish achievement, were it not for the premium Judaism places on free will and the unbelievable hardships Jews have endured. For 2,534 years, until Israel was created in 1948, Jews generally lived as minorities in widely dispersed enclaves (sometimes enforced ghettos) across much of the world. With notable, generally brief, exceptions, wherever they lived they were often persecuted, more often by Christians than Muslims, particularly in the second millennium. And while some Jews may have believed the hardships arose from their collective failure to keep up their end of the bargain (and was thus God's just retribution for these failings), for most Jews the advent of Emancipation and Enlightenment, the growth of Reform movements, and the horror of the Holocaust—which called into question the very notion that six million deaths could be the work of a just God—eroded the traditional sense of being chosen.

Moreover, why would a people that generally ceased proselytizing more than 2,000 years ago have been chosen by their God to become "a light unto the world" for their secular achievements?

A further notion of "chosen" deserves mention, linking it to *tikkun olam*. Though rabbinic in origin, and refined by the medieval Kabbalah, *tikkun olam* has become mainstream in recent years. It means chosen by God for the special responsibility of helping "repair a broken world." For some, the *tikkun olam* obligation arises as the Jewish response to original sin. For others, it involves a mystical conception of the need to reunite sparks of divine light that were shattered when God created the world. In either conception, Jews must help heal the broken world for the benefit of all mankind. In essence, Jews are chosen not for good fortune or for secular achievements, but to fulfill this duty.

Anti-Semitism: They Cheat, or the Deck Is Stacked in Their Favor

One article (item 105 in Part 2 of this book) describes Jan C. Biro's March 2011 paper citing pro-Jewish bias in the selection of Nobel Laureates. Biro's on-line resume lists a medical degree from an unnamed university and a PhD from Stockholm's Karolinska Institute. "The Jewish Bias of the Nobel Prize" is written in the form of a serious research paper with forty-seven endnotes. It is representative of many such anti-Semitic efforts that can be found on the Web—just more polite than most.

Biro alleges the disproportionate number of Jewish Nobel Prizes defies the stipulations of Alfred Nobel's intention in establishing the Prizes upon his death. Nobel's will states, "No consideration should be given to the nationality of the candidates." Biro also says Swedes view the Nobel Prizes as a PR opportunity for their small country, which would be unnoticed were it not for its annual Nobel ceremony." He also says, "Swedes are rather sensitive to corruption…but (they) can be moved by a nominee with many weighty supporters…(who have) a talent for networking." He adds (the Swedes are) "very responsive to all kinds of often stupid egalitarian argument (such as) the idea of giving one prize to a Jew and one to a Gentile."

His hypothetical (he says "plausible") example occurred in 2002 when Craig Venter, Francis Collins, and John Sulston were Nobel candidates. They were passed over, Biro says, because while the Selection Committee wanted to honor the Human Genome Project, Venter was disliked because he is "entrepreneurial," as was Collins because he is deeply religious. Instead, the Committee chose another research area and picked Sydney Brenner and H. Robert Horvitz for research on C. elegans (which Biro calls "a worm" to disparage the choice). To Biro, this is an example of pro-Jewish bias.

He goes on to say, "That Swedes are still entrusted to provide a prestigious prize is almost a joke," and then surprisingly adds that "Swedes do not care who the recipients are…and do not care about the gender or ethnicity of a laureate."

Toward the end of his paper, Biro returns to an early, uncompleted thought. He faults Swedes for failing to recognize that Jews think of themselves as a "nation." He seems unaware that Israel did not exist before 1948, and that many Prizes earned by Jews are associated with the countries in which they have lived before and since Israel's creation. He suggests instead that Jews should be considered a race, and with that, a single nation. And since their "nation" has already received so many Nobel Prizes, Swedes should recognize their bias and change it. He does not go on to say what he would do about Italians, Irish, Germans, Chinese, English, Russians, and others who have immigrated to countries that now count them as citizens, and thus as their own Nobel Laureates.

Since their inception in 1901, Nobel Prizes have been awarded by Swedes (Nobel was Swedish), and Norwegians (the Peace Prize). Nominations are taken from almost any group wishing to recommend a candidate, but it is the Swedish and Norwegian committees that make the decisions. The numbers of Jews in Sweden and Norway are trivial: 18,000 out of 9.1 million Swedes (two-tenths of 1 percent), and 1,500 Jews out of 4.9 million Norwegians (three-hundredths of 1 percent). It is unlikely they bias the selections.

Swedes may appreciate the recognition from hosting Nobel Laureates, but if there were no Nobel Prizes, neither Sweden nor Norway would be bereft of publicity or prestige. Finland, Denmark, Estonia, Latvia, Lithuania, Ireland, Luxembourg, and Switzerland are all smaller than Sweden in size and population. All of them are secure and well thought of. None are lazy, and they all have intelligent and well-educated citizens and successful economies. That Sweden and Norway need the publicity, or that needing the publicity has something to do with a bias favoring Jews is nonsense.

Those who read *The Golden Age* may recall my jibes at certain selections of Peace Prize winners, plus others for literature, and sometimes those for economics, but my book and most objective observers retain great respect for the ethics of the selection process and lack of racial or national bias, as well as the caliber of the physics, chemistry, and medical Nobel Laureates who are chosen.

We could do the same kind of analysis for every other domain of disproportionate Jewish achievement. Chess is a one-on-one competition, and so are most other sports and games in which Jews have done well. Representing 31 percent of the 2007 *Forbes 400* and 38 percent of *Business Week*'s 2003 to 2007 most philanthropic are the result of simple tallies based on net worth and public information on charitable giving. Enrollment in the Ivy League is similar. Dominance in social activism can be discerned with simple Web searches of the historical leadership of such organizations.

Kennedy Center honorees are selected in a complex Washington D.C. political process involving large numbers of congressional, White House, and other appointees. No single person or small group makes the selections. There is no room for confusion in identifying founders and leaders of banks and financial institutions, high tech enterprises, department stores, specialty retailers, movie studio entrepreneurs and heads, CEOs of broadcast networks and other kinds of enterprises.

Anti-Semitism long foreclosed Jews from being named *Fortune 500* CEOs until Irving Shapiro was selected to head DuPont in December 1973. Now it is mostly a matter of merit. Determination of the most significant real estate developers and managers is easy. Senators, congressmen and women are elected. Supreme Court Justices are picked by the President and confirmed by the largely non-Jewish Senate. Much the same is true of great visual artists, award-winning musicians, notable photographers, architects, and others.

Longer than the theory deserves, the prior comments hopefully convey a sense of this pseudo-scientific form of anti-Semitic bias and, hopefully, a logical response to it. Biro is not the only one perpetuating this point of view—the Internet is full of such comments. But most who read Biro's ideas will be struck by the illogic. He avoids the demagoguery of many other rants that attribute Jewish success and disproportionate achievement to cheating, fraud, conspiracies, and other nefarious behavior. In every case, the arguments are superficial and in error. Biro's paper at first appears professional, polite, and serious. It acknowledges Ashkenazi IQs and successful collaborations between "brilliant Jews and Gentiles." But in the end it is simply wrong. Envy is the source of nearly every contemporary allegation that Jews have cheated or have benefitted unfairly from a bias in their favor.

A Second-Generation Jewish Immigrant Phenomenon

It is impossible to read *The Golden Age* and not be struck by the incidence of second-generation immigrant Jews among the high achievers: Milton Friedman, Saul Bellow, Richard Feynman, Edwin Land, and on and on. All were sons of immigrants. For some commentators, this became the simple and accepted explanation for disproportionate Jewish achievement.

It was over lunch that a prominent Jewish publisher told me the theory I had not heard before. He explained it had great credibility among some in the Jewish community, including Nobel Laureates. Personally, he did not buy it, but like me, he found it interesting.

Roughly two million Ashkenazi Jews arrived in America from the Pale of Russia between 1880 and 1924. These are the ancestors of most American Jews. They fled an overwhelming oppression. "Convert, leave, or be killed" was thought to be Russian policy. It drove huge numbers to immigrate to America, Palestine, and elsewhere. Opportunities for education in the Pale were limited, thus many Jews arrived illiterate and were thought to have low IQs.

Within a generation, their children became astonishingly successful in the arts, education, science, medicine, and other fields. It was the parents and the culture driving the youth, and the young people driving themselves. They wanted a better life. This was a predictable human response to the oppression of the Pale and the opportunities in America. There was still anti-Semitism in America, but it was mild and much less evident than in other countries. Need met opportunity, creating a generation of high achievers who, with ambition, could move beyond the tenement, and perhaps beyond parents whose language and behavior might at times be a source of embarrassment. Such were the driving forces in a country that functioned mostly as a meritocracy.

Clearly, the second-generation theory has appeal, but it is not compelling to me, nor is it a complete explanation. It suffers from what logicians call the fallacy of *post hoc ergo propter hoc* (namely, "after this, therefore because of this"). Because it was common for high achievers to have been second-generation immigrant Jews does not make that the cause of the achievement. It may be a contributing factor, but there is more to it than that. While the second generation contained many high achievers, so too have the third, fourth and fifth generations, almost none of whom faced (nor did their parents face) anything like the poverty, illiteracy, and terrors of the Russian Pale. And for subsequent generations, America's opportunities were not so novel.

Furthermore, Jews were high achievers well before the American immigration. Jesus, St. Paul, St. Peter, Moses, Maimonides, Spinoza, Felix and Moses Mendelssohn, Offenbach, Pissarro, the Rothschilds, Disraeli, Meyerbeer, and Einstein are all counted among the most influential people of all time. None were second-generation immigrants to America. In his book *The Jewish Mind,* Raphael Patai noted the disproportionate number of Jewish scientists in Europe during the Middle Ages: between 1150 and 1300 CE, when 2.7 percent of Spain's population was Jewish, 41.2 percent of its leading scientists were Jews. In France, 25.4 percent of the scientists were Jews and in Germany, 21.4 percent. Clearly, Jews did not have to be second-generation immigrants to be disproportionate achievers in any of those countries.

One chapter in *The Golden Age* described the emergence of great Jewish western visual artists. Of the fifteen great Jewish visual artists listed by Charles Murray in his book, *Human Accomplishment*, only five were born in the United States. Six were Russian and the other four were Ukrainian, German, Hungarian, and Italian. Between 1850 and 1900, French Jew Camille Pissarro, was the only prominent Jewish visual artist. In succeeding fifty-year periods, the numbers of great Jewish visual artists have consistently risen. Today, 20 to 25 percent of all the great western visual artists are Jews. They are not second-generation immigrants.

And if second-generation immigrants are high achievers, why have Italians, Irish, Germans, French, and other immigrant groups not turned in comparable performances? The Irish and Italians were similarly discriminated against. Presumably, their next generations were also motivated to get ahead. After all, Jews were only about 10 percent of the huge 1880-1924 immigration to the United States., but other immigrant groups never touched the Jewish levels of achievement. One clue that something else was involved comes from Michael Barone's book *The New Americans*. He notes that in 1910, among first-generation Jews ages fourteen to eighteen, 56 percent were in school. For Italians, the number was 31 percent.

There is also the experience of the offshore Chinese. In every locale where the Chinese have been a minority, they have been disproportionately successful. Perhaps apocryphal, it is said the reason Singapore was carved out of Malaysia to become a separate island nation was that the Chinese were much more successful than the native Malays. A practical solution to resolve the envious anger of the majority Malays was to give the Chinese their own small country. Like the Jews, the Chinese have long placed a premium on education and hard work. This suggests that their culture, rather than second-generation status, drove their performance.

High levels of Jewish achievement also arose in nineteenth and early twentieth century Austria, Germany, and Switzerland. As the Jewish Emancipation and Enlightenment unfolded, the likes of Mendelssohn, Einstein, Freud, and others arrived on the secular scene making impressive contributions. We can debate whether or not his was a "contribution," but the name Karl Marx fits on this list as well.

And both before and after the Russian Revolution, Jews were disproportionate achievers there. Yuri Slezkine's book, *The Jewish Century*, delineates just how influential a relatively small number of Jews were in Czarist times, and later, in the Communist Party and the Soviet government (including the KGB). They were also among the leading lawyers, educators, scientists, and artists in the USSR. This is still true in today's Russia, albeit with substantially fewer Jews now than there were before the Soviet Union dissolved.

Finally, when one looks at Nobel Prizes over the decades, it is striking that while Jews have won 23 percent of all the Nobel Prizes, the rate since 1990 has climbed to 27 percent (including the period 2008 through 2013). This rise in the percent of Prizes going to Jews over the last twenty to twenty-five years contradicts the second-generation theory. These are not second-generation immigrants. The Golden Age of Jewish Achievement has not died with the second generation; it continues today.

Brains, Drive and Circumstance
(Malcolm Gladwell's *Outliers*)

As described in the Appendix, the title of Malcolm Gladwell's 2008 book *Outliers* telegraphed his premise. Outliers are those few among us who are unusually successful. Gladwell's theory is that brains and drive are vital, but they aren't enough. The stars must be properly aligned. Circumstances must offer up the third necessary ingredient in the form of opportunity.

Bill Gates was very smart and hard-working young man, but it could be argued that what made the difference was his good fortune to attend one of the very few schools at the time with access to a mainframe computer. He was an eighth grader in 1968; time-sharing was less than three years old. The PC was yet to be invented. With time-share access to a computer, Gates began programming. Later, he exchanged his work on software for access to a University of Washington computer. In short, says Gladwell, this very young, very smart, and very driven student just happened to be in the right place at the right time.

Gladwell reiterated this "stars aligning" theory with further stories about Joe Flom, the Jewish attorney who built the law firm, Skadden, Arps, Slate, Meagher & Flom, and Robert Oppenheimer, who headed the Manhattan Project, as well as many others—right place, right time.

That is what most readers and reviewers took away from the book. David A. Shaywitz's review in *The Wall Street Journal* said, "Intrinsic ability appears to be a necessary, but not sufficient condition for exceptional achievement...hard work is essential too.... Intrinsic qualities are required, but a lot of things also need to break just right, and a prodigious amount of good luck is necessary."

Despite the biographies of entrepreneurial, high-achieving Jews, *Outliers* seems to have missed an essential point about Jewish achievement. One cannot reasonably look at what the Jews have done in the Golden Age and conclude they were all in the right place at the right time. As detailed in *The Golden Age*:

— 23 percent of all Nobel Prizes—100 times their percent of the population.

— 21 percent of Ivy league students versus 2 percent of the U.S. population

— 51 percent of the Pulitzer Prizes for non-fiction

— 37 percent of the Academy Awards for Best Director

— 31 percent of the Forbes 400

— And on, and on, and on.

In short, *Outliers* makes the point that it takes more than brains and hard work to be successful, but the book's notion of fortunate circumstance as the third vital ingredient is completely inadequate to explain disproportionate Jewish achievement. The Jewish performance is much too broad in scope and deep in numbers. It is not possible that all these Jewish high achievers were in the right place at the right time.

A point missed by most *Outliers* reviewers was the fact that much of Gladwell's book, particularly the last half, tells fascinating stories about the vital importance of culture. Among those stories was the one covered in the prior chapter about David Greenburg, the newly hired head of Korean Airlines flight operations. Single handedly, he changed the dominant value for cockpit crews from deference to the captain into a requirement to directly challenge any captain whose actions were unsafe. For everyone in the cockpit, passenger and aircraft safety became the paramount value, and with that Korean became one of the world's safest airlines.

Gladwell also wrote about cotton farming in the American South during slavery, and how it differed from growing and processing sugar cane on Caribbean plantations in the same era. For Gladwell, Southern Blacks were taught only how to grow and harvest cotton. They were immensely disadvantaged compared to the slaves in the Caribbean whose absentee owners left them to grow, harvest, refine, package, administer, and ship the finished product. That difference in circumstance shaped a completely different cultural experience for Caribbean Blacks, and in that, Gladwell sees clues to help explain how his Black mother was so accomplished, and perhaps how someone like Colin Powell could become a four-star general and Secretary of State. In short, circumstances can help shape culture for the better, and culture matters.

Genes: Rabbinic Judaism versus Catholic Celibacy

Might a particular form of genetic natural selection have played a role in disproportionate Jewish achievement? The rabbi-versus-priest theory arose early in the twentieth century and was popularized by Ernest Van Der Haag in his 1969 book *The Jewish Mystique.*

The theory is that in feudal Europe, where most people were born to their station for life, the Roman Catholic priesthood was the one meritocracy. There, a person of talent could rise to a position of power in the only institution supposedly unsullied by nepotism. The downside was that some of Europe's best and brightest were choosing a career in which their genes would not be passed on.

Jews selected rabbis for their knowledge and intelligence, but generally required them to have a wife and children. Unlike priests, the rabbis could and did multiply. Hence, it followed, says the theory, that this must have been behind the growth of a very talented Jewish population versus the self-extinguishing Catholic clerical counterpart.

Perhaps this kind of natural selection made a difference, but celibacy did not exist in the Eastern Orthodox Church in the same way that it did for Roman Catholicism. While Eastern Orthodox monks are celibate, if an Eastern Orthodox man is married before becoming a priest, he can continue to serve while married. Reportedly, 90 percent of Eastern Orthodox priests are or have been married with children. And in the Roman Catholic Church, twenty-six early popes are known to have been married or sexually active. Abstinence as church policy was not widely adopted till the fourth century, and in succeeding centuries it was something of an on and off thing. Not until the First and Second Lateran Councils (in 1123 and 1139, respectively) were firm Church prohibitions adopted.

And in October 1517, Martin Luther nailed his Ninety-Five Theses to the All Saints' Church door in Wittenberg, Germany. It unleashed the Reformation, and with that, the end of celibacy for what would become Protestant ministers. Luther joined them by marrying a former nun. For nearly 500 years, ministers of numerous Protestant denominations have married and had families.

Since the Reformation, celibacy has had ever less effect on a largely Protestant and now increasingly secular Europe; it was never significant in North America. There is the further complication that the Ashkenazi population went through a bottleneck and was whittled down to very few families (perhaps 3,000) about one hundred years after the Reformation began (see Robert Pollack, "Some Genetics for Jews" – item 31 in Part 2). Clearly, if rabbinic Judaism fathered a disproportionately bright population, its greatest growth occurred well after the Reformation. The manifestation of disproportionate secular achievements arose in the nineteenth and twentieth centuries.

In short, Catholic celibacy may have played a small role in restraining the numbers of potential high achievers in Medieval Christian Europe, but the effect was brief, had less impact than it would seem, had no significant effect in areas dominated by the Eastern Orthodox church, and essentially none in America. While interesting, the theory is not compelling.

Genes: Survivor Skills Learned Over Thousands of Years of Persecution

This argument is straightforward. It says Jews have nearly always been persecuted. Incredible hardships over much of 4,000 years resulted in natural selection of the best and brightest. The Egyptians made Jews slaves and therefore they endeavored to escape. The Assyrians conquered the ten Northern Tribes and they were lost to history. No one knows whether they were assimilated or killed. The Babylonians defeated the Jews and forced many of them into exile. The Greeks fought them when they rebelled. The Romans did the same, killing one million Jews, destroying the Second Temple and dispersing most Jews from Palestine.

Muslims treated Jews as subservient and demanded *dhimmi* status (a tax for their protection). At times, Muslims would treat them tolerably, but then that would change and they treated them horribly. The pendulum swung back and forth. Christians did the same, generally treating Jews worse than Muslims, except in America. All things considered, with the possible exception of Gypsies, it has been more difficult for Jews for much longer than for any other of history's peoples—and yet they survived.

In short, "whatever doesn't kill me makes me stronger." Many of the weaker Jews were presumably lost to the pogroms, the Crusades, and countless anti-Semitic acts over centuries. Others simply opted out of Judaism. This form of natural selection through constant, horrific testing culled the weak from the strong. Those smart, tough, and talented enough to survive are the ones who have proven capable of making it through innumerable trials. And while not all Jewish offspring will be as capable, many will be. That is one way natural selection works.

As quoted in *The Golden Age*, Esther Rantzen, a then-prominent BBC personality said, "The slow often got wiped out. You always had to be a jump ahead of the pogrom. I am casting no aspersions on those who died, but, if you are persecuted for thousands of years, it is a very tough form of the survival of the fittest." One would be hard-pressed to imagine circumstances more challenging, and more likely to distill the best from the rest, than what Jews have been through.

This argument cannot be dismissed. It is not scientifically proven, but it has great intuitive appeal. And it has another aspect of interest: that is, to what extent have the hardships helped shape Jewish culture? Did the self-reliance required in the face of anti-Semitism, including obstacles to some kinds of employment, create a need to learn other kinds of survival skills and contribute to a different sensibility? I believe it did

These days, when affluent parents work to make life easier for their offspring, they may be ignoring the historical reality that hardship motivates more than comfort. Or, as a Jewish boss of mine used to say, "Steve, we learn more from our mistakes and difficulties than we do from our successes."

Certainly self-reliance was important, as were superb professional skills to distinguish oneself in an anti-Semitic world. Entrepreneurial skill was necessary when industries were foreclosed, and it would have been unwise to rely on the goodwill of others for a job. They could quickly turn against you if times turned bad. Education provided job skills and much more, including the ability to communicate and function across great distances and within multiple cultures, as did the Diaspora Jews.

But there are counter arguments. For example, we would expect the success of high achievers to make them targets of envy, rather than survivors of pogroms and the Holocaust. And, at the risk of being politically incorrect in augmenting the point that survivor skills help but are not the complete explanation, we can point to the Gypsies, who have been oppressed for just as long as Jews. They too went to the ovens at Auschwitz. They have certainly learned their own lessons of how to sur-

vive against oppression, but they have no comparable record of disproportionate achievement.

Complementing survival skills as contributing factors to Jewish
achievement are values such as the conviction that it is what you do in
this life that matters, the belief in a God who demands ethical behavior,
the premium placed on rationality and pragmatism, tenacity, verbal
skills, and much more. Survival skills are just part of a larger picture.

Genes: Nature/DNA and IQ Heritability

Over more than fifty years, studies have shown elevated IQ levels
for Ashkenazi Jews. Generally reported to be in the range of 106 to
112, the scores are one-third to two-thirds of a standard deviation
higher that the average for American and European Whites.

The evidence of identical twins raised apart, and the convergence of
their IQ scores as they age—despite having been brought up in different families and cultures—suggests a significant genetic influence. Yet
we also know that IQ scores of identical twins typically differ by about
one-half a standard deviation.

There is Dr. Robert Pollack's 2002 observation (Part 2) that the
world's Ashkenazi population dropped to something like 3,000 families
at its lowest point in the early 17th century. If for some reason that
small group of people had a significantly higher average IQ, it is possible that might help explain how today's Ashkenazis—all descendants of
that small smart population—inherited a genetic legacy for heightened
average IQ levels.

By this theory, nature is said to be more important than nurture.
Sometimes the argument also suggests that despite small numbers (12
to 14 million Jews in the world), their higher average IQ means Jews
are a larger proportion of those with the raw talent to achieve great
things where intelligence is critical, such as winning Nobel Prizes in science.

But linking disproportionate achievements to higher IQ runs into
problems. As pointed out in the prior section, and in reviews of Richard
Lynn's work later in this book, high IQ may be very important in earning a Noble Prize for physics or in becoming an international chess
champion, but in many domains, other traits likely count for more. Successful entrepreneurs may be smart, but they are rarely valedictorians or
members of Phi Beta Kappa. The same is true for sports stars, activist
leaders, authors, actors, musicians, politicians, real estate developers, or
Fortune 500 CEOs.

There is also the fact that even for Nobel Prizes for physics, medicine and chemistry, the math does not work. If one looks at the absolute numbers of Jews with very high IQs and compares those figures with non-Jews with equivalent IQs, the rate at which Jews earn these Nobel Prizes is still roughly five times higher than it should be. Something else is going on.

And there is Dr. Robert Pollack's argument that apart from distinctive DNA sequences of the Cohanim (and perhaps the Levites), there are many different strains of DNA in Jews, some of which are very common among Middle Eastern Arabs, including Palestinians, Syrians, Greeks, and other ancient Mediterranean lines. Pollack says, "There are no DNA sequences common to all (Ashkenazi) Jews and absent from all non-Jews." Jews are genetically close to many other cultures, including those whose accomplishments pale by comparison.

And even if inherited genes for intelligence are a significant factor in some domains of achievement, there are also ever more data points suggesting IQ may be more malleable than was earlier thought. It may be significantly influenced by environmental and cultural circumstances such as creation and enforcement of mandatory literacy within a culture.

Moreover, the latent potential of elevated intelligence may be wasted or go unrealized in no small measure because of cultural values. One example of this may be the Haredim. Genetically, there is no reason to think they are significantly different from their Ashkenazi (and to a lesser extent, Sephardic) brethren. In fact, their IQs are likely to be the same or nearly so, since they all share essentially the same genetic legacy. Yet despite this genetic and prospective IQ link, the Haredim appear to have almost no inclination to draw on this endowment to achieve greatness in secular domains.

Genes: Nature/DNA—the Cochran, Hardy & Harpending Theory

As briefly described in the prior section and in Part 2, Professors Gregory Cochran, Jason Hardy, and Henry Harpending published their academic paper "Natural History of Ashkenazi Intelligence" in the June 2005 issue of *The Journal of Biosocial Sciences*. The paper laid out an intriguing theory that ties Ashkenazi genetic ailments such as Gaucher's disease, idiopathic torsion dystonia and other genetic diseases more common among Ashkenazis than others, with elevated IQ and natural selection.

It was suggested the phenomenon might be akin to sickle cell anemia in people whose families came from Africa, parts of South or Central America, Caribbean islands, Mediterranean countries, India, and Saudi Arabia—malaria-prone parts of the world. The disease is inherited when both parents pass copies of the sickle cell gene to their offspring. If only one parent passes the gene, however, the offspring will not get sickle cell anemia. Instead, he or she will be genetically immune from malaria. The reason the gene has not only persisted but grown in frequency, is said to be the "natural selection advantage" it gives in keeping some portion of the population safe from malaria.

In like manner, presumed Ashkenazi disease risk and elevated IQ benefits were linked by Cochran, et al. Natural selection helped propagate the gene because Ashkenazis with high IQs prospered and had large families while those with low IQs were not successful. They had smaller families, or opted out of Judaism. The *Biosocial Sciences* paper suggested that the genes in question may enhance the numbers of neurons in the brain and the synapses that link them.

It also provided data on 255 Gaucher's patients in an Israeli hospital (eighty-one of which were reported to be in occupations averaging IQs of 120 or more) and it reported on a few other research papers from the 1970s that described elevated IQs among torsion dystonia and non-classic congenital adrenal hyperplasia (CAH) patients. Those papers suggested these patients and family members had higher IQs.

The Cochran paper unleashed a firestorm of criticism that continues to this day, with many prominent geneticists and others challenging the deductions.

Some said the examples cited for Gaucher's, torsion dystonia and CAH patients had flaws. The numbers of torsion dystonia and CAH subjects were very small, and the Gaucher's sample may have been unrepresentative. Some also found it strange that the longest studied (since 1881) of the Ashkenazi ailments, Tay-Sachs disease, provided no examples of elevated IQs in the paper.

Prominent geneticists, including Dr. Neil Risch of Stanford and UCSF, challenged the "natural selection" notion, saying there was no evidence the genetic mutations evolved though natural selection. Both before and after the Cochran paper, geneticists had published research saying the Ashkenazi genetic ailments arose at different times and show evidence of what are called "founder's effect" and "drift" rather than an increased frequency suggesting natural selection.

To date, no one is known to have done experiments to test the Cochran theory. Such an experiment would not prove nor disprove natural selection, but it should correlate (or fail to correlate) carriers of recessive genes for genetic ailments with elevated IQ, as compared with non-carriers. Among Ashkenazis the numbers of carriers of the mutations are high, and would not seem difficult to identify or recruit. IQ tests are inexpensive to administer and control groups would be easy to assemble. The expense would be for the whole genome tests and the evaluation of the data. Perhaps controversial or unpopular in some quarters, the experiment might yield meaningful insights, whether or not it corroborates the theory. But, until someone does these or other tests, all we can say is that the Cochran theory is interesting, controversial, and unproven.

Nurture and Nature: Botticini and Eckstein (Mandatory Education), Murray (Genes and IQ) and Cochran, et al.

In December 2005, Maristella Botticini and Zvi Eckstein weighed in with an article in the *Journal of Economic History*. In 2012 they went further with their book *The Chosen Few*. Botticini and Eckstein were among the first to provide a rigorous academic analysis of Rabbinic Judaism's unique mandate for literacy. The two authors pointed out that over a period commencing well before the Roman destruction of the Second Temple in ~70 CE, the Pharisees promoted education so that all Jews (probably only males in those early years) could study the Torah and the Oral Law. With the destruction of the Temple and the decline of the priestly Jewish religion of the Sadducees (who did not believe in the Oral Law), the Pharisees and Rabbinic Judaism became dominant. Their synagogues became schools, and they made education a mandatory duty for parents and communities. Jews became the first people in history known to do that.

Some Talmudic commentators have added that the move to literacy was at least in part motivated by remembrance of the lost ten tribes, presumably to assimilation following the Assyrian conquest. Literacy might help avert a similar fate for the remaining tribes in the dispersal (Diaspora) of most Jews from Palestine. Literacy was essential if Jews were to sustain the culture and religion of a dispersed population over the centuries. The religious trove had to be written down and canonized, and Jews needed to be able to read, write, discuss, and understand it in order for their common religion and culture to survive across the distances and time. Written tracts and literacy would keep Judaism alive. "The Word" would save "the people of the Book."

Judaism was transformed. Education flourished and by the time of the Muslim ascendency after 638 CE, "basic literacy among Jewish males was almost universal." As urban centers arose within the Muslim world, Jews were able to migrate to these communities where education gave them unique advantages in pursuits other than farming.

A tribe that was 80 to 90 percent farmers in the years between 0 and 400 CE was transformed to only 5 to 30 percent farmers by 638 to 1170 CE. They were now predominantly artisans, craftsmen, traders, merchants, doctors, and moneylenders. The imperative for education had dramatically changed Jewish culture.

The Botticini and Eckstein paper is a strong argument for Jewish culture, driven in part by the circumstance of the Roman Diaspora. It added new depth to the culture argument.

Drawing on this paper, and on the June 2005 Cochran, Hardy and Harpending (Cochran or Cochran et al) paper, Charles Murray, the Protestant Scots-Irish co-author of *The Bell Curve*, wrote his own paper titled "Jewish Genius" for the April 2007 issue of *Commentary*.

Murray began by describing his positive view of the history of Jewish achievement, including the remarkable creations of the Torah, Tanakh (Old Testament) and New Testament. He regarded them as complex, sophisticated texts that, as Thomas Cahill wrote in *The Gifts of the Jews* in 1998, provided "a way of looking at the meaning of human life and the nature of history that defines core elements of the modern sensibility." Murray talked about the importance of Jews in Moorish and Catholic Spain from 1150 to 1492 CE, and the explosion of disproportionate achievement commencing with Jewish Emancipation over the course of the nineteenth century.

He then asked, "What accounts for this remarkable record?" and responds by saying, "A full answer must call on many characteristics of Jewish culture, but intelligence has to be at the center of the answer...Jews have been found to have an unusually high mean intelligence as measured by IQ tests..."He goes on to say intelligence alone is not enough. "...imagination, ambition, perseverance and curiosity are decisive...but you have to be very smart to even have a chance of achieving great work."

His next question was, "How and when did this elevated IQ come about?" And from there he put forth his view that it had to be grounded in genetics. Perhaps, he said, it was a winnowing by persecution (but he went on to discount that), or a marrying for brains (a variation on the rabbi-priest theory). He discounted those as well.

Murray then referenced the Cochran paper. Here he was skeptical, in part because of the early urban character and occupations of Sephardic and Oriental Jews well before the rise of the Ashkenazim. He went on to explain the significant achievements of the Sephardim in Spain. This took him to the Botticini and Eckstein paper, and mandatory education. In Murray's view, mandatory education may have provided the impetus for elevated Jewish intelligence well before the 800 to 1700 CE timeframe focused on by Cochran and his colleagues.

Murray suggested a "natural selection" process for high IQs was more plausible than the Cochran theory. Murray's argument was rooted in the sharp decline in the numbers of Jews following the Roman conquest and Diaspora (down from roughly 4.5 million Jews to about 1.25 million). He said the decline could not be explained from one million deaths in the Jewish revolts against the Romans, nor by any natural phenomenon such as a plague.

In Murray's view, it was the educational demands to read, discuss, and debate the Torah and Talmud that led to a diminished population. These skills were useless for farmers, and expensive and time-consuming to obtain. As a result, he opined, many of the less talented (lower IQ) and less motivated Jews probably opted out. In this way, natural selection resulted in fewer but smarter Jews in succeeding generations, as the average IQ increased over time.

And while high IQ did not automatically ensure high achievement, Murray believed it substantially altered the odds. In short, genetic self-selection accounted for the higher IQs, and that facilitated disproportionate levels of achievement. Murray would certainly acknowledge that, if his surmise is accurate, it was the culture of Judaism—the premium placed on literacy and the demands of the religion—that led to the genetic natural selection, but for him, given enough generations, it was the genetic selection and higher IQ that mattered.

Murray's argument that Jewish literacy predated, and was a better explanation for, Jewish intelligence than the Cochran theory still rings true today. And the Cochran response, at least the one on the *Commentary*'s website, is unpersuasive. Murray has the better argument, in no small measure because it is based on the Botticini and Eckstein paper and Murray's knowledge of Jewish history and the record of their achievements.

Murray added a codicil that perhaps the inclination and genetic basis for elevated Jewish intelligence predated even the first century Rabbinic dictate. He noted the culling of Jews for the best and brightest during the Babylonian captivity and, before that, perhaps the heavy intellectual demands of Judaism dating from the time of Moses. He acknowledged this last point was speculation, but thought it was worth considering.

Murray makes solid points about culture, but for him genetics is still the core argument. In essence, intelligence is a necessary first condition for greatness and intelligence is largely genetic. Yet in describing the impetus at the heart of natural selection, his candidates (and those of Cochran's and others) seem to consistently point to natural selection driven by the intellectual demands of Torah, Tanakh and Oral Law/Talmud, the Rabbinic imposition of mandatory education and literacy, the culling of the best and brightest in the Babylon captivity, and the anti-Semitic constraints placed on Jews during the Diaspora. All of these arose from circumstances and culture. Consequently, it is not much of a leap to argue that over the course of centuries, what ultimately drove elevated Jewish IQ were a combination of those circumstances and Jewish culture.

Nature is the ultimate pragmatist. It's long-run rule is to propagate whatever works best. Mutations (variations) afford opportunities to find something new that may work "better" than whatever already exits. Anything "more fit" or that "fits better" is more likely to carry on, and what doesn't "fit" tends to recede. So when a particular cultural value such as treasuring education is more effective, over the long run it is more likely to lead to larger families whose genetic heritage arose from "what worked."

A few more points are worth raising. When *The Golden Age* was published, no one had meaningfully linked any individual gene or group of genes to significant elevation of intelligence in a replicated study. After completion of the Human Genome Project in 2003 and its refinements in 2005 and 2007, there were expectations genes for elevated IQ would soon be identified with significant insight as to how they work. To date (2014), that hope has not panned out.

Candidate genes have often not proven linked in subsequent studies. Epigenetics has yielded new complexities and insights, as have nucleosome wrapping, imprinting, and copy number variations, and more. In recent years we have also learned a great deal more about environmental influences and the malleability of IQ. Current claims for breakthroughs that tie individual genes to IQ are ever more modest. That may change as further genetic research makes strides, but new complexities continue to arise, the timeframe recedes, and the more we learn, the further the goal posts seem to get pushed out. Nevertheless, I think we can safely say that while genes and IQ contribute to the Jewish potential for disproportionate achievement, culture contributed both to the natural selection process for those traits and the outsized expression of those talents in the behavior of individual Jews .

To some extent, the Haredim (ultra-Orthodox) help illustrate this point. As mentioned previously, there is no reason to think the 9 to 10 percent of the World's Jews that are Haredim are genetically different— or that their latent intelligence is significantly different—from their fellow Ashkenazim and Sephardim. But their culture does not treasure Enlightenment (Haskalah) values. The Haredim have almost no interest in secular achievements, and little, if any, presence on *The Golden Age* lists of disproportionate high achievers.

Finally, we cannot (yet) directly manage the three billion base pairs in every cell of our being. We cannot turn them on, off, up and down, (except perhaps via future epigenetic tools). Nor can we today replace a gene with a variation we would prefer. Instead, we must play the hand we were dealt.

Genetics offers individuals a palette with more or fewer colors and better or worse brushes and canvases. Some things we might wish to do may not be possible with the brushes, canvases, and colors we have. But even with lesser endowments, some of us may turn out to be a Picasso or Van Gogh, having "overachieved" with our limited resources. Still others with greater gifts will deliver lesser works (akin to my awful paintings in third grade). Endowing an infant with a great paint set means nothing if the child never learns how to use it well. Culture, free will and personal motivation are the main tools we have at our disposal. They have an immense influence on what we do or do not do with the talents we have—and unlike genes, they are within our control.

CHAPTER 5

Culture Shaped by Historical Circumstance

With the passage of time since publication of *The Golden Age*, there have been major advances in genetic science and discoveries made possible by reduced costs for genetic testing. They have been matched by research and significant discoveries about culture and its impact on our lives. I also have the benefit of numerous comments and questions from presentations, conversations, and interviews after the book's release. What would I now say about culture as a primary driver of disproportionate Jewish achievement?

When I began my exploration, my first instinct was that Jewish culture was probably mostly shaped by religion. I was concerned the impetus for high achievement might dissipate as Jews become increasingly secular. As I learned more, I concluded it is more complicated than that. Huge numbers of Jews have long been secular. And for most secular Jews, what I think of as Jewish culture generally remains intact. Most continue to identify and think of themselves as Jews, and they have great respect for Jewish history and culture. Among Jewish high achievers, many are secular. Today I worry more about assimilation than the secularization of Jews.

A further shift in my thinking since *The Golden Age* is that I now add somewhat more weight to the impact of major historical events on Jewish culture. In no small measure, Jewish culture has been shaped by circumstances, and historical events beyond their control and those events greatly influenced how they have lived over the last two thousand years.

Consider, for example, some consequences of the Roman Wars:

— The Roman Conquest and destruction of the Second Temple in ~70 CE ended the era of the Sadducees' dominance of Judaism as an elite priestly religion of Temple sacrifices. They did not believe in the Oral Law. They were thought by the Romans to be complicit in the Jewish rebellion, and because of that, the Sadducees and the Temple were destroyed. The Pharisees (Rabbinic Judaism) survived them. In eclipsing the Sadducees, Rabbinic Judaism dramatically changed the religion and the culture. Over the following centuries, the Oral Law would evolve to become the written Talmud. And while both the Sadducees and the Pharisees promoted literacy, the Sadducees focused on educating the families of the priestly elite. The Pharisees, instead, promoted a more universal literacy. Rabbinic Judaism then imposed mandatory literacy on all Jews—and through that mandate, education became one of Judaism's primary cultural values. It has remained so for two millennia.

— The Roman-imposed Diaspora left Jews stateless for 2,000 years. They had no kings or lords. They had no armies. Instead, they had rabbis, who often served as both religious and civil leaders in their communities. Though Jews sent written inquiries and got answers from religious and legal scholars (the Responsa), there was no centralized authority akin to the Pope, and no Third Temple. Communities selected their own rabbis. Local synagogues often served as community centers and schools. Autonomy was mostly local. Only with the late nineteenth century Dreyfus affair did conventional political leadership begin to emerge, pointing ultimately toward statehood.

— Although Jews lived outside Palestine even before the Roman Conquest, the Diaspora spread nearly all of them around the Middle East, Europe and the Maghreb where they would live as relatively small minority enclaves among the much larger dominant populations. Jews became an international people, communicating and transacting religious, commercial, and family business across the globe. It contributed to their becoming among the world's most sophisticated businessmen of that era.

— Diaspora and mandatory education combined to convert Jews from a tribe of rural farmers and shepherds into an urban people spread over a vast geography. In addition to being religious and legal scholars, Jews became merchants, financiers, tax collectors, entrepreneurs, doctors, attorneys, and to practice many other skilled trades and professions (occupations in which individual skills truly make the difference). In many of these, not only are self-reliance and autonomy possible, they are often fundamental.

— At times, Jews operated at the verges of multiple cultures, such as the Moorish and Catholic cultures of Golden Age Spain. Jews served as intermediaries between them and learned from both. Later, Jewish financiers and merchants such as the Rothschilds did much the same between nation-states, such as France and England. They were trusted neutrals. The Rothschilds operated all over Europe before, during, and after the Napoleonic Wars. The breadth of Jewish exposure to other religions, cultures and ideas was thus remarkable and bordered on unique.

— Diaspora caused most Jews to become multilingual in order to live among the other cultures, pursue their work, and survive. Today, scientists say being multilingual can help sharpen the mind.

— Diaspora likely helped nudge Jews away from the Biblical prohibition of "usury" in its original sense (charging interest for borrowed money). Instead of loaning money to relatives and neighbors on adjacent farms for no interest, loans were now required for commerce, sometimes internationally. The use of someone else's money could no longer be free. Judaism changed its religious law to reflect this rational reality. In similar manner, forgiveness of loans on the seventh anniversary was abandoned.

— The Talmudic process, with all of its debates and interpretations, helped Jewish Law evolve as rational rules in light of changed circumstances.

— It is admittedly conjecture, but functioning in international urban settings may have also have further encouraged rationality. Survival and success in dealing with multiple cultures is likely to have been much more effective, drawing on pragmatism, diplomacy, and logic rather than parochial traditions, customs, and dogmatism.

— Finally, the demands of literacy not only provided Jews with the ability to pursue intellectually challenging and lucrative careers, it may also have caused many of the less able and less motivated Jews to leave the religion. Thus it may well have resulted in a natural selection process that culled Judaism for the best and brightest.

The Enlightenment and Emancipation

— The Enlightenment arose at the end of Europe's devastating and more than 120-year period of religious warfare. It opened up dialogue between Catholics and Protestants, and a shared exploration of science, reason, individualism and secular advancement. Not only did it help reshape the views of Catholics and Protestants toward each other, it brought Jews into those conversations. This was revolutionary. Without the Enlightenment, and the Jewish Enlightenment (Haskalah) that followed, there likely would have been no Jewish Reform movement in Europe, nor would there have been the Jewish Emancipation.

— Napoleon singlehandedly changed Jewish history. He emancipated French Jews and launched counterpart efforts over most of Europe. That, plus the Enlightenment and Jewish Enlightenment (Haskalah), encouraged Western Europe's Jews to enter the secular world. Central and Western European Jews were later joined by millions of Eastern European Jews who fled the pogroms of Russia's Pale.

Anti-Semitism, Oppression, and the Holocaust

— Nearly unceasing anti-Semitism over 2,000 years pushed Jews to perform and to survive on their own. They had to become entrepreneurial and professional. They had to survive by their wits and skills. They could count on none but their own.

— As Eric Hobsbawm said in his October 2005 paper "Benefits of Diaspora," (See Part 2), with the advent of Emancipation, given equal rights, at least in theory, a certain degree of unease in relations between Jews and gentiles has proved historically useful." His view was that even after Emancipation, tensions continued, and those tensions helped stir Jews to disproportionate levels of achievement. The interaction of a perceived hostile environment and Jewish culture contributed to the performance.

Immigration to America

— America gave Jews hope and a home. Far from perfect, it was at least a haven and it provided immense opportunities to succeed and thrive. A Jewish culture that treasured education, entrepreneurship, professional skills, and drive found a home where those cultural values were encouraged and reinforced.

Many of the events and circumstances I've just described were beyond the immediate control of Jews. Yet Jews helped shape those events. And it was the evolving Jewish culture that helped convert many of the challenges into opportunities to survive and, on occasion, flourish.

Among other areas in which my thinking is now more informed are the advances in genetics and genetic testing. We now know so much more about the Jewish people. We can confirm a significant Middle Eastern heritage for Ashkenazis and genetic linkages between them, the Sephardim, Mizrahim, the Haredim, and most other groups of Jews.

We know more about the differences between these four groups and the demographic changes going on within them. Some are growing, others are in decline. If current trends continue, it is likely to adversely affect the future of disproportionate Jewish achievement.

Finally, in recent years, we have learned much more about the interplay of nature and nurture. They seem ever less a dichotomy and ever more to be interacting forces.

Defining Culture

So let's first revisit what was meant by culture:

— Random House Dictionary provides two useful definitions of culture: "The behaviors and beliefs characteristic of a particular social, ethnic or age group; and in anthropology, the sum total of ways of living built up by a group of human beings and transmitted from one generation to another."

— In his book *The Wealth and Poverty of Nations,* Professor David Landes of Harvard University defined culture as the "inner values and attitudes that guide a population." He says, "If we learn anything from the history of economic development, it is that culture makes all the difference."

Jews are not monolithic. Differences in beliefs are not just tolerated, but considered healthy. Followers of Conservative, Reform, Orthodox, Kabbalist, Reconstructionist, Hasidic, and other past Jewish denominations (Sadducees, Essenes and Pharisees) have disagreed, sometimes vehemently, but most of them have a framework of shared views derived over their 4,000- year heritage. On balance, they agree much more than they disagree. In the same way that individual Native American tribes have differences but share a common heritage and culture, so do "mainstream" Jews.

And while Jews share values and beliefs with other cultures, theirs is a unique and distinctive combination.

The fourteen sections that immediately follow here describe elements of Jewish culture I believe have contributed to the Jewish "need to achieve." They are my own views based on what Jews have said and written about themselves, and have communicated to me personally, as well as what I have deduced from my research.

Ethical Monotheism

The first to believe in a single God, the Jewish conception of ethical monotheism is their gift to us all. From it came the Old Testament and much of Western civilization. Christianity and Islam now encompass half the world's people. Both began with Judaism.

David S. Ariel, president of Cleveland College of Jewish Studies, says: "There is no one authoritative Jewish conception of God, although all Jewish thinkers agree that God is one and indivisible... Judaism presents two interconnected sacred myths.... The first presents God as transcendent...a fearsome God who judges the world.... The other...views God as an accessible personal being...a nurturing and comforting parent...."

Whether transcendent or personal, both conceptions imply an absolute connection between ethical behavior and divine action. For Babylonians, Greeks, Romans, and other pagans, the "gods" were capricious, dealing a random, arbitrary fate to humans. As Ariel says, "The moral God of the universe is the fundamental axiom of Jewish belief." Human lives are not shaped by unpredictable, mercurial gods, but by their own actions. In Judaism, actions have consequences—a belief that bolsters achievement.

Progress

"In the beginning..." The first three words in the Bible envision a single point (a "big bang?") from which history began. Time is an arrow, not a circle. History does not repeat for Jews as it does for Hindus and Buddhists. Eastern passivity is transcended. Islam ("submission") and Inshah'Allah ("God willing") involve a theistic determinism most Jews reject. As Paul Johnson wrote in *A History of the Jews*, "No people ... ever insisted more firmly than the Jews that history has a purpose and humanity a destiny." Jews believe in a future different from and better than the past, and that God has given them a role in shaping that future. That is a powerful motivation to become engaged in making things better.

Free Will, Choice, Action, and Accountability

Faith and action are cherished in Jewish culture, but faith does not trump action. Admission to heaven is not based on faith, as it is in some religions. Choice and action are what counts. In the words of the ancient rabbis, "Everything is foreseen, yet freedom of choice is given." God creates options, but does not direct one's responses. From this flow freedom and accountability, a linkage that both ennobles and inspires as it mitigates victimhood. Almost no culture has more basis for feeling persecuted—and Jews do not forget their tortured history—but they rarely demonstrate the propensity of some cultures to see themselves as victims deserving of an entitlement. They take responsibility for themselves. Perhaps no comment on The Golden Age book tour was greeted with more heads consistently nodding in agreement than, "For most Jews, it's what you do in this life that matters!" That shared value gives urgency to one's life and endeavors.

Rationality, Modernism, and Verges

Though some Jewish denominations are traditional, even backward-looking, mainstream Judaism, particularly since the Jewish Emancipation, is pragmatic and forward-looking. "What works?" "What makes sense?" "How can this problem be solved?" As Johnson said in *A History of the Jews*, "Jews were the first rationalizers in world history. This...was to turn Jews into problem solving businessmen." "Above all, the Jews taught us how to rationalize the unknown."

Great Jewish thinkers from the Middle Ages to the age of Jewish Enlightenment, including Maimonides, Spinoza, and Mendelssohn, were rationalists. In some senses, the Talmud is the ever-changing application of Jewish Law to new circumstances as they arise. The commentary and responses are the rational process of great Talmudic scholars integrating differing points of view, debating them and thinking through the best way to deal with those new circumstances. In that sense, the Talmud is a body of work that will never be final, but will serve to help Judaism deal with the future.

Jews, for example, rationalized charging interest for loans among themselves long before Christians did. Islam still struggles with the issue. Thus Jews could practice finance when others could not. Dispersed from Argentina to India and North America to China, Jews had networks of family and "landsmen" around the world they could work with and trust. This was a huge advantage in international trade.

Throughout the Diaspora, Jews lived on what Pulitzer Prize-winning historian Daniel Boorstin called "verges." He attributed a great deal of American creativity and success to the country's being a place where different cultures, technologies, and political views encountered one another (at the "verges"). Each experienced interactions impossible in their own insular worlds. The encounters challenged their thinking, and therein stimulated change and growth. "In ancient, more settled nations, uniformity was idealized.... The American situation was different. The creativity, the hope of the nation was in its verges."

No culture has experienced more verges than Jews as they traversed the world. Thomas Sowell's book, *Migrations and Cultures*, speaks of Jews during Spain's Golden Age "standing at the crossroads of two great civilizations (the Moorish Islamic and Spanish Catholic worlds), Jews were peculiarly well situated to deal in the ideas and cultures of both...to advance themselves culturally and materially....They received knowledge from different directions (which)...stimulated their own thinking and (the) development of...Jewish culture...Maimonides was a product of such cultural crosscurrents."

Jews processed new ideas by integrating dissimilar facts and cultures and developed new insights that added to their collective knowledge and capabilities. Few cultures are as open to new ideas, as pragmatic about change, and so inclined to adopt solutions that work (or in Darwinian terms, solutions that "fit"). The never-ending development of Talmud, the resolution of usury, and the end of loan forgiveness after seven years are small examples of adaptation to changed circumstances and practical solutions to the problems at hand.

Tolerance for Competing Views

As the title of a collection of Jewish quotations says, *Two Jews, Three Opinions*. In his book *What Is a Jew*, Rabbi Morris N. Kertzer notes, "The most distinctive feature of the Jewish religion has been its hospitality to differences. In all of Jewish Law will be found both an austere interpretation and a liberal one—and the rabbis have ruled 'both opinions are the word of the living God.'" Hillel the Elder (70 to 10 BCE) and his contemporary Shammai (50 BCE to 10 CE) disagreed strongly about

Judaism. And though many prefer Hillel's views, Shammai's are also accepted as correct. The Talmud, in its commentary, represents something of a debate with different commentators offering up differing views.

As one illustration of this, consider the frequent role of Jews as leaders on different, often opposing, sides of major issues. Nobel Laureate Paul Samuelson was a leading Keynesian when he wrote his classic college textbook *Economics*. Fellow Jew Milton Friedman, also a Nobel Laureate, became the foremost economist to discredit much of the Keynesian dogma.

Paul Ehrlich made his reputation forecasting a dismal Malthusian future: the world would become overwhelmed by its burgeoning population. Ehrlich lost his famous $1,000 bet in a ten-year test of his hypothesis to economist and fellow Jew Julian Simon, whose outlook was decidedly more optimistic. Marx and Trotsky were among prominent Jews to theorize and devote their lives to Communism, yet among their fellow Jews were some of the most successful capitalist entrepreneurs of all time.

Noam Chomsky is a critic of nearly everything done by the Israeli government and the United States. Two of his constant adversaries are Alan Dershowitz and David Horowitz. At *The New York Times*, Paul Krugman and Thomas Friedman were strident critics of President George W. Bush; William Kristol and David Brooks often countered, presenting their own strong case for a more conservative view. J. Robert Oppenheimer ultimately opposed nuclear weapons, while former colleague, Edward Teller, developed the hydrogen bomb and supported the Star Wars missile defense program. Herbert Marcuse, I.F. Stone, and many fellow Jews strongly criticized the United States, often defending Socialism, while Norman Podhoretz, Charles Krauthammer, and other conservatives defended America and argued for a more muscular approach to the threats it faces.

In the end, such contrasts demolish simple-minded anti-Semitic stereotypes of Jews as monolithic, single-issue advocates of one dogma or another. On the contrary, what seems to engage the Jewish mind in an energetic involvement on all sides of an issue. The debates and differences of opinion are often vigorous, sometimes verbally aggressive, but rarely physically violent, unlike those that occur, for example, between the Sunnis and Shiites. Jews acknowledge that there may be more than one right answer, and are often tolerant of opposing views.

The drive to explore all sides of most issues, and the willingness and skill to debate them openly, is pervasive. Strong convictions and a willingness to communicate are as important as the tolerance for the views of others.

Assertiveness and Verbal Skills

Abraham challenged God. When God said he would destroy Sodom and Gomorrah for their wickedness. Abraham responded: "Will you actually sweep away the righteous with the wicked? Maybe there are fifty righteous people in the city.... Shouldn't the judge of all the earth do what is just?"

For most Jews, standing up and speaking out is valued—to see a wrong and not work to change it is irresponsible. Jews have a sense of duty and confidence about sticking up for their beliefs.

Such assertiveness is complemented by the premium placed on verbal skills and verbal self-confidence. One must be capable of thinking and reaching conclusions, and that skill must be coupled with a willingness to air those views, have them challenged, and challenge others in return. Yeshivas and Talmudic education stress thought and debate. Such skills were seen by some classmates to confer an unfair advantage on author Scott Turow when he was a student at Harvard Law School.

Bar mitzvahs and bat mitzvahs transition boys and girls from childhood to adulthood. In both ceremonies, the thirteen-year-old must stand before family and friends to publicly assert, "Today, I am a man" or "woman."

Speaking out and speaking well is important in Jewish culture. And in the significant numbers of Jews who practice in major law firms, hold political office, work in journalism, literature, the media, and entertainment, we see these skills manifested every day. In fact, there is a cultural expectation of verbal skill.

Education

When Muhammad called Jews "the People of the Book," the book in question already included all thirty-nine books of the Hebrew Bible, plus much of the Oral Law written into the numerous volumes of Talmud and Midrash. After Romans destroyed the Second Temple, killed a million Jews, and dispersed most of the rest to scattered small enclaves around the world, the need to write things down, and the ability to read and understand this trove, became fundamental to keeping the religion, the tribe, and the culture alive.

Jews thus became the first to demand that parents educate their children. Mandated when most Jews were still farmers, and well before the invention of the printing press, this was an expensive, time-consuming proposition for an end result—literacy—of little benefit to farmers.

But over the centuries that followed, as Jews became urban, and as their brethren moved to distant locales, literacy took on increasing importance while conferring the capability to work in careers substantially more challenging and lucrative than farming.

The duty to educate and be educated was absolute. In the twelfth century, the Jewish philosopher Maimonides , said, "Appoint teachers for the children in every country, province and city. In any city that does not have a school, excommunicate the people...until they get teachers for the children." This value was reinforced with the smartest and best educated Jews serving as rabbis. For much of 2,000 years, rabbis were more than simply religious leaders; in most communities they were the local civil authority and the revered head of the community. Intellectual skill, more than physical skill, conferred prominence.

Though circumstances made education difficult in the Pale of Russia in the 1700s and 1800s, a generally illiterate Jewish population still craved learning. Thomas Sowell's book, *Ethnic America*, notes that roughly half the Eastern European Jews were illiterate when they arrived in the United States. Once here, however, they "seized upon free schools, libraries and settlement houses in America with a tenacity...seldom approached by others. They not only crowded into public schools, but adult night schools as well (after long days of work).... And still, the Jewish daily newspaper, *Forward*, castigated them for not doing enough."

Though destitute and testing poorly on IQ tests when they arrived from the Pale, "Jews rose to have not only higher incomes than other Americans, but also more education and higher IQs. By the 1950s, more than one-fourth of Jewish males had four or more years of college, while less than 10 percent of the U.S. population...had that much education.... As of 1990, more than half of all Jews over age twenty-five were college graduates with 30 percent also completing postgraduate study. By contrast, 21 percent of the corresponding...(U.S.) white population had completed college with 9 percent completing postgraduate studies. Further, Jews not only have more education, but better education—from higher quality colleges and careers in more demanding and remunerative fields such as law, medicine and science."

The same thing happened elsewhere where Jews had the opportunity. In Australia, "Among young people between the ages of sixteen and twenty-two, nearly three-quarters of the Jews were full-time students, compared to about 20 percent of...the general population." In Argentina, "While Jews were only about 1 percent of the...population in 1980, they were 20 percent of the university student body." In early twentieth-century Germany, "one fourth of all law students and medical students…were Jews, though Jews were only 1 percent of the population." And in the Prussia of 1911–1912, where five of every 10,000 male Catholics were university students, (and thirteen of 10,000 Protestants), sixty-seven of every 10,000 Jews were in university.

These high levels of education, including advanced degrees from the best schools, allowed Jews to practice demanding scientific, literary, education, artistic, professional, and entrepreneurial careers. It facilitated their high achievement.

Jews continue to invest in their pursuit of learning, and thus in themselves. David Leonhardt's May 11, 2011 *Sunday New York Times Magazine* story "Is Your Religion Your Financial Destiny," with its chart akin to the one shown in item 106 – Part2, reaffirms that fact.

Family

Marriage and family have long been indispensable in Jewish life. A man without a wife was seen to be "without joy, without blessing, and without good." In *Ethnic America*, Sowell said, "Jews are more likely to marry…than others and less likely to divorce." Jewish fathers were also less likely to desert their families.

Jewish fathers have a duty to support their children, educate them and teach them a trade, and children have a duty to honor their parents. Scores of Jewish family rites link religious duties to love of home. These traditions strengthen both home and religion. Family support was critical in an environment where discrimination reinforced the need to take care of one's own. Traditions such as Shabbat (the Friday night and Saturday celebration of the Sabbath) kept the family close, while high expectations encouraged and pushed children to study and defer immediate gratification for longer-term goals. While I may have been out partying with friends on a Friday night in Spokane, my Jewish friends were home with their families engaged in a spirited conversation over dinner.

Jewish families also inculcated a drive to succeed in their young. Both "Italians and Jews," notes Sowell, "have had highly stable families, but the values of the Jewish family drive the individual toward upward mobility."

In many Jewish families, the day-to-day job of raising kids, instilling values, and encouraging academic performance has been the job of a loving—even demanding—Jewish mother. In his biography, Sherwin Nuland, author of *How We Die*, reflected on how vitally important his mother was. He perceived that she lived only for him. Even organized crime figure Meyer Lansky found his mother critically important in his life. She was the one person he did not want to disappoint.

Healthy Diet and Moderation in Drink

Traditional Jewish culture follows kosher dietary practices arising from Biblical injunctions about what Jews should eat and drink, and how these things should be prepared and served. All vegetables are kosher. Pork is prohibited, as are certain kinds of seafood. Blood must be removed, and dairy products must not be served with meats. Because they are creatures of God, animals must be killed in a humane fashion. Their death should not be taken lightly. For non-Jews, some kosher practices seem strange. Presumably, safety concerns about eating pork and shellfish 2,000 years ago are no longer warranted.

Orthodox Jews would respond that safer food is irrelevant. The Torah calls for kosher. Kosher "disciplines Jews toward holiness" in satisfying the basic need for food. It cultivates respect for the distinctive requirements of being Jewish, and once more we are drawn back to the Covenant. God requires it, and being Jewish means being different.

Many Jews enjoy alcohol, but most avoid excess. Recent research suggests there may be a genetic basis for such restraint. Drinking in moderation is also both healthy and a survival skill. Michael Barone has noted that among all immigrant groups, the rates of violent crime and alcoholism were lowest among Jews.

In his book *Ethnic America*, Sowell notes, "Like the Italians, Jews served wine with meals but seldom became drunkards. Drunkenness, boisterousness, or recklessness induced by drink could easily have become fatal in the precarious situation of most European Jews." He goes further in *Migrations and Culture*, noting, "...the unusually low rates of alcoholism...found in studies of Jews in Poland, Canada, Prussia, Australia, and the United States."

Skills, Autonomy, and Independence

Diaspora Jews were rarely farmers or landlords, and they were unwelcome in many established trades and industries controlled by locals. Still, they had to survive. If they were to provide for their families in a hostile world, skills were vital. Even those who dislike you will pay for your services if what you do is valuable and you do it better than other available sources.

Historically, Jews shied away from large organizations. Anti-Semitism made it unwise to trust the goodwill of others or serve an institution where a change in sentiment could put you at risk. Better to control your own destiny and succeed or fail based on your own performance.

The major paths open to Jews were the professions (such as doctor, lawyer, scientist, or entertainer) and working as merchants, financiers, and entrepreneurs. In each such field, skills are distinguishable and excellence is valued. Professions typically allow one to function outside large organizations and relocate if threats arise. Merchant and middleman skills were viewed as "beneath" most locals, while finance and lending were needed but prohibited by some religions. Jewelry and precious metals had the further advantage of being compact relative to their value. They could be moved quickly and quietly if circumstances warranted.

Jews created new industries where there were no established barriers. Their European legacy in the clothing industry had no peer in early nineteenth-century America, where they created the ready-to-wear industry from scratch. The feature-motion-picture business never existed before Jews started or shaped every major studio. More recently, they have created a huge number of new high-tech companies. When banks and law firms were already staffed by old-line, white-shoe Gentiles, Jews started their own firms—and later their own country clubs as well—when they found those doors closed to them.

Even the religion embodies autonomy. There is no pope, Christ, or priest serving as a religious intervener between the individual Jew and God, and each synagogue selects its own rabbi.

Hard Work, Tenacity, and Excellence

Jews rarely had family wealth to fall back on. Parents had to instill awareness that life was serious, play was not a priority, and determination mattered. Tenacity and superior talent made you valuable and discrimination costly. As Johnson has noted in his *History of the Jews*, "Where are the Edomites? Where are the ancient Hellenes and the Romans, the Byzantines, the Franks, the Mamelukes and the Ottomans? They have vanished into time, irrevocably. But the Jews are still in Hebron...Hebron reflects the long, tragic history of the Jews and their unrivaled capacity to survive their misfortunes." He goes further: "The Jews are the most tenacious people in history."

As a child, I was told a good definition of maturity was accepting (or believing in) the importance of deferred gratification. In part, this meant investing the time, energy and hard work towards the objective of accomplishing much more in the long term. Clearly, the Jews have believed in deferred gratification.

Determination and hard work were complemented with superior skills, and that excellence provided a sense of achievement. Financially rewarding, it was also a ticket to respect. But more, it was psychological compensation for the world's false view that you might be unworthy. In any meritocracy, Jews excelled.

Willingness to Be Different

The Biblical story of the Jews began with Abraham's willingness to be different. In the Covenant, "...the Lord said to Abraham, get thee out of thy country and from thy kindred, and from thy father's house, unto a land that I will show thee." It was an astonishing thing for a person to do 4,000 years ago. Abraham packed up and left virtually everything he knew. He had confidence in his God and in himself, enough to leave his home and go where God directed him.

Jews have followed seemingly strange religious practices. They often dressed and ate differently, spoke their own languages, kept to themselves, performed work no one else was willing to do, and generally refused to assimilate. This was not so much an accident of taste as a code of religious mandates keeping the tribe together—and apart from others. It lessened the likelihood of assimilation for a dispersed people. And while there was a price to be paid, the code survived for thousands of years. It only began to slacken with the growth of the Reform movement in Europe and the United States, and the subsequent shift to secularism. Meanwhile, among some of the ultra-Orthodox Jews, separateness, if anything, has grown. Stephan G. Bloom's *Postville*, written in 2000, offers a relatively recent (if notorious) illustration of this in Postville, Iowa.

Being perceived as "different" can be as liberating as it is uncomfortable. While the comfort of being in tune with the larger society may be absent, being different conditions Jews to stand apart and to live by their principles and their wits. Being viewed as an outsider only spurs a compulsion to demonstrate superiority, thereby overcoming negative stereotypes through superior performance.

In 1905, when Einstein proposed that the speed of light is constant, and because of that, both time and motion are relative to the observer, the concept was so revolutionary, so remarkably different from conventional wisdom, that years passed before his notions were accepted. $E=mc^2$ was equally revolutionary and hard to comprehend in the Isaac Newton paradigm of the times. Indeed, though Einstein developed four papers in 1905 and completed his general theory of relativity by 1916, it wasn't until 1922 that he received a Nobel Prize, and that was principally for his work on the photoelectric effect. Indeed, virtually every Nobel is an award for being different, for having thought through a problem in a new way that yields dazzling new insights.

Money

Jewish culture comes in for a good deal of both respect and derision when the subject is money. While a Scot may be kidded about being frugal in a charming sort of way, Jewishness can elicit a rather more broad-brush, often pejorative, treatment. To some, Jews are miserly or hoarding. Others see them as ostentatious. Still others see them using money as an instrument of control. Envy and anti-Semitic stereotypes come into play. Often missed is the disproportionate philanthropy of Jews to secular causes.

In a meritocracy, however, money is a reward for success, a scorecard of achievement, a proxy for status, and an insurance policy for survival. It goes to those with talent who work hard to earn it. It also provides the means to survive if, as in the 1930s, there is risk to you and your family. As a very concentrated and mobile form of wealth it provides a modicum of security in a very insecure world. One reason for Jewish involvement in diamonds and jewelry is the transportability of that form of wealth to augment security.

Thus, threatened for as long as Jews have been, wealth may be seen as insurance and a way to help compensate for discrimination.

Finally, money is the tool for providing charity. Many Jews feel a special duty to help those in need. Wealth provides the means to fulfill this responsibility.

In the end, money is more important in Jewish culture, and in more ways than for many other cultures.

While the above paragraphs are valid, I cannot end this discussion about money without also acknowledging the many Jews for which money has not been nearly so important. A good friend recently reminded me of the large number of Jewish professionals, such as physicians, teachers, and scientists—including most Nobel Prize winners—who have been remarkable achievers and never sought great riches. They have accomplished much, benefited many, and never become wealthy.

Justice and Charity

In 1987, Thomas Sowell wrote a remarkable book titled *Conflict of Visions*. In it he posited the notion of two prevailing social or political visions. Both want the best for everyone but differ sharply in their view of how the world works and how best to effect change. The "unconstrained view" sees a world where people can intervene directly to bring about desired social goals, and results can be directly prescribed. If you see an injustice, you can and should intervene to make things better.

The "constrained view" sees a nuanced world, complex beyond comprehension. It shares the unconstrained view's value for what is being sought, but sees most interventions as counterproductive, yielding unintended consequences that typically make things worse rather than better.

For those in the constrained camp, the unconstrained view is well meaning but flawed and elitist. It attempts to manipulate levers that don't work the way they are thought to work. For the constrained, the world is often self-corrective (Adam Smith's "invisible hand," the body's natural healing process, etc.). Intervention, if drawn upon at all, should complement the natural order rather than challenge it.

For the unconstrained, the constrained view is uncaring and aloof, ignorant of what can be achieved and, in not intervening, wrongfully abdicating responsibility. While the analogy may do a grave disservice to Sowell, the unconstrained might find and give fish to the poor because they are starving; the constrained instead might help them make a fishing rod.

Perhaps arising from the long history of anti-Semitism, Jewish culture strongly identifies with the underdog. Furthermore, many Jews believe they have a duty to care for and demand justice for others, as much as for themselves. And in *tikkun olam*, they were "chosen" to take action. The world and injustice will not heal themselves. "If not me, who? If not now, when?"

Jews are remarkably generous. Only 2 percent of the U.S. population, they were nineteen (38 percent) of *Business Week*'s 2007 list of the fifty most generous philanthropists over the previous five years. Those nineteen donated almost $23 billion over the five years to mostly secular causes. In 2010, Jews were five of the top six philanthropists and 19 of 53 named by the Chronicle of Philanthropy and in 2014 they were 18 of the top 50. Since "Temple times," the kuppah, or collection box, has been the community welfare box to which Jews were obligated to donate. Many Jews think of charity as an item to budget, just as they would the mortgage payment. It is an obligation (*tzedakah*), not an afterthought. One reason for accumulating great wealth is to help those in need.

In short, one sees in the activist liberal orientation of many Jews the consequence of long-standing cultural values akin to Sowell's "unconstrained view."[7] By intervening, they established trade unions, helped get Blacks the right to vote, cured polio, developed birth control pills, split the atom, pioneered psychotherapy, and effected thousands of other interventions that benefit us all.

———

With the Emancipation, Enlightenment and Reform movement, what was a long, interesting, and somewhat impressive performance by Jews exploded into an era of phenomenal secular achievement. Whether it arose from predominantly cultural or genetic origins, or some mix of both, there is simply no question that from roughly 1820 on, Jews moved from being an interesting footnote in the history of high achievers to center stage. Over the last 200 years, no group has accomplished as much relative to its population.

---

7. In his book, *Why Are Jews Liberal?*, Norman Podhoretz makes the point that for many secular Jews, being liberal has essentially become their religion. This despite, the fact, he says, that some secular liberal values directly conflict with values expressed in the Torah, Tanakh, and Talmud. In discussing Podhoretz' book with a close Jewish friend who is secular and liberal, he offered up the interesting notion that Jews have simply found liberal societies (and countries) to be the safest places on earth for them. That, he says, is because such places are so much less likely to be strongly anti-Semitic (think Golden Age Holland for Spinoza and other Jews as well as North America from 1654 on). In essence the idea is that liberal values have grown over time to become central and hospitable for Jews not only because they are consistent with some interpretations of *tzedakah* and *tikkun olam*, but also because they are associated with the safety of the Jewish people.

CHAPTER 6

A Summing Up: Genetics, Culture and Jewish Achievement

For many readers, a synopsis at this point may serve as a useful distillation—a summary of the major facts and analysis from the preceding Chapters and much of the Chronology that follows.

As author, my purpose in writing this book has been to present the most complete and objective compilation of the major facts and arguments surrounding the question of Jewish achievement. I sought to understand and clearly explain why Jews have proven to be the most disproportionate group of high achievers of the last 200 years.

In the end, of course, I have come to my own conclusions based on those facts, theories and analyses. I believe the strongest case squarely favors Jewish culture as the most important force behind the performance. I am not saying genetics do not matter. They do, but the more important force is cultural.

So what have I learned from this review of nature, nurture, and the recent dramatic progress in genetic and cultural research? What came of my exploration of the old arguments and the new research?

First, the genetic basis of the Jewish people is now clearer and more firmly established than ever before. This is a consequence of the Human Genome Project and the research that followed. Ashkenazis are now known, for a fact, to be genetically linked to their Sephardim and Mizrahim brethren. They are not Khazars who migrated west from Central Asia.

But at the same time, and due in part to genetic research, it's becoming evident that the dichotomy between nature and nurture is false. It is almost never just one or the other. Much more often, they interact. There are elements of both. Each affects and shapes the other.

The emerging science of epigenetics, largely developed following the Human Genome Project, has produced compelling evidence that while our genes may remain unchanged, several regulatory mechanisms—only recently understood—can turn some genes on and off or up and down. At times, these regulatory changes arise from straightforward environmental circumstances such as starvation, poor diet, chemicals, and other phenomena. Other times, it is as simple as a mother's warmth and caring, the involvement (or not) of a father in the life of a child, and many other influences we generally associate with nurturing.

While a clear and persuasive genetic case for traits such as intelligence was expected to emerge from the 2003 completion of the Human Genome Project, instead we learned the genetic basis for our traits is orders of magnitude more complex than was expected. Height, for example, may be influenced by perhaps 1,000 genes. And, no single gene is now thought to influence more than 1 to 3 percent of intelligence. Perhaps as much as a third of our genes are involved in the development of the brain. We have learned of the regulatory role of what was earlier thought to be vestigial "junk DNA." It is not "junk" at all. Instead, it is active in gene regulation. Similarly, epigenetics, copy number variations, imprinting, nucleosome wrapping and unwrapping, and other genetic phenomena affect the expression of our genes. Our understanding of the genetics of traits is lagging far behind where we thought we'd be by now. It seems almost ironic that more than ten years after the completion of the Human Genome Project, the best data we have on the genetics of traits are the result of the earlier twenty-year (1979 to 1999) study of identical twins raised apart.

Among the strongest arguments for genetics as the major driver of disproportionate Jewish achievement are the ones derived from the impressive research of Botticini and Eckstein, whose work has been summarized in many academic papers and in their book *The Chosen Few.* In short, they say that Rabbinic Judaism's demands for literacy following the destruction of the Second Temple in 70 AD led many Jews to opt out of the religion. Education was simply too expensive and time consuming for a tribe of mostly rural farmers who needed their offspring working beside them in the fields rather than in the classroom studying Torah and Talmud. The subsequent large decline in the numbers of Jews in the world could only be accounted for by the opting out of huge numbers of Jews to become Christians, later Moslems, and sometimes secular.

In essence, Jews self-selected for the best and the brightest, ending up as a unique urban tribe capable of pursuing intellectually demanding and rewarding careers. Particularly following the Enlightenment, the Jewish Emancipation, and the birth of the European Jewish Reform Movement, they had the wherewithal to become disproportionately high achievers. It is very likely that a form of Darwinian self-selection had a role in this outcome. Still, I would point out that it was the cultural value of the huge premium Jews placed on literacy and education that drove this culling for the best and brightest. Said differently, nurture (Jewish cultural values) led to nature, the possible culling that yielded a genetic predisposition for greater intelligence.

And yet it is not surprising that even people with highly similar genetics and potential can end up dramatically different in terms of how their lives are shaped and lived. The Jewish Haredim (Ultra-Orthodox) are mostly Ashkenazi—but in disdaining the Enlightenment, the Jewish Emancipation, the Jewish Reform movement, and a secular lifestyle, most American and Israeli Haredim have substantially less education, and tend to be closed-minded about evolution, the age of the universe, the literal truth of Torah, and much more. They also have much higher rates of poverty, and only rarely, if at all, are they counted among those whose human achievements are celebrated in the sense I described in *The Golden Age of Jewish Achievement.*

Said differently, a predisposition is simply not predestination. Ask any overachiever. Ask any person who overcame a deficit of any kind to become competent or outstanding in pursuing something important to him or her. It is in that sense that culture (nurture) can and often does trump genetics (nature). I talk more about this in the next section, *Further Reflections on Culture.*

Based on my compilation of the debate surrounding Jewish achievement, I believe the following cultural elements have had the greatest bearing on the track record of the disproportionate Jewish achievement:

— The huge premium Jews have placed on literacy and education for more than 2,000 years. Jews graduate from college at more than twice the national average. The data from other countries is similar. Jews tend to attend the best schools, get better grades and go on to pursue productive careers.

— Most Jews believe it is what you do in this life that matters. In that sense, many are driven to make a difference during their lifetime. They do not believe that a particular set of beliefs will get them into heaven. Every time I spoke about The Golden Age, I raised this point. And every time I would look out to see most of the heads in the audience nodding in agreement.

— Most Jews believe in progress. They are not passive, nor resigned. They think they have a duty to help improve things. They believe in free will and intend to exercise their minds and body to advance the ball in the direction(s) they feel are important.

— Jews have long maintained very strong family values. They divorce less. They are mostly members of two-parent families. The mother is loving, strong, demanding, and supportive. The father is equally engaged. Most religious holiday events, even for secular Jews, are major family events, as is Shabbat (Friday night dinner). Loyalty to family and kin is highly valued.

— Jewish lifestyle is generally healthy in terms of diet, and the approach to drugs and alcohol is moderate. An alcoholic Jew is a rarity. Kosher conformance has served many purposes, but historically, one of them has been to mandate healthy eating habits.

— Jews usually demonstrate high levels of self-discipline (deferred gratification). We see it in their diet, their commitment to formal education, their careers, and their drive to achieve.

— They encourage and develop their verbal skills and the inclination to speak up, make an argument, debate, and disagree if they feel strongly. Generally, reticence has not been esteemed. The Talmud is a religious tract, but it is also essentially an ongoing academic debate over the evolution of Jewish Law in light of changing circumstances.

— Jews stand up for what they believe in. They have "grit." They champion causes important to them. Wallflowers they are not!

— Ethical behavior has been inculcated in Jews by the Torah and Talmud. God demands it.

— Rationality is also embodied in the Talmud and in the lives of most Jews. One must deal with the facts on the ground and adapt. The Diaspora made anything less than this approach unfeasible. For most of 2,000 years, Jews had to exist as a small minority among other cultures, coexisting with countless other peoples, tribes, and cultures with substantially different beliefs and native languages. Staying alive demanded rationality and adaptability.

— Jews almost never adopt the mentality of victims deserving of an entitlement. God knows they have more right than most to have taken on that view, but they do not. They do not believe they are entitled. If anything, they help others who are downtrodden.

— And in the same vein, Jews feel a strong sense of duty to each other and to those less fortunate. Jews are among the most charitable and philanthropic of people.

In Part 2 of this book, you will find plenty of expert opinions that support these values as behavioral influences. You will also find entries that contradict this thinking, or suggest other reasons for Jewish achievement. One thing is beyond debate: throughout history, Jews have been faced with circumstances and adversity beyond their control, but to which they had to react. And react they did. Their culture and strength of character helped them to not only survive, but emerge as the most accomplished people of the last 200 years.

Perhaps in that is yet another lesson. We all seem to assume adversity and stress are negative influences in our lives and those of our parents, grandparents and offspring. It is not so simple. Those dangers and threats are challenges, as was anti-Semitism. Adversity may, instead, be an essential driver that helped push Jews to be high achievers.

There is nothing particularly Jewish about any or all of the cultural values celebrated above.

We can learn from their story.

CHAPTER 7

Further Reflections on Culture

In the Preface, I recounted my story of the closure of Spokane's public swimming pools for fear of polio when I was a child. Salk and Sabin were the high achievers who freed us from that scourge. They epitomize the reason for placing great value on individual human achievement—and for writing to encourage more of it.

Among the principal causes for Jewish achievement, the previous material makes the case that culture—namely what we as humans and members of groups believe, think, feel, fear, hate, and love—is a vital determinant of whether we do or do not aspire to achieve. It need not be achievement at the level of those in *The Golden Age,* but it is an urge to make things better, and to lead meaningful lives.

Our individual views of how the world works, what we can and cannot do, and our motivations, all arise in no small measure from our cultures.

Thomas Robert Malthus was an eighteenth century pessimist. His 1798 "Essay on the Principal of Population" predicted inevitable doom; population would soon outgrow its food supply. Despite Malthus being proved wrong, Paul Ehrlich expanded on this concept in his 1968 book, *The Population Bomb,* predicting certain mass starvation in the 1970s and 1980s—eventually losing a very public bet with economist and fellow Jew Julian Simon, who was much more optimistic about our ability to meet this challenge. The Malthusian view remains vivid despite more than 200 years of progress and innovations in plant breeding, soil use, and agricultural technology—all human achievements. They did not happen by accident.

Smallpox, chicken pox, diphtheria, malaria, measles, whooping cough (pertussis), pneumonia, tetanus, typhoid fever, yellow fever, and others all have been essentially solved through human achievement. Progress with HIV, heart disease, and many forms of cancer mark similar contributions.

More recently, the longstanding "peak oil" predictions of a world energy shortage have proven wrong as innovation in drilling techniques have dramatically altered forecasts, largely because one man thought about the problem in ways no one else had, and when everyone told him he was wrong, he stuck to his views.

In like manner, others who care, and who have the skills and values to commit themselves to solving problems, can make an enormous difference. Steve Jobs was such a person. Though many found him impossible to work with, he changed millions of lives for the better. His innovations improved products and productivity across almost every industry he touched, and created work and prosperity for many. Jobs did not take a large slice of the economic pie from anyone else. He made the pie bigger. He was a high achiever.

Human achievement is a testament to the view that life and history are not zero sum games. Innovative high achievers add to our potential and to the richness of our lives. Individual human achievement deserves to be treasured and encouraged.

Over the last 200 years, Jews have done this in astonishing fashion. There have been others before, as mentioned earlier: the seventeenth and eighteenth century Scots, the Golden Age Dutch, the offshore Chinese, the Renaissance Florentines and the early Greeks. Today, many Asians show a renewed inclination for high achievement. And there are the Sikhs, Basques, and others. No one knows if they share particular genetic traits, as some argued Jews do, giving them a gift for high achievement from their heightened intelligence. But we know they share many of the same cultural values—"cultural capital" as it were— of purpose, self-discipline, learning, family, community, and a commitment to contributing to a greater good.

In 2009, the Sonoma Valley Fund issued its Youth Initiative Study. As lead author, I saw our small community's academic problems up close. Our high school dropout rate that averaged 7 percent in the years from 1992–93 and 2001–02 had risen to 12 percent by 2009. With fewer than 35 percent of high school graduates qualifying to apply for admission to the University of California system, it appeared impossible that our community could sustain its longstanding population of 30 percent college graduates. Fewer than 50 percent of our youth were performing at grade level for English and math, and 10 percent or more of the Valley's children were significantly influenced by gang culture.

On a national scale, in March 2012, the Council on Foreign Relations issued its report *U.S. Education Reform and National Security*. It noted that while the United States spends more on education than other developed countries, our students are falling behind. American fifteen-year-olds rank fourteenth in reading, twenty-fifth in math, and seventeenth in science, compared with students in other industrialized countries. More than 25 percent fail to graduate from high school in four years. The number approaches 40 percent among African American and Hispanic students. ACT, the not-for-profit testing organization, found only 22 percent of high school students are meeting college ready standards in their core subjects and the College Board noted that even among college-bound seniors, only 43 percent meet these standards. Despite considerable spending on education, the United States is losing ground.

On January 31, 2012, *The New York Times* commentator David Brooks began his column by saying, "I'll be shocked if there's another book this year as important as Charles Murray's *Coming Apart*." To avoid issues of race, Murray chose to look only at White Americans and the worrisome gaps that have opened up in the last fifty years between those at the top, in the middle, and at the bottom of today's society. To simplify, the clear distinction is between those in the top 20 percent economically and those in the bottom 30 percent. And while the financial differences in terms of income and net worth are troubling, even more consequential are the differences in cultural values and aspirations.

The first part of Murray's book looks at those on top. Not only have their incomes more than doubled in real terms, so have their academic attainments. Those in America's fourteen most elite zip codes had average annual family income of $163,000 in 2000 versus $84,000 in 1960. In 1960, 26 percent held bachelors degrees; by 2000, that figure was 67 percent. Those fourteen exclusive zip codes are ever more cloistered and the lifestyle more rarified, much like an exclusive club. It was not like that in 1960 when we all lived much more like one another. There was no huge gap between those on top and those on the bottom.

While those on top have continued to do well, those in the bottom 30 percent have lost substantial ground. Murray's symbolic "Fishtown" had an average family income of $41,900 in 2000. They were mostly blue collar workers, and almost none had formal education beyond a high school diploma.

But while the snobbishness and exclusivity of the new elite is indisputably alarming, the unfortunate shift in values, particularly for those at the bottom, is even more so. The upper 20 percent (which Murray placed in the artificial town of "Belmont") have values one might term Victorian or bourgeois. That is no longer true of the bottom 30 percent in Fishtown. In 1960, 94 percent of those in Belmont were married, and 84 percent in Fishtown. By 2010, 83 percent of those in Belmont were married, but only 48 percent in Fishtown.

In 1960, only 2 percent of all American White births were to unmarried women. By 2008, of Belmont's births, 6 percent were out of wedlock—a small fraction of the 44 percent out-of-wedlock births for Whites in Fishtown. Of White men in their thirties and forties, those with only a high school education who said they were not available for work rose from 3 percent in 1968 to 12 percent in 2008 (remember, this was before the onset of the Great Recession). Among college graduates, the figure has stayed at 3 percent.

In terms of crime rates, Belmont showed no increase. In Fishtown, in 2009, violent crime was 4.7 times what it was in 1960. And in religion, those who profess no religion or attend church no more than once a year ("secular" as it were) and who lived in Belmont grew from 29 percent to 40 percent. But in Fishtown, that number grew from 38 percent to 59 percent. This is a far cry from the Puritan Ethic. What would Alexis de Tocqueville say if he came to America now?

In some ways, it is hard to know which of the two groups is the greater cause for alarm. It would be wonderful to be able to think of our upper class as contemporary replicas of Tom Brokaw's "Greatest Generation," refusing outrageous compensation, shunning greed, living more among those less fortunate, making sacrifices to help them, and serving as role models, but I know my generation is more selfish than my parents' generation, who lived through the Great Depression and World War II. The generation following mine is even more selfish.

But of the two, (the top 20 percent and lower 30 percent) the lower 30 percent worry me the most. Their cultural values are simply alarming.

The July/August 2012 *Harvard Magazine* wrote about this in, "When Having Babies Beats Marriage." Picking up on Murray, writer Kevin Hartnett noted: "(While) 94 percent of births to college-educated women today occur within marriage...57 percent of women with a high-school degree or less education are unmarried when they bear their first child."

Hartnett cites Katherine Edin's work, saying this is accounted for by obstacles that include the low quality of many of their existing relationships, the norms they hold about the standard of living necessary to support a marriage, the challenges of integrating children from past relationships, and an aversion to divorce—all contributing to the fact that we "sustain such high rates of inequality." To these I would add that we now know poor nutrition, scant nurturing, and lack of attention from caring parents can consign infants to significantly reduced opportunities to achieve their potential.

These are the stated obstacles. Still undetermined is why such views were largely non-existent until the 1960s, despite the much more difficult times of war and the Great Depression. To Murray, answers are in short supply. Perhaps tongue in cheek, he suggested the upper 20 percent should consider "preaching what they practice."

Murray sees part of the problem as being today's more meritocratic world, in which those with the highest IQs are best fit to meet its needs. Their skills, values, and drive are rewarded accordingly. Those without such talents can thus fall behind, he says, although Murray is more determinist than I am about the relentless inevitability of the rewards of high IQ in today's meritocracy.

Like Murray, I see an ever more competitive global economy. Lower labor costs channel jobs to places where they would otherwise not exist, and a lower cost of manufacturing allows buyers to save money and use it in more productive ways. The reductions in world poverty over the last quarter century are extraordinary. That is a very good thing.

We live in a world where technology replaces expensive labor to perform work more cheaply, quickly, and more effectively. It can put an immense squeeze on those in the middle, who fail to become or stay educated to meet evolving demand for skills. Like the changes when America transitioned from a nation of farmers to an industrial nation, the process is relentless. Productivity gains mean getting more from less. It is part of how Malthus and Ehrlich were proved wrong, but it dislocates those unwilling or unable to adapt.

In a way, this is akin to Darwinian natural selection. In the long run it has great benefits, since its paradigm is what works best. But in the short run, "creative destruction" can be very threatening for many people. Railing against the tide is futile—adapting is not. We must encourage education for a workforce for today, tomorrow and the coming years.

Cultures change. Deng Xiaoping eliminated the worst elements of Mao's authoritarian repression, replacing it with a culture that encouraged entrepreneurship—with a Confucian underpinning. New York City cleaned up graffiti and eliminated the extortion of thugs who intimidated drivers into paying them for running a squeegee across a windshield. Crime declined, and New York became livable again. Korean Airlines is much safer; Japan transformed itself in the Meiji restoration; so did South Korea in the last fifty years. But the changes—all to cultures—were not easy.

I am not a genetic determinist. Even as a lapsed Presbyterian, I don't think my future was "predestined" in my genes. Genes matter, but I don't believe they have been the most important force in my life. Moreover, genes are not "selfish." They simply do what works.

History's ebb and flow denies genetic determinism. Our DNA does not control our destiny. Einstein's conjecture about quantum uncertainty was likely wrong. God probably does play dice with the universe—even in mutations. That makes it all the more interesting.

Neither high nor low IQ confers selfishness or snobbishness; personal behavior and culture do. Nor does low or high IQ promote single-parent families, promiscuity, laziness or lack of desire to learn or work.

The DNA and IQ of Tom Brokaw's "Greatest Generation" are only a few generations removed from today. This is an insufficient period of time for significant genetic change. The Greatest Generation lived through severe economic hardship and global conflict, came home to become educated and get on with their lives, won a Cold War and became the most prosperous and advanced in history. Since then, something has changed. While it might be argued that it is relentless meritocracy or globalization, more likely over the last fifty years we've simply lost some of our cultural bearings.

Attempting to impose culture is futile, but cultures can be nudged. Leadership in shaping and promoting the right values can make an immense difference. If one seeks ideas about the values to encourage, there are four good places to start, beginning with item 186—the final entry in the Chronology (Part 2). David Brooks' "The Character Factory" elegantly captures the essence of this book's perspective. I also encourage you to learn more about traditional Jewish values, and to read Lawrence Harrison's writings on cultural capital, as well as Amy Chua and Jed Rubenfeld's comments about the values shared by high-achieving cultures.

Part 2
Chronology
of the Debate

CHAPTER 8

Tracing the Debate over Disproportionate Jewish Achievement

If *The Golden Age of Jewish Achievement* was filled with interesting bios that could be browsed from time to time, and which many readers tell me they found delightful and intriguing, Part 2 of this book hopes to do something akin to that with chronologically sequenced abstracts of events, books, articles, and studies. Most of them relate to the long debate over nature versus nurture, the impact and effects of culture, and questions about what drives human achievement, including Jewish achievement. Unlike the bios that could be browsed at random, these abstracts may be more meaningful if read in sequence. In reading it as a chronological flow, Part 2 provides a feel for the disconnected flow of events in the real world, including the breakthroughs, contradictory evidence, and setbacks.

Over the period covered by Part 2, there have been enormous advances in what we know about our genetics (nature) and culture (nurture). The pace of those discoveries is quickening, particularly since completion of the Human Genome Project. So too has recognition of disproportionate Jewish achievement and the debate over its causes.

Part 2 is selective, but it covers most of the key books and papers on these topics, particularly in recent times. Much of it draws on the work of researchers such as Dr. Angela Duckworth, academics such as Dr.'s Maristella Botticini and Zvi Eckstein, Dr. Nancy L. Segal who, as Assistant Director, worked closely with Thomas J. Bouchard Jr., who lead the Minnesota Study of Twins Reared Apart (MISTRA), leading scientific reporters at major publications, such as Nicholas Wade and Gina Kolata of *The New York Times*, Sharon Begley of *The Wall Street Journal*, and their counterparts at The Economist, whose work summarizes, better than the scientific journals, the research findings and their significance, particularly for an educated lay audience. It also draws on thought leaders who have worked these fields for many years, such as David Brooks, Charles Murray, Lawrence Harrison, and authors such as Richard Francis, who reported in depth on epigenetics.

Hopefully, together with the preceding material, the reader can perceive the ways in which the pieces have come together in this exploration of how Jews came to be disproportionately accomplished, and what we all can learn from that. I hope you find it interesting. To further assist readers, the pages immediately following also provide something of an index of ten major threads it covers, such as: Culture/ Environment, Jewish History, and the Genetics of Jewish Ancestry, Genetics and Race, Genetics and Traits, Genetics and the Brain/IQ, etc.

When you have finished reading it, you are likely to be impressed with the significant progress of recent genetic and cultural research. You will likely find recent genetic medical progress dramatic and important. The same will not be true, however, of genetic progress in understanding the links between genes and traits such as intelligence, drive, talents, and other aspects of our humanity. In explaining traits, genetic progress remains problematic.

In the end, I hope you will find this book provides the most complete compendium ever of the history, research, and analyses to explain not only the disproportionate Jewish achievements, but also the relevance of the genetic and cultural elements that shape and encouraged human achievement in us all.

Threads of Part 2 - Chronology of the Debate

Item	Date	Author	Title or Topic
1. Early Nature/Nurture			
1	10,000 BCE	Pease	Nurture Shapes Nature - Cross Breeding
70	1-Dec-05	Botticini & Eckstein	Mandatory Jewish Education/Literacy
50	1-Oct-03	Murray	*Human Accomplishment*
2	6-Dec-04	Pease	Lamarck
4	24-Nov-1859	Pease	Charles Darwin
5	1866	Pease	Gregor Mendel
6	11-Feb-05	Pease	Francis Galton
25	1-May-99	Wade	Darwin's Finches
2. Culture/Environment			
7	Mar 1899	Twain	"Concerning the Jews"
10	24-Mar-05	Silber	*Jewish Achievement*
11	29-Mar-05	Fraser et al	Other Early Acknowledgements
12	15-May-05	Dimont	*Jews, God and History*
13	22-May-05	Van Den Hag	*The Jewish Mystique*
15	30-May-05	Patai	*The Jewish Mind*
16	20-Feb-79	Bouchard	Studies of Twins Reared Apart
17	1-Jun-87	Shama	The Seventeenth Century Golden Age Dutch
18	9-Jun-05	Johnson	*A History of the Jews*
19	12-Jun-1990	Stevenson & Lee	Asian vs. American Parental Culture
24	20-Jun-05	Sowell	Trilogy on Culture
27	1-May-00	Harrison & Huntington	*Culture Matters*
29	22-Jun-05	Silbiger	*The Jewish Phenomenon*
30	1-Nov-01	Herman & Hart	The Scottish Geniuses
41	10-Feb-03	Buchwald	The Importance of Jewish Education
45	28-Mar-03	Begley	Asians and Westerners Think Differently
47	20-Jun-03	Begley	Identical Twins, Genes, IQ Heritability and the Flynn Effect
50	1-Oct-03	Charles Murray	*Human Accomplishment*
53	1-Jun-04	Slezkine	*The Jewish Century*
57	5-Nov-04	Begley	Buddhist Monk's Meditation
59	22-Mar-05	Mindin	The Haredim and Scientific Inquiry
60	10-Jun-05	Varadarajan	Indian American Success in Spelling Bees
64	5-Aug-05	Brooks	"All Cultures Are Not Equal"
65	6-Oct-05	Brooks	Adverse Effects of Low Cultural Capital
66	20-Oct-05	Hobsbawm	"Benefits of Diaspora"
69	16-Dec-05	Duckworth	Self Discipline, IQ, and Academic Performance
70	1-Dec-05	Botticini & Eckstein	Mandatory Jewish Education/Literacy
75	14-May-06	Kristof	Asian Academic Motivation
78	13-Aug-06	Brooks/Harrison	*The Central Liberal Truth*
80	1-Apr-07	Murray	Jewish Genius

Item	Date	Author	Title or Topic
81	25-May-07	Brooks	Skeptical Catholics and Protestants Do Well
86	1-Nov-08	Gladwell	*Outliers*
88	1-Apr-09	Harrison	*Jews, Confucians and Protestants*
89	30-Apr-09	Brooks	Effort May Trump IQ in Predicting Success
90	1-Jul-09	Gilder	*The Israel Test*
92	1-Nov-09	Senor, Singer	*Start Up Nation*
93	1-Dec-09	Pease	*The Golden Age of Jewish Achievement*
95	1-Mar-10	Wade	Human Culture as an Evolutionary Force
97	4-May-10	Brooks	"Limits of Policy: Culture, Ethnicity, Group Psychology and Behavior"
98	6-May-10	Brooks	"Leading With Two Minds: Petraeus and the Army"
99	1-Jun-10	Cohen	Culture and Crime: Richard Cohen Sees the Light
101	6-Oct-10	Resmovits	"What? Not All Jews Are Geniuses? - Jews and MacArthur Fellowships"
104	16-Feb-11	Kagan	"The Costly Neglect of Child Rearing Practices"
106	15-May-11	Pew Charitable Trust	Correlating Religion, Education, and Income
108	19-Jun-11	Winter/Bird	"God's MBAs - The Mormons"
117	1-Feb-12	Kohut	*A German Generation*
119	6-Mar-12	Kandel	Experience Affects the Brain
120	18-Mar-12	Bhattacharjee	Multiple Language Skills Might Make You Smarter
124	22-Apr-12	Hurley	Building a Smarter Brain: Jaeggi and the N-back Exercise
128	12-Jun-12	Berger	The Haredim (Ultra Orthodox) Aid Jewish Population Growth
129	18-Jun-12	WSJ/NYT	Asian Immigration Exceeds Hispanic Immigration - A First
130	1-Jun-12	Segal	Identical Twins: *Born Together - Reared Apart*
132	1-Jul-12	Botticini & Eckstein	*The Chosen Few: How Education Shaped Jewish History*
139	20-Dec-12	Chen	"Asians: Too Smart For Their Own GoodÚ
140	22-Dec-12	Economist	Cleverer Still - High Scoring Womens and Men's Math Scores and The Flynn/ Effect
142	25-Dec-12	Brooks	The Collapse of Jewish Academic Achievement - The Ron Unz Essay
143	25-Dec-12	Cherlin	Unmarried Poor: Bad Values or Bad Jobs - The Effect on the Children
144	19-Jan-13	Economist	Staying Focused: Characteristics of Successful Children
146	5-Feb-13	NYT	Visual Analysis of Science Test Scores in 65 Countries
149	23-Feb-13	Economist	Japan's Prisons and Their Prisoners
150	28-Feb-13	Brooks	"The Learning Virtures : Cultures of Learning"
151	5-Apr-13	Kozak	Tiger Students
155	2-May-13	Chandler	"The Best Little Boy in the World"
156	10-May-13	Kohut	Values Despite Hardships
157	26-Jun-13	Allen	*Men on Strike*
159	24-Jul-13	Abravanel	Abravanel's Speech to Ferdinand and Isabella
145c	17-Sep-13	WSJ	Orchids, Dandelions, Dopamine and DRD4
162	1-Sep-13	Pew	U.S. Jewish Identity

Item	Date	Author	Title or Topic
163	9-Oct-13	Jewish Journal	Jewish Scientists Score Nobel Prizes - An Israeli Teacher's Analysis
166	20-Oct-13	Belefsky	The Roma: Primitive or Just Poor?
167	23-Oct-13	Economist	Amsterdam: Literacy, Liberality, and Commercial Success
168	3-Nov-13	Hurley	"Jumper Cables for the Brain"
169	30-Nov-13	Economist	Nurturing Nature - Robert Plomin and Individualized Education
170	7-Dec-13	Economist	"Finn-ished"
172	23-Jan-14	Brooks	Help For Underprivileged Children
173	25-Jan-14	Gopnik	Time to Retire Nature vs Nurture
176	4-Feb-14	Chua & Rubenfeld	*The Triple Package*
177	10-Feb-14	Brooks	"The American Precariat"
178	17-Feb-14	Brooks	Prodigal Son: A Precariat Follow-up
181	18-Apr-14	Dweck	Self Theories - Professor Carol Dwecks Stanford Class
182	3-May-14	Wade	*A Troublesome Inheritance: Genes, Race, and Human History*
184	5-May-14	Ehrenfreud	Study Ties Hard Work to Asian Student High Grades
186	31-Jul-14	Brooks	"The Character Factory"

3. Jewish History and the Genetics of Jewish Ancestry

Item	Date	Author	Title or Topic
3	11-Dec-1807	Pease	Napoleon's Grand Sanhedrin - Early Praise for Jews
6	11-Feb-05	Pease	Francis Galton
8	1-Aug-03	Joly/NKVD	*The Protocols of the Elders of Zion*
14	29-May-05	Koestler	Khazars as The Thirteenth Tribe
21	1-Jan-97	Nature	Jewish Genetic History - The Cohanim
26	1-May-99	Wade	Jewish Genetics - The Cohanim and the Lemba
28	1-May-00	Natl Academy	Jewish Genetics - Common Jewish Origins and Khazars
31	1-Mar-02	Pollack	"Some Genetics for Some Jews"
34	10-May-02	Wade	Jewish Genetics and Mitochondrial DNA
36	1-Nov-02	khazaria.com	Khazars - Again
43	4-Mar-03	Wade	Jewish Genetics: Might Mutations Benefit Natural Selection?
49	27-Sep-03	Wade	The Khazars (yet again)
62	1-Jun-05	Chochran et al	"Natural History of Ashkenazi Intelligence"
70	1-Dec-05	Botticini & Eckstein	Mandatory Jewish Education/Literacy
72	14-Jan-06	Wade	Ashkenazi Genetics: Middle Eastern Mitochondrial DNA is Found
79	8-Dec-06	Goldstein	A Genetically Demonstrable Jew That Israel Says Is Not
87	5-Dec-08	Wade/Begley	Jewish and Moorish DNA in the Spanish and Portuguese
91	1-Jul-09	Goldstein	Ashkenazim Are Khazars - Shlomo Sand
100	9-Jun-10	Wade	Jewish Genome Wide Scanning Links Jews, Discredits Khazar Theory
126	15-May-12	Oransky's	A Case for Genetic Jewishness and Is There a Jewish Gene? - Harry Ostrer"

Item	Date	Author	Title or Topic
132	1-Jul-12	Botticini & Eckstein	*The Chosen Few: How Education Shaped Jewish History*
137	9-Dec-12	Sanders	Genetic Testing Helps Samaritans
159	24-Jul-13	Abravanel	Abravanel's Speech to Ferdinand and Isabella
182	3-May-14	Wade	*A Troublesome Inheritance: Genes, Race, and Human History*

4. Genetics and Race

Item	Date	Author	Title or Topic
6	11-Feb-05	Pease	Francis Galton
20	1-Sep-94	Murray	*The Bell Curve*
22	1-Aug-97	Wade	Ashkenazi Genetic Ailments
35	1-Jul-02	SF Chron	*Taboo*: Black Athletes and Racial Differences
38	1-Jul-02	Wade	Is Race Biologically Meaningless?
44	1-Apr-03	Wade	Race and Medicine (Again)
68	11-Nov-05	Wade	Race, Genetic Variance, and Medicine (again)
70	1-Dec-05	Botticini & Eckstein	Mandatory Jewish Education/Literacy
82	11-Nov-07	Harmon	"Racial Genetics of Medicine, IQ? And Fears of Misuse"
83	11-Nov-07	Lynn	Jewish Achievement: The Role of Intelligence and Values
85	21-Mar-08	Hotz	Differences in Genetic Variations in Different Populations
182	3-May-14	Wade	*A Troublesom Inheritance: Genes, Race, and Human History*

5. Twin Studies

Item	Date	Author	Title or Topic
6	22-May-05	Pease	Francis Galton
16	20-Feb-79	Bouchard	Studies of Twins Reared Apart
47	20-Jun-03	Begley	Identical Twins, Genes, IQ Heritability and the Flynn Effect
84	11-Mar-08	O'Connor	Genetic Differences in Identical Twins
130	1-Jun-12	Segal	Identical Twins: *Born Together - Reared Apart*
169	30-Nov-13	Economist	Narturing Nature - Robert Plomin and Individualized Education

I

6. Epigenetics

Item	Date	Author	Title or Topic
2	6-Dec-04	Pease	Lamarck
4	"Nov 24, 1859"	Pease	Charles Darwin (Pangenesis)
6	11-Feb-05	Pease	Francis Galton (Darwin's Pangenesis)
32	12-Apr-02	Begley	Genetics of Chimps & Humans - Epigenetic Regulation of Genes?
37	21-Jun-02	Begley	Thoughts and Behavior Can Trigger Physiological Responses
39	20-Sep-02	Begley	Genetic Variance, the Environment, and Effects on Violence?
54	16-Jul-04	Begley	Epigenetic Effect of Maternal Styles of Rat Mothers
55	23-Jul-04	Begley	Identical Twins: One Schizophrenic, the Other Not?

tem	Date	Author	Title or Topic
56	17-Sep-04	Begley	Maternal Behavior and Dietary Effects on the Unborn
63	5-Jul-05	Wade	Some Identical Twins Grow Ever Less Identical: Epigenetics?
71	13-Jan-06	Begley	Genes, the Environment, Shyness, Violence, and Intelligence
73	24-Feb-06	Begley	Parental Behavior May Alter Genetic Expression in Adoptees
76	7-Jul-06	Begley	Environmental Influence On Genetic Expression of Agression
84	11-Mar-08	O'Connor	Genetic Differences In Identical Twins
85	21-Mar-08	Hotz	Differences in Genetic Variances In Different Populations
102	8-Nov-10	Begley	"Sins of the Grandfathers: Trans-Generational Epigenetic Effects"
107	13-Jun-11	Francis	*Epigenetics* : The book
109	22-Aug-11	Begley	Sad Moms and Stressed Parents Can Scar Kids
119	6-Mar-12	Kandel	Experience Affects the Brain
121	7-Apr-12	Economist	Epigenetics and Cancer
122	15-Apr-12	Economist	Rhesus Macques and the Epigenetics of Induced Stress
125	12-May-12	Ridley	"How Dickensonian Childhoods Leave Genetic Scars"
134	9-Sep-12	Shulevitz	"Why Fathers Really Matter"
145a	21-Jan-13	Kolata	Epigenetic Gene Regulation and Disease
145b	10-Feb-13	Bronson	"Why Worry: Stress, Panic and Test Taking"
145d	6-Aug-13	Reynolds	Exercise and Methylation (Epigenetic Changes)
145c	17-Sep-13	WSJ	Orchids, Dandelions, Dopamine and DRD4
145e	14-Dec-13	Economist	"Poisoned Inheritance - The Folate Studies"
173	25-Jan-14	Gopnik	Is It Time to Retire Nature Versus Nurture?

7. Other Genetic and Genetic Regulatory Phenomena

33	10-May-02	Begley	The Placebo Effect
61	24-Jun-05	Begley	Imprinted Genes
77	25-Jul-06	Wade	Nucleosomes: Another Regulator of Gene Expression
84	11-Mar-08	O'Connor	Genetic Differences in Identical Twins
125	12-May-12	Ridley	"How Dickensonian Childhoods Leave Genetic Scars"
133	5-Sep-12	Kolata, et al	ENCODE: Much Junk DNA Is Found Not To Be Junk After All
138	1-Dec-12	Economist	"The Origin of Species: Perhaps It's Not All Junk DNA After All"
160	17-Sep-13	Zimmer	More Than One Genome Per Person?
164	12-Oct-13	Sapolsky	Shuffling Genes in Our DNA
175	3-Feb-14	Ouellette	*Me, Myself, and Why*

8. Genetics and traits

4	24-Nov-1859	Pease	Charles Darwin
5	8-Feb-05	Pease	Gregor Mendel

tem	Date	Author	Title or Topic
16	20-Feb-79	Bouchard	Studies of Twins Reared Apart
47	20-Jun-03	Begley	Identical Twins, Genes, IQ Heritability, and the Flynn Effect
48	16-Sep-03	Wade	The Genetics of Perfect Pitch
62	1-Jun-05	Cochran et al	"Natural History of Askenazi Intelligence"
80	1-Apr-07	Murray	"Jewish Genius"
95	1-Mar-10	Wade	Human Culture as an Evolutionary Force
130	1-Jun-12	Segal	Identical Twins: *Born Together - Reared Apart*
145b	10-Feb-13	Bronson	"Why Worry Stress, Panic Test Taking"
158	19-Jul-13	Kolata	A Gene For Fatness?
160	17-Sep-13	Zimmer	More Than One Genome Per Person?
169	30-Nov-13	Economist	Narturing Nature - Robert Plomin and Individualized Education
174	1-Feb-14	Sapolsky	A Gene For Height or Smarts? Don't Bet On It!
179	23-Feb-14	Clark	Your Ancestors, Your Fate?
182	3-May-14	Wade	*A Troublesome Inheritance: Genes, Race, and Human History*

9. Genetics and the Brain/IQ

4	24-Nov-1859	Pease	Charles Darwin
6	11-Feb-05	Pease	Francis Galton
9	18-Mar-05	Pease	IQ Testing Begins
16	20-Feb-79	Bouchard	Studies of Twins Reared Apart
20	1-Sep-94	Murray	*The Bell Curve*
23	1-May-98	Wade	Gene Variance for IQ
40	24-Sep-02	Wade	Reduced Brains Size
43	4-Mar-03	Wade	Jewish Genetics: Might Mutations Benefit Natural Selection?
47	20-Jun-03	Begley	Identical Twins, Genes, IQ Heritability and the Flynn Effect
50	1-Oct-03	Murray	*Human Accomplishment*
52	14-Feb-04	Lynn	"The Intelligence of American Jews"
62	1-Jun-05	Cochran et al	"Natural History of Askenazi Intelligence"
70	1-Dec-05	Botticini & Eckstein	Mandatory Jewish Education/Literacy
74	30-Mar-06	Wade	Brain Development & IQ
80	1-Apr-07	Murray	"Jewish Genius"
83	11-Nov-07	Lynn	Jewish Achievement: The Role of Intelligence and Values
94	22-Feb-10	Science Daly	Mapping IQ and the brain
96	22-Apr-10	Science Daly	Genetics of low IQ
110	5-Sep-11	Lynn	*The Chosen People: Jews Intelligence and Achievement*
111	19-Oct-11	BBC	Malleability of IQ in teens
113	26-Oct-11	Science Daly	Genetics of brain development
114	26-Dec-11	Begley	Perhaps Not All Superior Mathematicians Are Male
116	19-Jan-12	Naik	IQ Decline in Scots
118	24-Feb-12	Science Daly	Genes and IQ links elusive
119	6-Mar-12	Kandel	Experience Affects the Brain
123	15-Apr-12	Science Daily	Pooled Brain Scan Research Explores Diseases and IQ

tem	Date	Author	Title or Topic
130	1-Jun-12	Segal	Identical Twins: *Born Together - Reared Apart*
132	1-Jul-12	Botticini & Eckstein	*The Chosen Few: How Education Shaped Jewish History*
140	22-Dec-12	Economist	Cleverer Still - High Scoring Womens and Men's Math Scores and The Flynn Effect
146	5-Feb-13	NYT	Visual Analysis of Science Test Scores in 65 Countries
147	16-Feb-13	Naik	A Genetic Code for Genius
148	23-Feb-13	Economist	How Brains are wired
160	17-Sep-13	Zimmer	More Than One Genome Per Person?
161	21-Sep-13	Gopnik	Malleability of IQ
163	9-Oct-13	Jewish Journal	Jewish Scientists Score Nobel Prizes - An Israeli Teacher's Analysis
168	3-Nov-13	Hurley	"Jumper Cables for the Brain"
169	30-Nov-13	Economist	Narturing Nature - Robert Plomin and Individualized Education
175	3-Feb-14	Ouellette	*Me, Myself, and Why*
180	7-Apr-14	Chang	Predicting IQ at Six Months of Age
182	3-May-14	Wade	*A Troublesom Inheritance: Genes, Race, and Human History*
183	5-May-14	Winslow	"New Blood Can Benefit More Than Organizations"
185	10-May-14	Economist	The 3% Solution - a Potent Study of Genetic Variation in Cognitive Ability

10. Genetics and Medicine - Slow Beginnings & Later Big Breakthroughs

16	20-Feb-79	Bouchard	Studies of Twins Reared Apart
22	1-Aug-97	Wade	Ashkenazi Genetic Ailments
42	28-Feb-03	Begley	Disease Risks from BRCA 1 and BRCA 2
47	20-Jun-03	Begley	Identical Twins, Genes, IQ Heritability and the Flynn Effect
58	14-Jan-05	Begley	Family History Beats Genetic Variation
67	5-Nov-05	Begley	The Haplotype Map: Silver Bullet or Not
68	11-Nov-05	Wade	Race, Genetic Variation and Medicine (again)
82	11-Nov-07	Harmon	Racial Genetics of Medicine, Perhaps IQ And Fears of Misuse
85	21-Mar-08	Hotz	Differences in Genetic Variances in Different Populations
103	14-Nov-10	Begley	Family Medical History Matters
115	10-Jan-12	WSJ/NYT	Expectations For $1,000 Human Genome Scanning Tests
123	15-Apr-12	Science Daily	Pooled Brain Scan Research Explores Diseases and IQ
127	18-May-12	Wade	Rare Genetic Mutations: More Complex Than Was Expected
130	1-Jun-12	Segal	Identical Twins: *Born Together - Reared Apart*
131	7-Jul-12	Kolata	Breakthrough in Treating Adult Acute Lymphoblastic Leukemia
135	10-Sep-12	Kolata	Lung Cancer Genetics Point To Tailored Treatments

tem	Date	Author	Title or Topic
136	4-Oct-12	Kolata	Catching Infant Genetic Defects Within Days of Birth
141	24-Dec-12	Flinn & Vance	How Much Are 30,000 Human Genomes Worth?
145a	21-Jan-13	Kolata	Epigenetic Gene Regulation and Disease
152	15-Apr-13	Green	Post Human Genome Project Progress
153	28-Apr-13	Eisenberg	Tools for Finding Genetic Variations
154	2-May-13	Kolata	Genetic Linkages of Cancers
160	17-Sep-13	Zimmer	More Than One Genome Per Person?
165	16-Oct-13	Winslow	Genes and Mutations Tied to Cancer
171	15-Jan-14	Bus Week	Illumina

CHAPTER 9

Early Recognition and Theories of Achievement

1. Nurture Shapes Nature – Cross Breeding
We know that since ancient times, people have crossbred varieties of plants and animals in the hope of improving the strains. Mules, for example were created more than 3,000 years ago in Mesopotamia (*Epigenetics*, p 116) and the ear of corn we eat today is far larger, tastier, and more nutritious than any part of the tiny teosinte plant from which it is thought to have originated 7,500 to 12,000 years ago in Central America (Wikipedia). It is remarkable how many species of plant and animal strains mankind has improved upon over those thousands of years, when so little was known about genetics. Nonetheless, through hit and miss and lessons learned from experiments, humans bred strong oxen, beautiful tulips and tasty foods. Huge numbers of plants and animals were domesticated and tended to over thousands of years.

2. Lamarck
Jean-Baptiste Lamarck's *Recherches sur l' Organisation des Corps Vivants* was published in 1802. A military hero, Lamarck (1744 to 1829) was the first to use the term "biology" in today's sense of the word. The breadth of his academic work is stunning, and while we might have begun with earlier pioneers and papers, Lamarck is particularly interesting since, among other aspects of his work, in it we see how scientific theories arise, come into fashion, are challenged, recede, and sometimes return again, in altered form. Lamarck's 1802 book and two additional tomes, *Philosophie Zoologique*, in 1809, and the seven volume *Historie Naturelle Des Animaux Sans Vertebres* (1815 to 1822), laid out a new theory—Lamarckian evolution—covering plants, animals, and humans. Before Lamarck (1744–1829) and Charles Darwin's grandfather, Erasmus Darwin (1731–1802), most people thought species were fixed. Some species, dinosaurs for example, might occasionally disap-

pear due to a natural disaster of one kind or another, but new species never arose and certainly they did not evolve.

Lamarck openly promoted the notion that organisms evolve from simple to complex and adapt, as though striving for perfection. He thought humans were at the apex of this process. He believed evolution arose from an inheritance of acquired characteristics as plants and animals adapted to their environment, and passed along whatever was gained to the next generation. Lamarck thought giraffe necks, for example, became longer as the giraffe stretched more and more to reach higher leaves. The father's longer neck was then passed along to the offspring.

It did not take long for a contemporary French scientist, George Cuvier, to take on Lamarck with a few simple examples. (Children of cowboys were not bowlegged. Children of weight lifters did not inherit large muscles. And a dog that loses his tail does not sire tailless puppies.)

In today's terminology, Lamarck was arguing that nurture (the environment and what we do in that environment) shapes nature (genetics and DNA). He was called out for his error of method (how his theory operated) and for the lack of reproducible proof. Lamarck was wrong about how the process works; nonetheless, the pendulum has swung back and forth from time to time. Recent scientific discoveries, such as epigenetics, are reviving memories of Lamarck, albeit rather more in spirit than in detail. More on that later.

3. Napoleon's Grand Sanhedrin, Early Praise for Jews

In early 1807 Napoleon convened the Grand Sanhedrin. At it, Jewish leaders formally ratified the answers of an earlier Assembly of seventy-one "notable" Jews to twelve questions he had posed, including their loyalty to France. With ratification of those satisfactory answers in hand, Napoleon unleashed the Jewish Emancipation. It unfolded throughout Central and Western Europe over the next eighty years or so.

In an 1847 speech to the British House of Commons, Lord Ashley spoke about the "very powerful intellect (of Jews)" in proportion to their numbers. He noted their range of accomplishments encompassed music, poetry, medicine, and astronomy, and further, that "in every field, they were more than a match for their competitors. (Lynn, *The Chosen People* p 3)

In 1853, the French weighed in with Count de Gobineau who, in discussing intellectual and cultural achievements, said, "the Aryans (Northern Europeans) and Jews were the two most intelligent people."

4. Charles Darwin

On November 24, 1859, Charles Darwin's *On the Origin of Species by Means of Natural Selection, or the Preservation of Favoured Races in the Struggle for Life* (later shortened to *The Origin of Species*) was published. One of history's more extended authorial efforts (twenty-two years), Darwin sailed with the *HMS Beagle* from December 1831 to 1836 on a groundbreaking coastal mapping and naturalist survey of South America, and upon returning home, commenced writing in mid-1837. He was only pushed to complete the book when he got word in 1856 that Alfred Russell Wallace might beat him to the punch.

In some sense, the book arose from "nurture" since Darwin's grandfather, Erasmus, was one of the first to believe in evolution taking place over millions of years. But Erasmus had not thought it through with great clarity, and his authored views appeared only in an obscure 1794 publication. Arguing for evolution would have been risky at that time.

When Darwin pulled his thoughts together after the voyage of the *Beagle*, it changed the world and how we think about it. As summarized by the biologist Ernst Mayr in his 1982 book, *The Growth of Biological Thought*, Darwin was saying:

— "Every species is sufficiently fertile that if all offspring survived to reproduce its population would grow (fact).

— Despite periodic fluctuations, populations tend to remain roughly the same size (fact).

— Resources such as food are limited, and relatively stable over time (fact).

— A struggle for survival ensues (fact).

— Individuals in a population vary significantly one from another (fact).

— Much of this variation is inheritable (fact).

— Individuals less suited to the environment are less likely to survive (survival of the "fit," rather than survival of the "fittest"), and less likely to reproduce; individuals more suited to the environment are more likely to survive and more likely to reproduce and leave their inheritable traits to future generations, which produces the process of natural selection (inference).

— This slowly effected process results in populations changing to adapt to their environments, and ultimately, these variations accumulate over time to form new species (inference)."

It was a remarkable work and is now widely accepted.

Understandably, Darwin is less well known for his theory of Pangenesis, which was part of his last book, *Variation in Plants and Animals Under Domestication*. This was something of a Lamarckian notion in which somatic cells would adapt to their environment and throw off particles ("gemmules" or "pangenes") that would course through the body. The particles would contain information about the parent cells, and this information would be passed along to succeeding generations. Those characteristics would be found in the offspring. Darwin's Pangenesis theory would later be undone by his cousin, Francis Galton (see below).

5. Gregor Mendel

In 1866, Gregor Mendel, an obscure Augustinian monk, published the results of his research into the crossbreeding of common pea plants. At the time, Mendel, age forty-four, was serving as a teacher/scientist at the Abbey of St. Thomas in Brno, a city now in the Czech Republic. Before joining the Abbey, he had grown up on a farm, kept bees, and gardened. As a gymnasium student he studied practical and theoretical philosophy as well as physics. And later, as a teacher and scientist, he studied astronomy and meteorology. He was not what one might imagine upon learning he was a monk. But his abbey gave him access to 4.9 acres of plantings in an experimental garden, and he worked with peas (29,000 plants) to learn how different characteristics were passed from one generation to the next. The notion of dominant and recessive genes (and resulting phenotypes) arose from his work.

Before Mendel, most thought offspring got an averaging of sorts from parents (dark skin and light skin would yield medium skin). Mendel saw that was incorrect since the peas he worked with were bimodal in several characteristics. They had either purple or white flowers, their seed color was yellow or white, the pod color was yellow or green, etc. He saw no "averaging" of these colors (characteristics), and that drove his research. Through the successive generations of peas he witnessed, the dominant gene produced more of its color in successors, but the recessive colors did not disappear—they just happened less frequently. Mendel figured out intuitively that if the offspring inherited the recessive gene from both parent plants, it explained why the less frequent coloration remained possible. In short, two dominant genes mean the dominant characteristic persists as does one dominant and one recessive gene. But two recessive genes result in the recessive trait being expressed.

So the parent's traits (in the form of a gene or genes) are passed along unchanged[8] to offspring, and the offspring gets a copy from each parent. Whether that trait (gene) will show up in the offspring depends on a random process that determines whether the offspring will get two dominant genes, two recessive genes or one of each. Both the recessive and dominant genes will pass along to successive generations, even if the recessive gene remains unexpressed.

No one really noticed Mendel's paper when it was published. Had it received recognition, it would have further undermined Lamarckism and Darwin's Pangenesis, but only in 1900, sixteen years after his death, was his work rediscovered and then recognized as important.

6. Francis Galton

In 1869, Francis Galton's book *Hereditary Genius* was published. This was the first contemporary book to analyze genius and greatness and, as noted above, Galton was Charles Darwin's cousin. A polymath, Galton was an inventor, anthropologist, tropical explorer, proto-geneticist, statistician, geographer, eugenicist, meteorologist, and psychometrician.

Perhaps the Darwin/Galton apple didn't fall far from the tree. Galton wrote 340 books and papers, created the statistical concept of correlation, promoted "regression to the mean," coined the expression "nature versus nurture," was the pioneer in statistical study of human differences and of the inheritance of intelligence. He was also the first to recognize that the study of twins, particularly identical twins raised apart, could yield valuable insights into the heritability of traits, including intelligence.

In the book, Galton noted the intelligence of Jews and commented that Jews "appear to be rich in families of high intellectual breeds."

Less accepted since the end of World War II was his influence in what came to be known as "eugenics," a term he coined in 1883.

Galton worked with his cousin Darwin to test the theory of pangenesis using experiments with rabbits. In those tests, he transfused blood between different breeds of rabbits, but was unable to see any of the characteristics that might have been expected in the offspring. Darwin conceded, saying he never meant to imply the process worked through

---

8. More recent findings indicate the word "unchanged" needs to be clarified. The emerging field of Epigenetics (described later) is the reason refinements are needed.

the bloodstream, but pangenesis died after the experimental results were known. Galton also rejected Lamarckism, and ultimately is remembered as a firm believer in heredity. In that field, his work was pioneering and is well thought of.

7. Mark Twain – "Concerning the Jews"

In March 1899, Mark Twain's *Harpers'* article, "Concerning the Jews" (quoted earlier in the Introduction) drew considerable American attention to Jews and their record of disproportionate achievement. Written about halfway through the forty-five year immigration of roughly two million Jews into America from the Pale of Russia, and as a prominent author, Twain's views were widely read. His comments on European anti-Semitism were also of interest. And despite some errors involving Jewish military experience (which he later corrected), and some mildly pejorative comments, he described his own positive views about Jewish beliefs and values as reasons behind the remarkable per-formance. There was no mention of anything like genetics or heredity.

CHAPTER 10

The Twentieth Century: Science and Sharp Debate

8. *The Protocols of the Elders of Zion*

In August/September 1903, a book that would become known as *The Protocols of the Elders of Zion* was published in Russia. Proof of its fraudulent origin (a "literary forgery" of an 1864 French political satire by Maurice Joly), was available as early as 1921 and it was easy to see by comparing the text of both documents. Nonetheless, *The Protocols* took on a life of its own. It said Jews were set on a conspiracy to take control of the world. All their brilliance was being used in service to their greed and connivance. They were willing to lie, cheat and do anything they had to in order to succeed. In the United States, *The Protocols* were reissued in English and shortly thereafter the Bolsheviks took power in the Soviet Union. Jewish involvement with Communism tied Bolshevik plotting and Communism's aims to *The Protocols.*

Henry Ford believed the lie and spent his own money to distribute 500,000 copies. (Not as well-known was Ford's court-ordered retraction and apology in 1927, when he explained he had been duped by his assistants.) To this day, *The Protocols* are still cited, and in recent times have been the subject of purported "documentaries" on Egyptian television that later ran in other Arab countries. As Jews were ever more seen to be high achievers, anti-Semitism gave rise to a possible cause—cheating and connivance. Their performance only made some non-Jews more envious and angry.

9. IQ Testing Begins – Binet, Stanford, Terman, and Eugenics

In 1904, the French government was interested in learning which of its students might need special assistance. To that end, it commissioned Alfred Binet and his colleague, Theodore Simon, to prepare a test to determine intellectual capability. This led to the creation of the first credible test.

Binet was also the first to set the average for test-takers at 100. And he was first to compare test results based on age. For example, an eight-year-old child scoring on par with the average ten-year-old child was said to have an IQ of 125, (10/8 = 1.25), while a ten-year-old scoring on par with the average eight-year-old was said to have an IQ of 80 (8/10 = .80).

Later, as more tests were developed and "standardized," the 100 point IQ "average" was augmented with a standard deviation of 15 points. Namely, 68.2 percent of those taking the test would score between 85 and 115, while 95.4 percent would score between 70 and 130, and 99.7 percent would score between 55 and 145. Said differently, only about 16 percent of those tested should score above 115 (or below 85), only 2.2 percent should score above 130 (or below 70), and only about 0.1 percent should score above 145 (or below 55).

Binet was cautious about what the test could and could not do. He saw it as having a single purpose—the task set by the French government—and he did not assume it measured an inherent ability (intelligence) that would not and could not change. Instead, it showed which students might need more help now. But what he did was so revolutionary, and the single score so simple to digest, that it led to widespread interest and the development of many similar tests.

In 1916, the Stanford-Binet Intelligence Scales was published. It drew on a translation of the Binet test, but unlike Binet, Lewis M. Terman, the Stanford University test developer, thought IQ was fixed and hereditary. Stanford-Binet became the standard in America for decades.

Around the same time, the U.S. Army developed its own test, which it administered to more than two million new recruits. After World War I ended, variations of that test were used on immigrants as they arrived at Ellis Island. Despite obvious language limitations, those results led to calls for immigration restrictions. And perhaps in error, there were reports that Jews arriving from the Pale of Russia performed poorly on the tests and thus were thought to have low IQs. This was quickly disproved by the admission rates of second generation Jews into Harvard (20 percent of the students), Columbia (40 percent) and Hunter College (80 percent).

Ironically, the high Jewish admission rates at Ivy League schools ultimately led to a *de facto* form of discrimination against Jews. This was the first use of "diversity" as a policy in Harvard admissions. In this case, diversity was to be geographic—namely, admitting more students from Iowa and California so there would be fewer students from New York's lower East Side.

That form of diversity was later eclipsed by the adoption of the Scholastic Aptitude Test (SAT), which was based on the Army's tests. When James Conant reformed Harvard admissions to a meritocratic selection process in the 1930s, (he was wary of legacy admissions and the predominance of the "white shoe elite establishment" among Harvard's students), the SAT became a core part of admissions decisions. In no small sense, the SAT is an IQ test used to predict likely college success, and it has been widely used that way for more than eighty years.

Some test designers, including Stanford's Terman, proved to be supporters of eugenics, which encouraged selective breeding to "better the human race." In the 1930s, eugenics would become associated with the Nazis and what they did to Jews, Gypsies, homosexuals, the mentally disabled, and others. IQ tests, though useful and very much refined over the years, became controversial and tainted by their association with eugenics.

10. The First *Jewish Achievement* Book – Dr. Mendel Silber

In 1910, Modern View Publishing Co., in St Louis, Missouri, published Dr. Mendel Silber's book, Jewish Achievement. In its Introduction, Jewish publisher Abraham Rosenthal expressed his purpose: "The knowledge of the achievements recorded of Jewish men in the following pages nourishes effort and fosters emulation." Silber (also Jewish) added "… it is probably the only book in which the reader may find a survey of the entire field of Jewish contributions to the world's progress."

In identifying more than 1,000 Jewish high achievers, Silber organized his discussion into chapters that spelled out the wide range of activities in which Jews were high achievers. They included: agriculturalists, jurists and statesmen, painters and sculptors, composers and players, actors, architects, singers, scientists, physicians, philosophers, astronomers, mathematicians, historians, poets, authors, journalists, soldiers, sailors, bankers, financiers, philanthropists, travelers, explorers, and, chess players.

In talking about what drove performance, Rosenthal mentioned "providence," "historical and fateful experiences,…(the) griefs and joys of Jewish faith,…hidden wells, and secret springs that drive the Jew on to achievements that benefit humanity."

Silber used each chapter to describe his own views. The more than 2,000-year history of Jewish Law contributed to the numbers of outstanding lawyers and jurists. The parts of the Talmud devoted to farming helped explain Jews' long history as farmers and their contemporary prominence in agriculture. The "Word" expressed in the Torah, Tanakh and Talmud helped to spur great Jewish authors. Broad international experience, knowledge of languages, and a corresponding ability to communicate with those from many countries (all products of the Diaspora) were said to contribute to scientific capability. And, the long history of Jews serving as physicians helped explain their importance in modern medicine. Jewish emphasis on education contributed to Jewish skills as astronomers and mathematicians. Other chapters had comparable explanations.

11. Other Early Acknowledgements – Fraser, Jacobs, and Veblen

In 1915, John Fraser, a British author, wrote *The Conquering Jew*. In it, he wrote of Jewish genius, documented their achievements in America, Great Britain, Germany, Austria, France, Russia, Southern Europe, and elsewhere. He clearly felt Jews were more intelligent than Gentiles.

Joseph Jacobs said much the same, though his effort was focused on Germany, a rigorous statistical analysis of Jews (*Studies in Jewish Statistics: Social, Vital, and Anthropomorphic*, D. Nutt, London, 1890) and their careers. From that he concluded they were heavily involved in intellectually demanding careers and gave his own cultural arguments explaining why that was so, including the premium on education, the urban lifestyle and similar factors.

That same year, Thorsten Veblen wrote about Jewish success. Interestingly, he attributed the success to their separation from most of the people in the countries where they lived. He thought isolation freed them and allowed them to be more creative because they were not constrained by the conventional thinking of the times. And because he held that view, he was skeptical that Jews would continue to be high achievers if they ever got their own country. In light of history since 1948, it is clear he recognized the disproportionate performance early, but was wrong in his projection of what would happen if Israel came into being.

12. *Jews, God and History* – Max Dimont

In 1962, Max I. Dimont, a 1930 Jewish immigrant to the United States from Helsinki, Finland, wrote *Jews, God and History*. Israel was then only fourteen years old and the 1967 Six-Day War and Yom Kippur War were yet to be fought. Dimont's book focused mostly on the survival of the Jewish people and all they had been through over four thousand years. And in the telling, he dealt with high achievement. He said it arose from a number of sources: the premium placed on education, including abstract concepts; the basic role of the Torah and Talmud/Jewish law as part of that education (Yeshivas and Talmudic debate sharpened the mind); the sense that one had to be twice as good as non-Jews to survive and prosper; and the hardship since the Roman conquest—all of that combined with the Diaspora experience.

13. *The Jewish Mystique* – Ernest Van Den Haag

Non-Jew Ernest Van Den Haag's 1969 book, *The Jewish Mystique*, appears to be the first widely read exposition citing Roman Catholic celibacy, versus Jewish rabbis' large families, as a cause for disproportionate Jewish achievement. Namely, over many generations, natural selection diminished the best and brightest among Catholics (those who went into the priesthood and remained celibate) while enlarging the proportion of bright Jews (since rabbis were expected to marry and have large families). The theory predates Van Den Haag, appearing in academic papers written in the 1950s and 1960s (see Patai's *The Jewish Mind*, p 576), but Van Den Haag's book popularized the notion.

Ultimately, Van Den Haag went much beyond that single theory's inherent argument for heredity/natural selection based on cultural values. He discussed the importance of other elements of Jewish culture at length and cited the relative lack of emphasis placed on education by Sephardic Jews, as compared with Ashkenazis. He saw that as a major reason for diminished Sephardic average IQs and their lagging record of high achievement. He also wrote about "Jewish character." He never brought it all together into a coherent theory but he implied both nature and nurture were causative.

14. Khazars as *The Thirteenth Tribe* – Arthur Koestler

In 1976, Arthur Koestler's book, *The Thirteenth Tribe*, was issued. In it, Koestler, a secular Jew, introduced the controversial theory that Ashkenazi Jews had not descended from Jews of Mideast antiquity, but instead, were Khazars, a Turkic people from the Caucasus who converted to Judaism in the eighth century. Though he said he hoped his theory, when proven, would help reduce European anti-Semitism, instead, it later unleashed a firestorm from various groups who found it useful in making their own anti-Semitic arguments. These included Arabs and Palestinians who wished to discredit Ashkenazi claims to Palestine dating back to ancient times.

15. *The Jewish Mind* – Raphael Patai

Raphael Patai's 1977 book, *The Jewish Mind*, combined history with several chapters devoted to Ashkenazi IQ and disproportionate

Jewish achievement. It was Patai who first explained, for popular audiences, the critical importance of the Jewish Emancipation in spurring significant Jewish involvement in European secular life. His often-quoted passage on this point was cited in Chapter 1.

As a Jewish scholar with a doctorate in Semitic Languages and Oriental History, Patai's work focused on ancient and contemporary cultural development of the Jewish people and their history. His chapter devoted to Jewish Intelligence explained what IQ is, compared IQ test results of different groups, and covered environmental conditions he thought encouraged and discouraged high IQs among a population. He used part of that chapter to write about heredity, but devoted the majority of it to the often-difficult circumstances in which Jews had lived and the cultural values they held.

In the end, Patai made the case that Jewish excellence and genius arose from: 1) the "pressures of Gentile persecution, or at least discrimination, which made for the survival of the most intelligent; 2) the advantages enjoyed by the best scholars in mating and procreation; that arose from 3) the religious and cultural traditions that considered 'learning the highest value' in terms of Torah and Talmudic study, and intellectual aspirations and demands on children to achieve academic success; 4) the 'extremely stimulating character of the home environment; 5) the 'age old preference for urban living;' 6) the results of which were, because of Gentile proscriptions, to eke out a living in commercial occupations that required language, mathematical skills, and intelligence; and 7) to survive in the challenging Gentile cultural atmosphere; all of which tended to raise Jewish intelligence and increase the numbers of gifted among the Jews."

In short, Jewish circumstances and Jewish values combined to contribute to a natural selection process for higher IQ, and with that, high achievement ("environmentally induced genetic development"). The essential thrust of Patai's writing was the importance of Jewish cultural values, and to quote him, the Jewish people "act to adapt themselves to reality or to adapt reality to themselves" (*The Jewish Mind* p. 338; and Jamie Glazov, *Front Page Magazine.com,* December 3, 2001).

16. The Studies of Identical Twins Reared Apart – Thomas J. Bouchard, Jr.

Chapter 1's section, The Twin Studies and Heritability, describes how, in early 1979, University of Minnesota Professor Thomas Bouchard learned of two identical twins that had been raised apart since they were four weeks old. Recently, they had been reunited and their remarkable similarities, together with the extensive press coverage the story received, gave Bouchard an insight to how he might assemble a large group of twins like them. His intention was to rigorously study the similarities and differences of identical twins raised apart and with that to better understand the respective roles of nature and nurture in shaping us as humans.

As early as the 1860s, Francis Galton had anticipated the usefulness of identical twins, particularly identical twins raised apart, as subjects for studying the heritability of traits. In 1925, geneticist Hermann Werner Siemens published research on identical and non-identical twins in Germany and in 1937, 1962, and 1965, scientists in Chicago, England, and Denmark, respectively, did other studies. But each study was small in terms of the numbers of twins and the completeness of the inquiries and analysis.

In the two Jims, Bouchard saw an opportunity to launch a major study, and the heightened public interest they garnered gave him an idea of how to track down more twins who had been separated at birth or shortly thereafter. Ultimately, eighty-one pairs of identical and fifty-six pairs of fraternal twins "reared apart" were enrolled, along with an equivalent number of identical and fraternal twins who had been reared together.

When Bouchard applied for grants to study the twins, he noted, "Our findings continue to suggest a very strong genetic influence on almost all medical and psychological traits." By February 1980, this became the Minnesota Study of Twins Reared Apart (MISTRA). Formally, MISTRA lasted twenty years, but the analysis and use of its data continues to this day. According to the Web Of Science (WOS), Bouchard's articles and book chapters have now been cited more than 5,500 times in the scientific literature of others, and MISTRA itself published more than 150 scientific papers and book chapters.

Today, identical twin studies are the principal source for IQ heritability estimates of roughly .4 to .7 (with heritability rising with age). As time has passed, a consensus has grown, sharing the view that intelligence is significantly influenced by genetics.

Bouchard's timing was interesting. Only 20 years earlier, Tay Sachs was found to be a genetic disease, as later so would other so-called Ashkenazi predisposed diseases, plus sickle cell anemia, cancer, and many others not necessarily of higher incidence in Ashkenazis. Moreover, the Pavlovian model of "conditioned behavior" was proving false. It was becoming ever clearer that we humans are not "blank slates at birth, but instead we are born with certain predispositions. And while the role of genetics in behavior was subject to major disputes (witness the treatment of Edward O. Wilson, author of Sociobiology, who was doused with water by protesters at a scientific convention), the nature-nurture debate was increasingly in the spotlight. It was all very heated and subject to a great deal of "politically correct" criticism.

For more on MISTRA, see item 130 below. It covers Dr. Nancy Segal's 2012 book, *Born Together—Reared Apart*, a well written retrospective review of the entire MISTRA project written by a key member of Bouchard's team.

17. The Seventeenth Century Golden Age Dutch

In June 1987, Harvard Professor Simon Schama's book, *The Embarrassment of Riches*, was published. A Cambridge-educated historian, Schama wrote about the Dutch Golden Age and the ambivalences and tensions of that remarkable era. More recently, he has had great notoriety (nearly all of it positive), for his two-volume *The Story of the Jews* and the associated five-part PBS series available on DVD.

Roughly spanning the seventeenth century, the Dutch Golden Age began as the mostly Protestant (Calvinist, Mennonite and Lutheran) Dutch fought for religious, political, and economic freedom from Hapsburg Catholic Spain. By mid-century, after nearly eighty years of war, they achieved their independence. Most of the Protestant Dutch living outside the boundaries of the new Republic then moved to present-day Amsterdam, which quickly became a major world center for culture, commerce and learning.

Dutch tolerance allowed Catholics who wished to remain in the Netherlands to do so. Most lived among fellow Catholics in their own neighborhoods, as did most Jews (some Ashkenazi, but mostly Sephardic immigrants from Portugal). Spinoza's grandfather first fled Portugal for France, and later moved to Rotterdam as part of the large wave of Portuguese Sephardic Jews fleeing Iberian repression to live in a more tolerant society. Spinoza lived among his fellow Sephardics until he was excommunicated, after which he lived alone. Other refugees included the French Huguenots, some English Puritans, and Renaissance Humanists.

Despite the tiny geography (slightly smaller than New Jersey) and a population of only 1.5 to 1.9 million, Dutch science, military and naval skills, art, publishing, and trade, grew to become among the world's most acclaimed of the time. The world's first multinational enterprise was the Dutch East India Company and its success eclipsed the Portuguese and Spanish in developing commercial opportunities in Japan, China, Indonesia, the Americas, and Europe. The counterpart, The

Dutch West India Company, ordered New Amsterdam's Governor, Peter Stuyvesant, to admit Jews fleeing the Inquisition in 1654. Like the Jews, the Dutch developed international trading skills and extensive knowledge of other places and cultures. They were successful capitalists 150 years before Adam Smith published *Wealth of Nations.*

Dutch intellectual tolerance was a magnet that attracted thinkers and scientists from all over Europe, particularly to the University of Leiden (established in 1575 by William, Prince of Orange, leader of the Dutch Revolt in the 80 Years' War). Rene Descartes lived in Leiden for twenty-one years and Spinoza was born and raised in Holland. Christian Huygens, the astronomer, physicist, mathematician, and clockmaker, and Anton van Leeuwenhoek, who famously improved the microscope to study microscopic life and discovered bacteria and blood cells, were among the eminent Dutch scientists of the time.

The Dutch also were Europe's leading publishers, issuing religious, philosophy, and science books too controversial to have been produced elsewhere in Europe, and its chambers of rhetoric fostered literary activities. Among the great painters of the Age were Rembrandt van Rijn, Johannes Vermeer, Jacob van Ruisdael, and Frans Hals.

This was a literate, mostly Calvinist-oriented meritocracy affording little respect to landed nobility but great tolerance for others' religious views. Status was accorded to successful merchants, scientists, artists, and thinkers. Equality before the law was important, as were incorruptibility and the wisdom of judges.

For Schama, a major part of his book dealt with the tensions the Dutch faced in living with both their immense material success and the piety and high ethical standards they expected of themselves. He suggested the Dutch spirit could be summed up in their motto *Luctor et Emergo,*—"I struggle and emerge."

18. *A History of the Jews* – Paul Johnson

Paul Johnson's 1987 book, *A History of the Jews,* arose from his earlier book, *A History of Christianity.* Johnson, who is Roman Catholic, said he discovered "the magnitude of the debt Christianity owes to Judaism" in writing the earlier book. He wanted to explore and understand the history of the Jewish people and tell others what he learned.

It is not clear if he read Patai, who is not cited, but clearly he picked up on the importance of the Jewish Emancipation, referring to it as "an event of shattering importance in World History." And without documenting the disproportionate achievements, he wrote about many Jewish high achievers in very positive terms.

Johnson's perspective is that of a historian. And while he talked about the heritage of rabbis and successful people marrying and having large families, suggesting the possibility of inheritance as an explanation, the bulk of his exposition made a strong case for Jewish culture and values as the driving force.

19. Asian vs. American Parental Culture

In 1990, H.W. Stevenson and S.Y. Lee's paper, "Context of Achievement: a Study of American, Chinese, and Japanese Children" was published in *Monographs of the Society for Research in Child Development*. It was not the first nor last report on the subject, but it remains widely cited as a major source—something of a precursor to the Tiger Mom book (*Battle Hymn of the Tiger Mother*) and the phenomenon arising from its 2011 authorship by Yale Law professor Amy Chua.

The 1990 paper explained what were seen as the causes for the high achievement of Chinese and Japanese children versus American children. It looked at first and fifth grade children in the Minneapolis, Minnesota area, Taipei, Taiwan, and Sendai, Japan. There were 1440 subjects in all: 240 first graders and 240 fifth graders in each city, from twenty different classrooms at both grade levels. The first graders were also revisited later when they were in the fifth grade. The children were all given achievement tests in reading and math. The mothers, children and school principals were all interviewed, while the teachers filled out questionnaires.

Throughout the study it became clear the Asian mothers put much greater emphasis on their children's academic success. They were more heavily involved in the educational process and had higher expectations of their offspring. There was a major difference in the parents' and children's beliefs about the relative influence of effort and ability on academic achievement. For Chinese and Japanese mothers, this was their major pursuit. American mothers, instead, attempted to provide experiences that fostered cognitive growth rather than academic excellence. Asians also tended to provide more realistic assessments of their children's academic, cognitive, and personality characteristics than did American mothers, who tended to overestimate their child's abilities and expressed greater satisfaction. Asians also stressed the importance of hard work, whereas American mothers gave greater emphasis to innate ability.

20. *The Bell Curve* – Charles Murray

In September, 1994, Harvard psychologist Richard Herrnstein, who passed away the month before the book was issued, and American Enterprise Institute Fellow Charles Murray published *The Bell Curve*. The book was focused on two key points. First, that intelligence is a solid pre-dictor of later outcomes such as careers chosen, income, job performance, and conversely, unwed pregnancy and crime. The predictive power of IQ was stronger than the socioeconomic status of one's parents and even one's education. Second, the authors said that America is increasingly becoming a meritocracy in which those with higher intelligence become more successful, and with that, more isolated from general society and from those with below-average intelligence. Murray and Herrnstein saw the stratification as a dangerous trend that needs attention. This point was raised again in Murray's more recent book, *Coming Apart* (2012).

The first of those two concepts is particularly germane to this book. *The Bell Curve* says IQ or "g" (general intelligence) is real, meaningful, and that in general, is a decent predictor of future achievement. Herrn-stein and Murray support that case by correlating intelligence with important indicators of achievement. And while intelligence may not matter in some domains of achievement, such as athletics, it clearly does matter in others, such as winning a Nobel Prize in physics.

The authors also say that both genetics and environment affect intelligence. Using data from a huge number of sources, they suggest the genetic heritability component is likely on the order of .4 to .7.

There is no detailed discussion of Jewish achievement in the book, but Herrnstein and Murray note that Ashkenazi Jews had scored the equivalent IQ of 112.6 on the Armed Forces Qualifying Test adminis-tered to 10,000 Americans as part of the Federal National Longitudi-nal Study of Youth. Data from that study were at the core of *The Bell Curve* analysis. The result was consistent with other studies putting Ashkenazi intelligence roughly 0.8 standard deviations above the aver-age of 100 for European and American Whites.

The book ignited a firestorm of criticism, most of it undeserved. In devoting several chapters to data on different ethnic groups (Asians, Whites, Blacks, and Hispanics) and mentioning IQ differences between the various groups, including Jews, the match was lit. Most of the ensuing arguments were ill informed, angry and often ludicrous. And in the years since, much of what was actually said by Herrnstein and Murray has held up well. We now talk of different kinds of intelligence, but the so-called "g" factor for general intelligence has not been discredited. Students still take SAT tests and except for rare cases, such as Lani Guinier's recent crit-icisms in her book, *The Tyranny of the Meritocracy*, their predictive power has not come into question.

And in America, Asians, and Jews continue to show the highest IQs as groups. Behind them come Whites, then Hispanics, then Blacks. And the separation of those with high IQs at the top of our society, and those with low IQs at the bottom, has continued to worsen. If anything, that situation has reached alarming proportions. For me this truth has almost nothing to do with latent ability, but mostly arises from a failure to esteem education, inculcate self-discipline, raise most offspring in two-parent families, and instill other cultural values generally akin to those of Jews and other high achieving groups described in Part I.

Among those who wrote to support Herrnstein and Murray throughout the controversy was Thomas Bouchard of the Minnesota Twin Studies. He joined John B Carroll, Hans Eysenck, Arthur Jensen, Richard Lynn, Robert Plomin, and forty-seven other experts in intelligence from leading universities around the world in signing a twenty-five-point response to misstatements made by critics of *The Bell Curve*. They arranged for it to be published in *The Wall Street Journal*.

21. Jewish Genetic History Research – The Cohanim
In January 1997, Dr. Michael Hammer of the University of Arizona published one of the earliest research papers written about Jewish genetic history, in the British science journal *Nature*. Hammer reported on his tests of DNA collected from 188 Jewish males, exploring whether or not Jews who say they are from the Cohanim priestly class are related, and if so, when the Cohanim line originated.

Hammer looked at the Y chromosome, (unique to males), and reported that he had found a common mutation marker (YAP-) in 98.5 percent of the Cohanim and in a significantly lower percent of the non-Cohanim. Moreover, in analyzing the history of that mutation, it was possible to say the common ancestor of the Sephardic and Ashkenazi Cohanim went back 106 generations, roughly 3,300 years. This may simply be a coincidence, but for some it suggested the possibility that Moses' brother Aaron might, in fact, have been an ancestor for many or most of the Cohanim.

22. Ashkenazi Genetic Ailments – Nicholas Wade
In August 1997, Nicholas Wade, a science reporter for *The New York Times*, wrote one of the earliest of his many stories about results from genetic research, some of which have focused on Jewish genetics. Over the years, Wade, also deputy editor of the journal *Nature*, contributed more than 1,000 science stories to *The New York Times*. As a result, his reports are a good chronological guide to important research breakthroughs in these areas.

In the August 1997 story, Wade indicated that Johns Hopkins biologists had discovered a genetic mutation associated with colon cancer in 6 percent of Ashkenazi Jews. If confirmed, the mutation would double the risk of colon cancer (from 18 to 30 percent versus 9 to 15 percent) for those Ashkenazis carrying the mutation. Because such information can encourage anyone with the mutation to be tested more frequently (and be treated early if polyps are found), the report was seen to illustrate the medical advances that might arise from the Human Genome Project. Perhaps it helped assuage some Jewish fears about genetic research on matters of race and ethnicity by focusing on its potential benefits.

23. A Gene Variance for IQ?

In May 1998, Nicholas Wade reported that psychologists had found the first gene thought linked to heightened intelligence. Working in London, an American and two British doctors had studied fifty students with IQs measured at 160 points or more. When they compared the DNA of these students with children of average IQ, they discovered a genetic variant of a gene on chromosome six was twice as common among the high-IQ children. The effect was small, however, "perhaps accounting for about 2 percent of the variance, or 4 IQ points." This was seen to be consistent with the view that perhaps "50 or more" genes might influence general intelligence. The work was considered credible, in part because of the credentials of the researchers, and this was said to be the first time a gene had been associated with some specific aspect of cognition and behavior. This first association of a gene with heightened IQ was seen to have scored a point for nature in the nature versus nurture debate.

24. Thomas Sowell's Trilogy on Culture

In 1998, Thomas Sowell, PhD, completed his trilogy: *Race and Culture* (1994), *Migrations and Culture* (1996), and *Conquests and Culture* (1998). An immense fifteen-year effort by the outspoken economist and Hoover Fellow, it was a remarkable testament to the importance of culture. Sowell has long been articulate and controversial because he and a few other Black intellectuals have been willing to defy stereotypes. In the trilogy, Sowell wrote of the difference culture makes to different peoples. He noted, for example, that:

— The Chinese went from intellectuals and world leaders during the Ming Dynasty, to isolated, impoverished and backwards through the era of Mao, until today when they are again dynamic and have become the world's second largest economic power. All this in roughly 500 years. Political leadership and cultural values drove these changes, not changes in IQ.

— The Scots went from impoverished and backward, largely illiterate, and a defeated people, to producing some of the most important geniuses of the eighteenth and nineteenth centuries: Watt, Smith, Hume, Clark Maxwell, Lord Kelvin, and others.

— The Japanese went from an isolated feudal society in 1853 to a naval military power able to defeat the Russian Navy fifty years later. From there they went on to dominate Asia, lose World War II, and restore themselves to become, today, the world's third largest economy.

Among hundreds of data points Sowell used to illustrate the power of culture, he also pointed out that:

— In the early 1920s, 6 percent of Hungary's population was Jewish as was 11 percent of Poland's, but Jews were more than half the physicians in both countries.

— The Chinese were 5 percent of the population of Indonesia, but they owned an estimated 80 percent of the country's capital.

— During the 1960s, the Chinese minority of Malaysia earned more than one hundred times the number of engineering degrees, as compared with the Malay majority.

— In the Austrian Empire of 1900, the illiteracy rate of adult Poles was 40 percent. For Serbo-Croatians, it was 75 percent, and for Germans, 6 percent.

— In the 1960s, the majority of Nigeria's population lived in its northern provinces, but that majority accounted for only 9 percent of University students and 2 percent of Nigerians studying abroad.

Education, exposure to other peoples (as opposed to isolation), geography and its influence on exposure and commerce, and urban (as opposed to rural) lifestyles were just a few of the influences that affected the cultural milieu and values which Sowell identified as contributing to differences in performance. And when discussing geography and resources, he advanced the notion that these were instances in which natural circumstances influence cultural values. In *Migrations and Cultures* (p 376) he says, "Over long spans of history, the racial reshuffling of the relative technological ranking of different races and nations makes it hard to conclude that such standings are genetically determined."

25. Darwin's Finches

In May 1999, Nicholas Wade wrote two articles on genetic research for *The New York Times*. The first indicated researchers had developed genetic data on the famous Galapagos Island finches to prove Darwin's theory of "adaptive radiation," a form of natural selection. The research analyzed DNA from the thirteen different Galapagos Islands' species of finches and found they all originated from a single ancestral species. Each species had adapted to the varying conditions on the different islands to become a new species.

The phenomenon, and particularly how quickly finches adapt to climate change, were chronicled in Jonathan Weiner's 1994 Pulitzer Prize winning book, *The Beak of the Finch*. The new research corroborated Darwin's adaptive radiation theory of natural selection as well as the work of Peter and Rosemary Grant, the two Princeton researchers featured in Weiner's book who had observed the changing finches on the Galapagos island of Daphne Major since 1973. "Survival of the fit" (if not necessarily the "fittest") was clearly demonstrated in the Galapagos finches.

On August 5, 2014, *The New York Times* Science section ran a story by Weiner on Peter and Rosemary Grant's ongoing work. Both are now 77 and yet new insights keep coming. They continue to study a family of new finches that arose from "Big Bird"—a hybrid of two finch species—who first arrived on Daphne in 1981. His lineage now extends through seven generations and may ultimately prove to be its own long lasting species. The Grants have had a front row seat for all of this, been honored with every major prize in evolutionary science, and are thought by some to have done the most important evolutionary biology research of the last fifty years.

26. Jewish Genetics – The Cohanim and the Lemba

Wade's second article reported on a new study to be published in *The American Journal of Human Genetics* by Dr. David Goldstein of Oxford University. Some of Goldstein's research focused on refining Dr. Michael Hammer's techniques. Goldstein explored Y chromosome data relating to the paternal genetic linkages to the priestly Cohanim.

In the process, he said he developed a tool to distinguish Jewish from non-Jewish populations. He chose to use this tool, and his

Cohanim test, to look at the Lemba, a Bantu people of Southern Africa. The Lemba have long said that an ancient ancestor named Buba led them from Judea to Southern Africa. They claim Jewish ancestry, wear yarmulkes, circumcise their male children, keep a day of Sabbath, do not eat pork or pork-like meats, and have Semitic names. Nevertheless, many had long discounted the Lemba claim of Jewish ancestry. Then "Goldstein reported that 9 percent of Lemba males carry the Cohanim genetic signature and, of those who said they were related to Buba, 53 percent" carry the signature. Another tribe had established its Jewish bona fides.

CHAPTER 11

2000 to 2005: The Genome, New Data, and New Theories

27. *Culture Matters* – Lawrence Harrison and Samuel P. Huntington

In May 2000, Lawrence Harrison and Samuel P. Huntington's book, *Culture Matters,* was published. Not simply the work of the two authors, the book also compiled papers presented at an April 1999 Harvard symposium.

The symposium's blue chip presenters included: Harvard Economics Professor David Landes; Harvard Business School Professor and international competitiveness expert Michael Porter; economist Jeffrey Sachs; political scientist Francis Fukuyama; political social scientist Seymour Martin Lipset; cultural sociologist Orlando Patterson; sociologist Nathan Glazer; and others. The papers and the book focused on "How Values Shape Human Progress" and explored a wide range of topics linking values and progress, geography and culture, and cultural change.

In the book's foreword, Huntington said, "Perhaps the wisest words on the place of culture in human affairs are those of Daniel Patrick Moynihan: 'The central conservative truth is that it is culture, not politics, that determines the success of a society. The central liberal truth is that politics can change a culture and save it from itself.'"

Huntington pointed out that in the early 1960s, the per capita gross domestic product of Ghana and South Korea were comparable. They had "similar divisions among primary products, manufacturing, and services…with South Korea producing a few manufactured goods." Both received comparable levels of foreign aid. Thirty years later, South Korea was the world's fourteenth largest economy and well on its way to consolidating democratic institutions. By1990, Ghana's economy was only one-fifteenth the size of South Korea's.

135

Following World War II, South Korea went through its own variation on Japan's experience in the Meiji Restoration. No longer a colony of Japan nor ruled by its own military, it was nudged by the United States toward democracy. The positive elements of Confucian cultural values were unleashed without the constraints of authoritarianism.

Today, South Korea, an area about the size of the state of Indiana, with few natural resources, has a population of forty-nine million. Literacy is 97.9 percent. The unemployment rate is 3.4 percent. Its debt, at 33.2 percent of GDP, is among the lowest in the developed and developing worlds. It has become a huge success. And at $1.5 trillion (USD), its economy is now twenty times Ghana's.

28. Jewish Genetics – Common Jewish Origins and the Khazars (again)

In May 2000, the on-line National Academy of Science published a paper by Dr. Michael F. Hammer and eleven colleagues. It reported on the DNA evidence for common Jewish origins of six Diaspora communities. The research established that the Ashkenazi, Roman, North African, Near Eastern, Kurdish and Yemenite Jews were not significantly different from each other. They share a common Middle Eastern genetic ancestry, and have low levels of "admixtures" from other populations (about 0.5 percent in each generation among Ashkenazim.) This confirmed that Jews had rarely married non-Jews. The only exception was the Ethiopian Jews, with a significantly higher admixture of non-Jewish Ethiopians.

Only present day Palestinian and Syrian populations showed DNA data akin to the seven Jewish communities. The data also suggested that the shared lineage might be traced as far back as 4,000 years ago. Once more, data was discrediting the Khazar theory of Ashkenazi origins. As the report's abstract noted, the seven Jewish communities are "descended from a common Middle Eastern ancestral population ... and have remained relatively isolated from neighboring non-Jewish communities during and after the Diaspora. In reporting on this paper, Nicholas Wade noted that research on the Y (male) chromosome links all males to "a single genetic Adam who is estimated to have lived about 140,000 years ago."

29. *The Jewish Phenomenon* – Steven Silbiger

Steven Silbiger's late-2000 book, *The Jewish Phenomenon,* made the case for culture. Writing as a Jew, he laid out seven principles behind

Jewish success. He lauded immense respect for learning; openness to and encouragement of debate (with consequent verbal and writing skills); a willingness to take unpopular positions; being comfortable with being seen as different; and an emphasis on creativity, professional, and entrepreneurial skills. Silbiger saw these as important character traits that explained Jewish success, and as such, "teachable lessons" for both Jews and non-Jews who aspire to comparable success.

30. The Scottish Genius(es) of the Seventeenth and Eighteenth Centuries

Michael Hart's 1987 book, *The 100,* ranked his own list of history's 100 most influential people. In it, he made the observation that "no fewer than five (of the 100) came from Scotland" and all five of those, born between 1723 and 1881, were "in the top half of the list." They were James Watt, James Clark Maxwell, Adam Smith, Alexander Graham Bell, and Alexander Fleming. In his final comment, Hart noted, "Since the Scots constitute only about one-eighth of one percent of the world's population, this represents a truly astonishing concentration of talent and achievement."

In November 2001, Arthur Herman laid out his views in *How the Scots Invented the Modern World.* He credited John Knox, father of the Scottish Reformation, who, in 1559, led efforts to overthrow Scotland's Catholic Church. Knox, Herman said, "wanted to turn the Scots into God's chosen people." The Reformation had made the Bible available to Scots in "the vernacular" and no priest was needed as an intervener between God and man. But literacy was a must if a Scot was to read and understand it. Education was pushed by the Presbyterian Church, and in 1696, Scotland's Parliament passed a law establishing a school in every parish that did not already have one (most already did). By 1750, when the English literacy rate was 53 percent, Scotland's rate was 75 percent. In 1763, Edinburgh had six publishing houses in a city of 60,000.

Knox insisted that power be vested in the people. Though the Crown would come and go, Scottish protestant churches were always self-governing. They selected their own leaders and ministers. And Presbyterian and Calvinist values were strict in demanding parishioners meet God's demands.

The Scots were never strangers to adversity. Often ruled harshly, particularly after losing wars to England, they lived through economic calamity. Between 1696, when the Darien Company was founded, until after its 1705 failure, the Scottish economy was devastated in ways much worse than the current economic travails of countries such as Spain and Portugal. In 1704, the Bank of Scotland failed following three years of famine and the so-called "Lean Years" of 1697 to 1703, marked by more than 10,000 Scottish deaths.

Like the Jews, Scotland had their own Enlightenment as secularism leavened the demands of religion. And fundamental to Scotland's emergence as a society of disproportionate high achievers, according to Herman, was the Scotts' view of history as progress. He argued that from the Scottish perspective: "Societies, like individuals, grow and improve over time. They acquire new skills, new attitudes, and a new understanding of what individuals can do and what they should be free to do. The Scots would teach the world that one of the crucial ways we measure progress is by how far we have come from what we were before."

31. "Some Genetics for Some Jews" (and Ashkenazi History)– Robert Pollack

In the spring of 2002, Robert Pollack, PhD, a highly respected molecular biologist at Columbia University, wrote "Some Genetics for Some Jews: A Jewish Look at the Human Genome" for the *Conservative Judaism Journal*. Though not enthusiastic about the "genetic revolution," Pollack's essay was a superb explanation of Jewish and Ashkenazi population change over recorded history and its ramifications for Jewish genetic history. The same history is also germane to any exploration of disproportionate Jewish achievement and its causes.

Jewish Demography – 1000 BCE to 2001 CE

Year	World Population	Number of Jews	% of World Population
1000 BCE	100,000,000	2,000,000	2.00%
500 BCE	150,000,000	300,000	0.20%
70 CE	270,000,000	4,500,000	1.67%
600 CE	200,000,000	1,250,000	0.50%
1600 CE	625,000,000	1,250,000	0.20%
1939 CE	2,000,000,000	16,500,000	0.83%
2001 CE	6,000,000,000	13,000,000	0.20%

Pollack said the numbers of Jews in the world have varied widely over the last 3,000 years. He noted that at the time of David's establishment of history's first Jewish state about 3,000 years ago, the Jewish population rose from 500,000 to approximately two million. Almost one person in fifty (2 percent of the world's population at the time) was Jewish. This was the population peak for Jews as a percent of the world's population.

After Babylon conquered the Jews about 2,500 years ago, the number of Jews dropped to approximately 300,000 and still later, under Greek rule, Jews were only one in 500 of the world's population (one-fifth of 1 percent). Before the Roman Conquest in 70 CE, the Jewish population had risen to four to five million, or one person in sixty (1.67 percent of the world's population.) But following the Roman Conquest and the Diaspora, by 600 CE, Jewish numbers fell to roughly one person in 200 (one-half of 1 percent). From that time until the year 1600, the total number of Jews ranged between 1 and 1.5 million while world's population doubled. By 1600, Jews were back down to one in 500 of the world's population (one-fifth of 1 percent), the same percentage as followed the Babylonian conquest.

From that low point, Jews exploded to seventeen million by 1939 (eight-tenths of 1 percent of the world's population). The Holocaust then destroyed one-third of them. Since the end of World War II, the Jewish population has remained essentially flat while the global population has tripled. The result is that today, Jews are only two-tenths of one percent of the world's population.

Perhaps the most amazing aspect of Pollack's demographic history is what he says about Ashkenazis. Until sometime around 800 CE, they were not even identified as a distinct Jewish group. They grew in numbers but suffered through European Crusades, anti-Semitic persecution and pogroms. And by 1500, Pollack estimates, the numbers of Ashkenazis could be counted in the tens of thousands in a world of a million or so Jews. From that point, the Ashkenazim contracted still further to an estimated 3,000 families by 1600. Then it all reversed—an astonishing population growth commenced, and continued over the next 350 years or so. Pollock estimates that by 1939, the Ashkenazim were 95 percent of the world's 17 million Jews (more than 16 million Ashkenazis).

Pollack also discussed the "founder effect" ramifications of this history. Namely, with such a large population arising so quickly from so few "founding" families, and with almost no intermarriage except among fellow Ashkenazis, all those who arose from this small base share essentially the same genetic heritage.

As he says, "Given the great number of versions of each gene available in the human species at large, long runs of identical versions of genes in two unrelated people will never occur by coincidence. But because the surviving population of Ashkenaz was so terribly small in the mid-1600s, and because it grew in an uninterrupted way from such small numbers, a large fraction of Jews today share long stretches of genes with each other.... The utter sameness of the DNA...means that every Jew whose ancestors come from Ashkenaz—about nine of every ten Jews alive today—is the descendent of no more than about 3,000 families who survived the pogroms of the mid-1600s."

And with that, he concluded any genetic defects of the founders, coupled with high rates of intermarriage among the Ashkenazim, tend to carry the defects through to succeeding generations. It leads to the elevated incidence of ailments such as Gaucher's disease, Tay Sachs, idiopathic torsion dystonia, and others at much higher rates for Ashkenazis than any other group.

In the end, it must be said that Pollack was very concerned about the notion of race and the risk that genetic research could result in the return of dangerous racial stereotyping. Perhaps two sentences in his March 7, 2003 essay, "The Fallacy of Biological Judaism" best summarizes his view: "there are not DNA sequences common to all Jews and absent from all non-Jews. There is nothing in the human genome that makes or diagnoses a person as a Jew."

32. Genetics of Chimps and Humans – Sharon Begley

On April 12 2002, Sharon Begley, *The Wall Street Journal* science columnist, wrote one of her early reports covering research in genetic science, its medical applications, its influence on individual traits, and the environmental and cultural factors that shape human behavior. A Yale graduate and winner of numerous industry awards for her science reporting, Begley is author or co-author of three books. In addition to *The Wall Street Journal*, she has written about science for *Newsweek*, Reuters, *The Daily Beast*, and others. Like Nicholas Wade, Begley is a highly credible reporter to follow if one is tracking the unfolding developments in behavioral and genetic science.

Begley's April 2002 column dealt with the research that compared DNA in the brains of chimps with that in humans. She noted that 98.7% of chimp DNA is identical to human DNA. In samples of DNA taken from the brains of three deceased chimps and three deceased humans, only 175 of the 34,000 gene sequences were significantly different. She noted, "What distinguishes ours from theirs is which genes turn on and how much. (Genes make proteins; a gene turned to 'high' makes more of its protein than one turned to 'low'.) The kinds of proteins produced by the chimp genes differ from ours by only 7.6 percent. The amounts of those proteins differ by 31.4 percent." After discussing regulatory genes and genes that turn other genes on and off, she notes,

"Whether genes are on or off, and how high they are turned on, often depends on what your senses are taking in, what you're feeling and even what you're thinking."

Begley did not use the term "epigenetics" in her commentary. Nonetheless, the phenomenon she describes sounds very much like what, over the last few years, has become an important part of today's genetics—namely, that regulatory mechanisms, often arising from the environment, turn genes on and off or up and down without changing the gene itself as a mutation would.

33. The Placebo Effect (and the Brain?) – Sharon Begley

In a May 10, 2002 article for *The Wall Street Journal,* Begley looked at the placebo effect. She noted that in 2001, *The New England Journal of Medicine* had featured a paper that dismissed the effect entirely. That, in turn, led to medical meetings which referred to the placebo effect as "medical myth," "an urban legend," and "a scam."

Begley went on to document research over the ensuing months that completely undermined the *Journal's* argument. Her reports demonstrated that the effect was not "nothing" but instead it involved genuine physiological changes triggered by the patient's belief that real medicines were being administered. In one study reporting on comparable outcomes, whether patients received the drugs or the placebo, psychiatrist Andrew Leuchter of UCLA noted, "People who get better on the placebo have a change in brain function just as surely as people who get better on antidepressants." The same outcome occurred in Parkinson's patients who got equivalent releases of dopamine from the placebo and the drug. It turns out that expectations can influence outcomes.

34. Jewish Genetics and Mitochondrial DNA – Nicholas Wade

In May 2002, Nicholas Wade wrote a column in *The New York Times* linking the May 2000 Michael Hammer paper (see item 21 above) with a more recent paper by Dr. David Goldstein of Oxford University and others, reporting on an examination of the mitochondrial DNA of Jewish women. Different from paternal DNA found on the Y chromosome, mitochondrial DNA allows the tracing of the maternal genetic history.

Published in *The American Journal of Human Genetics,* the Goldstein paper indicated that among women in the nine Jewish communities studied (from Georgia to Morocco), the female genetic histories were very different from the males and there were very few genetic signatures on the mitochondrial DNA. This suggested that there were a very small number of founding mothers, likely non-Jewish local women who married single Jewish traders that had immigrated to the countries of their non-Jewish wives. Those wives converted to Judaism. Then after these founding non-Jewish wives, the barriers went up and there was almost no further intermarriage. If there had been, Goldstein said, there would be much greater diversity in the mitochondrial DNA of subsequent generations.

There was a good deal of commentary by various experts on what all this might mean, particularly in light of Jewish matrilineal descent which is thought to have been adopted sometime between 200 BCE and 500 CE. And as one might expect, the work of both Hammer and Goldstein once more ignited heated discussion about the validity of race, particularly for a people for whom the issue of "race" has brought so much pain.

35. *Taboo:* Black Athletes and Discussions of Racial Differences

Several months later, the *San Francisco Chronicle* ran a Scott Winokur story covering a controversy stirred by the recently published book, *Taboo: Why Black Athletes Dominate Sports and Why We're Afraid to Talk About It,* by Jon Entine (a Jewish American) and Alondra Oubre (an African American). Winokur said it was furor. Espousing the notion that "Blacks are biologically different, as are Asians, and Whites of all ancestries," caused Entine to be labeled an "ill-informed popularizer of essentially racist pseudoscientific notions, an explosive hack, and an idiot." In short, talking about race, even to say positive things about Black athletes, was taboo. Around that same time, public television aired several programs set in academia, with professors leading the charge that 'there is no such thing as race'.

36. Khazars – Again!

In November 2002, regular contributors to the *khazaria.com* web site posted comments saying reports that discounted the importance of the Khazars' contributions to Ashkenazi Jews were wrong. As one commented, it is "foolish for anyone to argue that Jews worldwide are a 'race' or a 'single ethnic group.' " On December 8, 2002, Steve Olsen wrote a major story for the *Washington Post* about "genetic tests now being rushed to the market…(with) the potential to do great mischief." Further, he said, ancestral pride would not be such a dangerous thing were it not linked so closely to issues of race and ethnicity." As noted above, the era of 'there is no such thing as race,' was underway and aspects of genetic and DNA testing quickly became highly controversial topics to discuss.

37. Thoughts and Behavior Can Trigger Physiological Responses – Sharon Begley

A June 21, 2002 Begley column in *The Wall Street Journal* focused on thoughts and behaviors that trigger physiological and genetic changes. She first noted an anonymous contributor to *Nature* magazine who reported a noticeable increase in the growth of his beard when anticipating a romantic liaison (which had "loosed a flood of testosterone causing the growth"). After a brief mention of stress experienced by medical students, inducing alteration in genes expressed in their immune systems, she went on to describe how the receptors for stress hormones in mice pups are expressed—or not—as a function of maternal handling and licking. Michael Meaney of McGill University reported, "Rats that got less maternal handling grew up timid and withdrawn in novel situations." In essence the issue was the turning on and off of genes based on an environmental influence (a more or less affectionate parent).

38. Is "Race" Biologically Meaningless in Medicine? The Debate – Nicholas Wade

In July 2002, Wade reported on a paper in *Genome Biology* by then Stanford geneticist Dr. Neil Risch. It challenged a 2001 editorial in *The New England Journal of Medicine* that had opined, "Race is biologically meaningless." Risch responded that racial genetic differences have medical significance, since some differences among genes affect susceptibility to diseases and responses to drugs.

In effect, and as suggested in Wade's May 2002 column, as the Human Genome Project unleashed ever more research reports, political sensitivities and worries born of the early twentieth century eugenics movement and historic persecutions based on race (of Jews and others), were coming to the fore.

Nonetheless, it was clear that important genetic differences exist, and Risch was arguing that these needed to be studied and understood. He noted that hemochromatosis, an iron metabolism disorder, occurs in 7.5% of Swedes but not in Indians and Chinese. Lactose intolerance is common, but arrives later in life for Northern Europeans. Sickle cell anemia afflicts Blacks and Tay Sachs afflicts Ashkenazis. Dr. David Goldstein (see item 34 above) weighed in to support Risch, as did Dr. Stephen O'Brien, a geneticist at the National Cancer Institute, who said, "Neil (Risch) and his colleagues have decided the pendulum of political correctness has taken the field in a direction that will hurt epidemiological assessment of disease in the very minorities the defenders of political correctness wish to protect."

39. Genetic Variance, the Environment, and Effects on Violence? – Sharon Begley

Begley's September 20, 2002 column in *The Wall Street Journal* reported on a study of 442 White male New Zealanders born in 1972. It noted that a gene on the X chromosome that makes monoamine oxidase-A (MAOA) comes in two varieties. One produces low gene activity; the other high activity. MAOA, she said, breaks down neurotransmitters, including serotonin and dopamine.

The New Zealand study looked at boys who had been maltreated, and discovered that adult violence among the maltreated boys was far more likely among the 55 who carried the low activity MAOA. They were twice as likely to engage in persistent fighting, bullying, theft, cruelty, and vandalism. Moreover, the low-MAMO population who were not abused as kids showed no increased risk to grow up antisocial or violent. Terrie Moffit of King's College, London, the leader of the study, wrote, "Genes can moderate children's sensitivity to environmental insults. Some genotypes may promote resistance to trauma."

40. Genes, Reduced Brain Size, and Consequences for IQ – Nicholas Wade

On September 24, 2002, in *The New York Times*, Wade reported on a British pediatrician who, together with a Harvard Medical School neurogeneticist, had discovered a gene mutation that led to reduced brain size (microcephaly) in a population of 24 Pakistani families living in England. A "one-letter" change in the gene caused it to make a smaller-sized protein involved in brain development, and with that, fewer neurons. It was one of five genes thought to contribute to smaller brain size, but no research had yet determined precisely how it works.

Though not mentioned in Wade's article, prior research had suggested a correlation between brain size and IQ. Thus the more recent study would potentially suggest another means by which genetics might affect IQ. In noting a coincidence of terminology (the gene's proteins primarily consist of what are called "IQ domains"), the British doctor said the reduction of so-called IQ domain units and the smaller-sized brain was "a proof of God's existence since only someone with a sense of humor could have arranged for the correlation."

41. The Importance of a Jewish Education

The February 10, 2003 weekly radio message of Rabbi Buchwald and the National Jewish Outreach Program was titled, "The Primacy of Jewish Education." Early in his talk, he noted that donations to building or furnishing a tabernacle or temple, or erecting another type of religious edifice, had to be voluntary. People should contribute as much "as their heart's desire." But, "when it comes to lighting a menorah... the light and wisdom of holiness...the light of Jewish education, donors have no choice. Jews must contribute. There is no choice in the matter."

He went on to chronicle a Golden Age unmatched since Spain of the twelfth and thirteenth centuries, and provided statistics and names as though he had just finished reading *The Golden Age of Jewish Achievement*.

His fear was that the Golden Age was receding. Assimilation and loss of Jewish values, he said, risked "losing the magic that in so many ways propelled the exceptional achievements of our people." Among these values were excellence in education, extreme charitability, stability of marital and family life and abhorrence of violence. And it was not just assimilation that was at fault; it was the quality of education he decried. "It is now absolutely indisputable, that aside from Yeshiva and intensive Day School education, every other form of Jewish training for young people in America has proven to be an unmitigated disaster."

42. Disease Risks From BRCA1 and BRCA2 Genetic Mutations – Sharon Begley

The February 28, 2003 Begley column in *The Wall Street Journal* raised the issue of "penetrance" of a gene. Namely, she noted the experience with mutations in the BRCA1 and BRCA2 genes associated with breast cancer and ovarian cancer. Why, she posited, do 13 to 44 percent of women with the gene not get breast cancer and 56 to 72 percent not get ovarian cancer? In short what are the factors that cause a gene to trigger the expected malady or not? Clearly, she suggested, there is no "one for one" relationship.

43. Jewish Genetics: Might Mutations Benefit Natural Selection? – Nicholas Wade

On March 4, 2003, Wade reported in *The New York Times* on a study by Stanford geneticist Dr. Neil Risch, in which he sought to learn if some diseases common to Ashkenazis exist because they confer a natural selection benefit, or occur simply as a matter of chance.

The natural selection notion (see also item 62), suggests some genetic mutations confer benefits that offset—or more than offset—the risk of coincident harm. Sickle cell anemia is one example. The genetic mutation that causes the disease in Blacks when inherited from both parents, confers protection from malaria when inherited from only one parent, hence a natural selection benefit which causes the mutation to persist.

Risch looked at four lysosomal diseases: Tay-Sachs, Gaucher's disease, Neimann-Pick disease, and mucolipidosis type-IV. He examined the dates the diseases first occurred, their frequency, and their geographical distributions, and compared the data with comparable information for other, more common diseases causing Ashkenazi mutations. The premise was that if a natural selection benefit was conferred, the incidence of the four mutations would have grown and become ever more common because of a benefit it conferred.

The absence of increased frequency led Risch to suggest these ailments arose and continue to exist as a matter of chance, and not because they provide a natural selection benefit. Wade's piece pointed out that geneticists now say the Ashkenazi disorders commenced at different times: roughly 2,200 years ago for the blood clotting disorder known as Factor XI deficiency, 900 years ago for three of the four lysosomal diseases, and 500 years ago for a third group of mutations.

44. "Race" and Medicine (Again) – Nicholas Wade

A few weeks after his column on Risch and mutations, Wade reported that the debate over whether "race" has a valid role in medicine cropped up again. This time Dr. Richard S. Cooper of Loyola Stritch School of Medicine argued it should not be used. While he acknowledged that some rare diseases are particular to certain populations, most diseases, he said, are not. He worried that "if medical geneticists were to prove that race is a valid biological concept, then social and political aspects of race, some not so benign, might also seem validated." He said that, for example, APOE4, a genetic variation found in all populations, contributed to Alzheimer's disease.

Dr. Neil Risch responded that even common diseases can involve variations based on race. APOE4 genes from both parents, he noted, raises Alzheimer's risk 33 times in Japanese populations, 15 times in Caucasians and only six times in Africans.

This time around, *The New England Journal of Medicine* opined, that it would be "unwise to abandon the recording of race when we have barely begun to understand the architecture of the human genome and its clues to the genetic basis of disease." Risch said that anxiety among minorities was valid, but despite early fears, "Jews had taken charge of the information about diseases more common in Ashkenazis and now accepted its usefulness."

The following June, *The American Journal of Gastroenterology* published a report titled, "NOD2/CARD15 Genotype and Phenotype Differences Between Ashkenazi and Sephardic Jews with Crohn's disease." It reported on a study of 180 Jewish Crohn's patients, 73 ulcerative colitis patients and 159 ethnically matched controls involving three mutations. The carrier rates for those mutations were 41.1 percent for all Jews versus 10.7 percent for the controls. Further, Ashkenazi Crohn's patients had a carrier rate of 47.4 percent versus 27.5 percent for Sephardics. Again, the incidence rates of disease risk were confirmed to be different between different groups, even including differences between the Ashkenazim and Sephardim.

45. Asians and Westerners Think Differently, But Its Not Hard Wired – Sharon Begley

A March 28, 2003 Begley column in *The Wall Street Journal* focused on different patterns of thinking by Asians and Westerners. A study by Richard E. Nisbett of the University of Michigan had looked at the cognition patterns of thought and noticed that Westerners typically focused on specific elements when presented with an image. Asians, instead, tended to see a bigger picture and relationships between elements. Westerners preferred abstract universal principles while East Asians sought rules appropriate to the situation.

Interestingly, they found these cognition patterns are not hard wired. Asians living in the West and Westerners living in Asia were found to have "gone native" in terms of their thinking patterns, while those in Hong Kong, with its combined Chinese and British history, showed thinking patterns intermediate between East and West.

46. The Human Genome Project Announces Completion (almost)

In April 2003, the Human Genome Project announced it had essentially completed its task to sequence the human genome two years ahead of schedule. Launched in 1990, the $3 billion international scientific effort was initiated by the U.S. Department of Energy and the U.S. National Institutes of Health. It had been expected to take fifteen years. The project set out to come up with a generic map (or sequence) of the three billion base pairs on the human genome with an estimated 20,000 to 25,000 genes. Because each human's sequence is unique, the project map is not a representation of everyone's (or anyone's) genome, but is a reference genome of various anonymous donors. In May 2006, a further milestone was passed when the sequence of the last chromosome was published in the journal *Nature*. And in September 2007,

Craig Venter, chief executive of Celera Corporation, the private company that competed to complete the sequencing, released the first complete sequence of an individual genome—that of Venter himself.

47. Identical Twins, Genes, IQ Heritability, and the Flynn Effect – Sharon Begley

Begley's June 20, 2003 column in *The Wall Street Journal* reported on the genes and other factors that "make up a high IQ." She explained that dozens of studies of thousands of identical twins had shown that DNA must play a significant role in IQ. The studies looked at twins raised by birth parents, as well as other twins separated at (or near) birth and raised by adoptive parents. The studies showed that the IQs of identical twins are more similar, even when raised apart, than other sibling pairs—and more similar to their biological parents than their adoptive parents. Generally, the studies suggested that genetic influences account for about 50 percent of the differences in intelligence from one person to another.

Despite this evidence, tracking down the genes responsible for that outcome has proven daunting. Begley quoted Robert Plomin, a behavioral professor at King's College, London who called this "the most complex and controversial of all complex traits." In short, while IQ is estimated to be 50 percent heritable, no one can yet demonstrate which genes account for it and how.

The May 1998 discovery of a gene thought to be linked to heightened IQ (see item 23 above) could not be replicated in a Kings College follow-up study. That same gene was found in 19 percent of the high-IQ children and 24 percent of those with average IQ.

Part of this, Begley suggested, has to do with our lack of understanding about how the brain works. For example, we don't have any idea how Einstein's brain was different from yours and mine. Another issue is that intelligence may be driven by a large number of other influences such as motivation, which in turn is driven by yet other genes. And still further, "No one gene makes more than a tiny difference."

Environmental circumstances, she said, could also contribute to the ~50 percent that is thought to be heritable. Namely, the positive reinforcement of early signs of higher IQ by parents, teachers, fellow students and others may encourage the kind of studious behavior, critical thinking, and other skills—in effect "bootstrapping" the person to behavior that improves results measured by IQ tests. That could, she said, help explain another phenomenon, namely that measurable heritability of IQ increases from 40 percent in childhood to 60 percent or more as adults.

She quotes James R. Flynn, a professor at the University of Otago, Dunedin in New Zealand, saying, "It isn't that genes grow stronger. Instead, a slight genetic edge at birth snowballs by nudging people to choose intelligence-enhancing experiences. The result is a potent multiplier."

Flynn is well known to such debates as the discoverer of the so-called "Flynn Effect," showing that IQ results overall have been on an upward trajectory for decades, at roughly eighteen points per generation in the Netherlands, Belgium, Israel and Argentina. Americans have gained the equivalent of twenty IQ points. "Genes," said Flynn, "don't change fast enough to explain this, but which genes are 'turned on' might."

With this comment, Begley expanded most readers' knowledge of epigenetics, the emerging science that explores the phenomenon of genes being turned on and off or up and down. Before epigenetics, many people thought of genes as being either on or off, with all genes being either inherited or occasionally inherited, and later mutating. Begley quoted Plomin saying, "the holy grail in this field is identifying what experiences turn on the genes that influence intelligence."

Begley concluded her comments with the observation that "it's already clear that, with so many genes involved in IQ, genetic engineering for it (intelligence) isn't in the cards. If we care about intelligence, she said, "we must seek ways to nurture it not in the genes we pass on to our kids, but in the world we make for them."

48. The Genetics of Perfect Pitch – Nicholas Wade

On September 16, 2003, Wade's column in *The New York Times* was about perfect pitch, based on a story in *Nature Neuroscience* by Dr. Robert J. Zatorre. Dr. Zatorre had observed the rarity of perfect pitch (where one can identify a musical note without any reference point and can assign 70 notes or more). Most of us, instead, have relative pitch, and can identify six to eight notes from a starting note. Zatorre noted a possible genetic basis with an 8 to 15 percent chance that if one sibling has perfect pitch, the other will too, and further, Asians are much more likely to have it than other ethnic groups. But among the curious aspects is that apparently if absolute pitch is not an attribute by age nine to twelve, it will never be. Why this is so remains a mystery. It should be noted that at the time Zatorre made his observations, conjecture about genes being turned on and off was uncommon in articles on the topic.

More recently, UCSF has an ongoing research project to map the location of genes for perfect pitch. Interestingly, none of the eight

Ashkenazis in the study with perfect pitch show a genetic link to the four regions along the human genome associated with perfect pitch in other study subjects.

49. The Khazars (yet again) – Nicholas Wade

On September 27, 2003, the Khazar/Ashkenazi connection cropped up again in a Wade column in *The New York Times*. It reported on a recent *American Journal of Human Genetics* article. Among the article's authors was Dr. Michael Hammer, who was part of an earlier study that tied the Ashkenazi Cohanim genetic signatures to Middle Eastern roots dating back approximately 3,000 years (item 25). This is roughly the time of Moses and Aaron from whom the Cohanim are said to have originated.

In the new report, 52 percent of Ashkenazi Levites appear to carry a genetic signature—a set of variations known as R1a1 located on the Y chromosome. The variation is said to have originated in Central Asia from one or a few men who lived there only about 1,000 years ago. The same signature is also found among men of Middle Eastern origin, but it is much less common. The Levites are the second ancient caste of hereditary Jewish priests. Levites are said to date to Levi, the third son of the patriarch, Jacob, who lived long before rabbinic Judaism became the dominant sect after the Roman conquest in 70 CE.

50. *Human Accomplishment* – Charles Murray

Murray's October 2003 book, *Human Accomplishment*, did not focus on Jewish achievement. Murray, who is not Jewish, aimed his book at the entire scope of human accomplishment from 800 BCE to 1950 CE. But Murray singled out just one group—Jews—for singular discussion in depth (p. 275-293 & 603-4). In his writing, he documents some of the more impressive achievements, and in the course of his research, he developed an impressive list of history's most important Jews, which he kindly allowed me to include as an exhibit in *The Golden Age of Jewish Achievement*. A number of his tables and part of his discussion in *Human Accomplishment* laid out the disproportionate performance.

He cited Patai, and like Patai he opined on the importance of the Jewish Emancipation. Murray devoted some of his writing to the high levels of Jewish IQs and the probable importance of IQ in explaining disproportionate achievement. And he wrote with equal clarity and force about the devotion to learning, strong families, the pressures of anti-Semitism requiring Jews to survive in hostile environments, the large families of Jewish rabbis, good diet, similar Jewish cultural values, and other environmental circumstances. In the end, he said, "Almost all of the current evidence regarding the causes of group differences is circumstantial and inconclusive. The debate will not have to depend on circumstantial evidence much longer, however. Within a few decades we will know a great deal about the genetic differences among groups ... the room for argument will narrow substantially."

51. The Pygmalion Effect: Expectations Influence Outcomes – Sharon Begley

A November 7, 2003 Begley column in *The Wall Street Journal* discussed the "Pygmalion Effect"—namely that expectations may influence outcomes. She wrote that 479 studies have found teachers' expectations affect student performance, and that despite all the studies documenting the phenomenon, very little is known about it.

In a typical experiment, she said, elementary teachers were told that a group of students had done extraordinarily well on a test known to be predictive of remarkable future academic gains. After a few months, the students achieved statistically significant gains over other students. In fact, there was no such test, and the students in the group included some whose results ranged widely (as did those of the rest of the students not included in the group). But the teachers saw the students as "better adjusted, more affectionate, and less in need of social approval." As a consequence, they were treated differently. Psychology professor Robert Rosenthal at the University of California, Riverside, said the teachers taught the selected students "more warmly" and "tended to give greater opportunities for responding and more differentiated feedback to these students—rather than a pat."

Interestingly, a comparable test was done using twelve experimenters, each of whom was given five rats. Six were told their rats were of a strain that "learned like long-tailed geniuses; the other six were told their rats were dolts." Five days were allocated to train the rats to run a maze and the differences were clear from day one. The "genius rats" just kept getting better. As you may expect, the rats were all the same. The observers noted the experimenters working with the "smart rats" felt "more relaxed and enthusiastic as they worked with them...and handled them more." The "smart rats" did 65 percent better than their peers.

52. "The Intelligence of American Jews" – Richard Lynn

On February 14, 2004, the now-retired Professor of Psychology, Richard Lynn, who has taught at the University of Ulster, Coleraine, Northern Ireland, the University of Exeter, and the Economic and Social Research Institute in Dublin, wrote a paper titled, "The Intelligence of American Jews." Lynn, a Cambridge graduate, issued his first book in 1972 and has written on achievement, intelligence and IQ variations between different populations since the 1980s. Anyone who has closely followed the debate over Jewish achievement has read some of his papers. Among his early efforts was a late 1970s paper noting elevated IQ in East Asians, five points higher than Whites.

Lynn's 2004 paper aggregated vocabulary scores of Jews, non-Jewish Whites, Blacks and others from American *General Social Surveys* done by the National Opinion Research Centre for the years 1990 to 1996. With 1,500 individuals in each year's survey, the combined results provided sufficient representation of Jews (150 were tested) to allow a high level of confidence in the statistical significance of the results. Lynn indicated that the vocabulary test results, which are a "good measure of verbal intelligence," showed Jews "obtained a significantly higher mean vocabulary score...equivalent to an advantage of 7.5 IQ points" (one half a standard deviation) above non-Jewish American and European Whites.

53. *The Jewish Century* – Yuri Slezkine

In June 2004, Yuri Slezkine's book, *The Jewish Century,* was published. A Russian immigrant to the United States (Slezkine teaches Russian history at the University of California, Berkeley), he brought to his book an intimate knowledge of the history of Russia and the Pale (from which the bulk of America's and Israel's Jews immigrated between 1880 and 1924). Slezkine's work was an invaluable resource for me in writing *The Golden Age*—in part because he laid out the remarkable data on disproportionate Jewish achievement in tsarist Russia, when few Jews were allowed into Russia proper (only 50,000 lived in Moscow and St. Petersburg versus the 5.2 million consigned to the Pale). Then he documented the same disproportionate performance after most Jews had left the Pale for the Soviet Union, America, Palestine, and elsewhere.

In the Soviet Union, Jews were just as disproportionately high achievers in political, scientific, legal, and cultural circles as they were in other parts of the world. The Soviets placed a red "J" on every Jew's passport, representing a theoretical Jewish nationality. That, together with meticulous Soviet recordkeeping, provided complete and accurate data for Slezkine to use in documenting their disproportionate success.

Second, Slezkine explained what he saw as the motivation behind the high rates of achievement. He noted the discrimination and circumstances of the Pale. Jews could typically not own land, could not enter civil service, faced quotas on academic admissions, and could not serve as an officer in the military. Their economic role was that of "middlemen" between Christian farmers in the Pale and the urban markets for their goods. Jews bought and sold; provided credit; managed and leased estates and processing facilities; "kept taverns and inns; supplied manufactured goods (as peddlers, shopkeepers, or wholesale importers); provided professional services (most commonly as doctors or pharmacists), and served as artisans (from rural blacksmiths, tailors, and shoemakers to highly specialized jewelers and watchmakers)."

Meanwhile the few Jews in Russia proper were "dominant in banking, and they financed much of Russia's railroad construction, its gold mining, oil production, river transportation, and commercial fishing. They were also prominent in its timber and sugar industries, and for a long time controlled most of its grain trade."

Within both Russia and the Pale, Jews had unique skills and talents that demanded education and specialized training. As they moved to the Soviet Union and America, they brought these talents to their new homelands, along with the motivation arising from their history of discrimination, and the kinship of their fellow Jews who they felt they could trust in business and finance.

Most of them saw opportunities to excel and achieve success with less risk that success might be persecuted. And as more of them became urban, rather than rural as so many were in the Pale, they thrived in the rapidly changing and modernizing world from 1880 to the end of World War II. Their skills were valuable and their motivations strong.

Ultimately, Stalin's Russia turned on the Jews, particularly after the creation of Israel (Stalin felt he could no longer count on their loyalty) and during the anti-Semitism of late Soviet times. After the fall of the Soviet Union, and by the time Slezkine finished his book, the Jewish population in Russia had dwindled to 230,000. Israel and America had taken in most of those who left.

54. Epigenetic Effects of the Maternal Styles of Rat Mothers – Sharon Begley

A July 16, 2004 Begley column in *The Wall Street Journal* reported on research by Professor Michael Meaney of Montreal's McGill University. Meaney looked at the effect of different maternal styles of mother rats on their offspring. Earlier, (see item 37 above) Meaney had reported on neurotic offspring whose mothers had rarely licked and groomed them when they were growing up.

In the new study to test whether that outcome may simply be

genetic—with a neurotic mother passing neurotic DNA to the infant rat—scientists switched the rat pups, putting the offspring of attentive moms with standoffish moms and vice versa. It turned out that it was the mother's behavior and not the genes that mattered. Pups born to standoffish mothers reared by attentive mothers grew up "less fearful, more curious, more laid-back, taking stress in stride."

The maternal behavior affected molecules in the pups' brains that "catch hold of stress hormones," increasing the numbers of these receptors and reducing the numbers of stress hormones released. With that, the pups grew into mellow adults. The conclusion was that all pups are born with "molecular silencers" on their stress receptor genes that can be removed by attentive maternal behavior or left in place by standoffish mothers.

Meaney said, "In the nature/nurture debate, people have long suspected that the environment somehow regulates the activity of genes. The question has always been *how?* It took four years, but we've now shown that maternal care alters the chemistry of the genes." When challenged by a skeptic not to publish Meaney's research report, the journal *Nature* disagreed and published it anyway.

Begley noted that the genetic code—the "As, Ts, Cs, and Gs—were all there and the sequence was untouched, but certain molecules "glom onto the DNA" and the silent gene becomes active or the active one is hushed. This, again, was the emerging field of epigenetics.

55. Identical Twins: One Schizophrenic, the Other Not? – Sharon Begley

Begley followed her July 16 column a week later with a report in *The Wall Street Journal* on identical twins (sharing identical DNA), where one of the twins was schizophrenic and the other was not. In this case, the genetic "silencer" she described in the prior column (see item 54 above) affects dopamine in the brain. The silencer was almost absent, and with that the gene was operating at full speed. In another pair of twins, both of whom were schizophrenic, it was noted the silencers were also missing. Even cancer, she reported, might sometimes involve the epigenetic "un-silencing" of genes that can cause cancers in ways different from that of outright mutations do.

56. Maternal Behavior and Dietary Effects on the Unborn – Sharon Begley

On September 17, 2004, Begley wrote in *The Wall Street Journal* column about adult diseases that could be traced back to the womb and the fetal, infant, and childhood factors that shaped 50 to 60 percent of the likely incidence of heart disease and diabetes. Diet and nutrition play a significant role in how it unfolds, and she noted that a version of a gene called PPAR-gamma-2 raises the risk of type-2 diabetes, but only for "scrawny newborns." Encouraging pregnant mothers to eat better, take care of themselves and provide good nutrition for infants can literally turn on and off the genes that are helpful or harmful.

57. Buddhist Monk's Meditation Effects on Brain Waves – Sharon Begley

A November 5, 2004 Begley column in *The Wall Street Journal* covered a report to be published the following week in the *Proceedings of the National Academy of Science*. The report focused on brain scans performed by a team led by neuroscientist Richard Davidson of the University of Wisconsin, Madison. The issue was whether conscious behavior could change neuronal brain activity. While physical experience and outside influences were known to cause changes, no one had studied whether changes could also be induced by "internal mental signals."

Five neuroscientists were invited to spend five days with dozens of Tibetan Buddhist monks at the home of the Dalai Lama in Dharamsala, India. Brain scans of the meditating monks were projected onto screens in the room as monks with varying levels of meditation experience all focused on compassion. The five neuroscientists were skeptical until they witnessed the "dramatic increases in high frequency brain activity, called gamma waves, during compassion meditation."

And while younger, less experienced monks were impressive, most of the older monks "showed extremely large gamma wave increases never before reported in the literature of neuroscience." The left prefrontal cortex, which is home to positive emotions, was active in ways not seen before, and that activity "swamped activity in the right prefrontal area, home more to anxiety and negative emotions." Conscious mental activity can indeed change the brain.

58. Family History Beats Genetic Variance in Predicting Disease – Sharon Begley

In a January 14, 2005 column in *The Wall Street Journal*, Begley described the surprising failure of DNA "association studies" to show high correlations between some gene variants and diseases. Previous predictions about the incidence of diseases associated with certain genetic variants were proving to be too high. The BRCA1 or BRCA2 breast cancer risk, previously said to be 82 percent, was being changed in studies to be 73, 65, 56, and 36 percent in different studies and in some of those cases, it appeared the linkage was closer to family history than it was to DNA variations. Similar results were being reported for ADD1 (hypertension), APOE (schizophrenia), BLMH (Alzheimer's), GSTM1 (breast cancer), PON1 (coronary artery disease) and others.

Joel Hirschhorn of the Broad Institute at Harvard and MIT said he "counted more than 600 reported associations between a DNA variation and a disease. Only 166 had been studied at least three times; only six had been consistently replicated."

59. The Haredim (ultra-Orthodox) and Scientific Inquiry

On March 22, 2005, Alex Mindlin wrote a story in *The New York Times* titled "Religion and Natural History Clash Among the Ultra-Orthodox." It was about the scathing criticism of the young Haredi Israeli Rabbi Nosson Slifkin by twenty-three of his fellow Haredim rabbis who took issue with Slifkin's scientific writings. Slifkin, author of nine books before he was twenty-nine, was teaching a course in biblical and Talmudic zoology near Jerusalem.

In his lectures and books, Slifkin said some biblical creatures are mythical, including the unicorn and phoenix. So too are assertions that geese grew on trees (as is said in The Bible), that the earth is 5,800 years old, that lice can be killed on the Sabbath because they do not sexually reproduce, and that the Talmudic basis for distinguishing some animals as kosher or non-kosher are scientifically inconsistent. Evolution, he said, did not disprove the existence of God and the Big Bang Theory might well be consistent with Genesis. These and other of Slifkin's arguments were driving his counterparts crazy. They sought and obtained commitments from publishers and retail outlets to stop carrying his books—which of course only increased their sales.

The debate highlighted the division within different subsets of the Orthodox community. Some of them are skeptical of scientific inquiry, disdain college, and discourage education (except traditional Torah and Talmudic education). The reporter, Mindlin, described those who were leading the campaign against Slifkin as "the most unworldly segment of the Haredim (ultra-Orthodox) community, in which contact with the secular world, including secular education is shunned." It is also an insight into the cultural differences between different parts of the Jewish Ashkenazi community, in which all may share a common genetic heritage but not all share the same cultural values or perspectives.

A codicil may be in order here for those unfamiliar with the Haredim (a term considered more respectful by the Haredim, than "ultra-Orthodox"). The Haredim provide another perspective on the debate about the Jewish culture of achievement. As a group, these sects of Judaism are among the most conservative. They include a broad range of Hasidim, streams of Lithuanian-Yeshiva Ashkenazim, and Oriental Sephardim.

Of the 1.0 to 1.4 million Haredim worldwide (9 to10 percent of the world's 13 to 15 million Jews), an estimated 20 percent are thought to be Sephardic and the rest Ashkenazi. It is estimated that approximately 500,000 to 800,000 live in Israel, ~500,000 in the United States, and ~50,000 in the United Kingdom, as well as smaller communities in Canada, France, Belgium, the Netherlands, Switzerland, Austria, South Africa, and Australia. While there has been no significant growth in the world's Jewish population since the Holocaust, the Haredim are doubling every twelve to twenty years. Families of five to eight offspring are not uncommon.

Generalizations are difficult because of the number and variety of sects, but for the most part, the Haredim are dedicated students of Torah, Talmud, and Halakha (Jewish Law). They typically restrain their young people from secular studies, and limit their use of modern technologies such as television and unfiltered access to the Internet. Historically, the Haredim's relations with Reform, Conservative, Modern Orthodox, Zionist and secular Jews are limited and often quite strained—in part, because the Haredim see these other groups as deviating from authentic Judaism.

In writing the above paragraph, I am reminded of a comment made by a secular Sephardic friend of longstanding who, when discussing a mutual Haredim business colleague, said "Steve, he dislikes me much more than he dislikes you."

60. Indian-American Successes in Spelling Bees

In *The Wall Street Journal* on June 10, 2005, Tunku Varadarajan reported on the success of Indian-Americans in spelling bees. A week earlier, Anurag Kashyap, a thirteen-year—old, had won the fifth spelling bee by an Indian-American in the last seven years. In fact, Indian-Americans had taken all three top places in the competition, even though Indian-Americans are only 0.66 percent of the U.S. population.

Varadarajan said that one reason for the disproportionate success was because this ethnic group has "pushier parents than any other people, all very eager—no, make that desperate—for their kids to succeed at school or anything that looks remotely like school." He said it was a "cultural trait bequeathed to broader Indian society by the Brahminical upper stratum. Success at letters is the sweetest sort of success, the achievement nonpareil. For a millennia, India was the land where the poorest scholar was held in higher esteem than the richest businessman."

Varadarajan went on to say that certain Asian cultures tend to produce child prodigies. They involve determined parents who press their kids when they are very young. In these cultures, there is no "childhood" as we know it in the west. As a result, the United States is a beneficiary: our immigration laws let in the cream of the Indian crop of doctors, engineers, and mathematicians. Thus the spelling bee winners are the children of "parents who themselves competed—probably at a ferocious level—to get into the best Indian schools and then to get here...." Varadarajan closed by saying, "Only part of his success, I'm pleased to report, is attributable to matters deoxyribonucleic."

61. Imprinted Genes – Sharon Begley

A June 24, 2005 Begley column in *The Wall Street Journal* introduced "imprinted genes." They involve the equivalent of what was previously called a "silencer" on a gene or genes. But in this case, the silencers are specific to genes coming from either the mother or the father. In essence the normal gene is there, but the silencer keeps it from ever being expressed. The only functional copy comes from the maternal (or paternal) side, since its gene is not imprinted and the copy received from the other parent is. But if the only active (non-imprinted) gene is defective, then a healthy copy from the other parent cannot take over.

Begley illustrated imprinting with three genes on chromosome 10, all with the paternal gene imprinted (silenced). The genes involved late Alzheimer's, male sexual orientation, and obesity. Thus, for example, if the paternal gene has a mutation that would otherwise cause Alzheimer's, the fact that it is silenced means it will never be expressed. That form of Alzheimer's will not be inherited from the paternal line. But on chromosome 2 and 22, maternal genes associated with schizophrenia are imprinted. So if the father's line has a family history of schizophrenia, the risk the offspring will have it is higher since the mother's gene cannot take over.

Because the imprinting is an epigenetic phenomenon, Begley raised the possibility that imprinting might be changed by environmental conditions. For example, toxic chemicals might cause the silencer tag to be removed with possible trans-generational consequences. "Two points," she said, "to readers who say 'Lamarck lives!'"

She expected a new technology, MethylScope, to be used to map all imprinted genes and identify differences between normal and cancerous cells. "The ink is barely dry on the human genome project," she said, "but already researchers are onto the 'second genetic code,' or the pattern of silencers on our DNA."

62. "Natural History of Ashkenazi Intelligence" – Cochran, et al

In June 2005, University of Utah professors, Gregory Cochran,

Jason Hardy, and Henry Harpending issued their paper titled, "Natural History of Ashkenazi Intelligence." To say it unleashed a firestorm is an understatement. In thirty-one single-spaced pages of analysis and eight pages of sources, they made an argument correlating genetic ailments with high IQs in Ashkenazi Jews.

The authors argued that limited career options were available for Medieval Ashkenazis. Among these were "entrepreneurial and managerial roles as financiers, estate managers, tax farmers and merchants." In all cases, high IQs were said to be essential for success. Those limited career options, coupled with the financial and other rewards that came from being very good in these pursuits, encouraged genetic natural selection for those who were most capable. That success also led to larger families, while those who were less successful had small families or simply opted out of Judaism. The consequence was an inevitable rise in average IQ among a more select group of Ashkenazis.

But, this "natural selection for high IQs among Ashkenazim... (came with) associated costs." ("Natural History..." p. 9) In this case, the "regime of strong directional selection...that (was) otherwise fitness reducing rose in frequency. In particular, we propose that the well-known clusters of Ashkenazi genetic diseases, the sphingolipid cluster and the DNA repair cluster in particular, increased intelligence in heterozygotes. Other Ashkenazi disorders are known to increase intelligence." (*ibid* p. 1)

This was akin to sickle cell anemia. If the gene is inherited from both parents it is devastating, but inherited from only one, it can be a protective blessing. In the Ashkenazi case, genetic expression of the mutation from both parents led to tragedy, but from one, they argued, it would enhance brain development in neuron and synaptic growth. Ashkenazi offspring were smarter.

Within days, *The New York Times, The Economist, Jerusalem Post, Jewish Telegraphic Agency,* and numerous publications ran coverage, meetings were convened, and talk shows discussed this hot topic at length. Some were convinced; others were skeptical. Many were extremely uncomfortable. The debate continues even now nine years later.

63. Some Identical Twins Grow Ever Less Identical: Epigenetics? – Nicholas Wade

On July 5, 2005 in *The New York Times*, a story by Nicholas Wade reported on how the DNA of identical twins can develop quite differently over the years. Dr. Manel Esteller of the Spanish National Cancer Center in Madrid led a team of researchers whose work was to appear that day in *The Proceedings of the National Academy of Sciences.*

Color photographs of chromosomes ran with the story to show how identical twins, who are born with the same genes, begin, over time, to display at first "subtle differences," which later become ever more obvious. One image incorporated into the story showed chromosome 1 for identical twins at age three and then at age fifty. The differences were obvious and striking.

That identical twins begin to look different, develop different ailments, and have different personalities is no great surprise. My wife, a mirror image identical twin, gives me first-hand experience with this. Several years ago, my sister-in-law developed chronic lymphocytic leukemia. My wife has never had it. Instead, she had spinal meningitis at three months of age and appendicitis as an adult, whereas my sister-in-law has never had either one.

Historically such differences have been attributed to environmental causes. The Esteller paper added epigenetics to the equation. Part of the study looked at two kinds of epigenetic change. One was the addition of "acetyl groups to histone proteins that act as a scaffolding and as a control system for DNA." The other involved the "methyl group of chemical handles added or attached to genes." Methyl tends to inhibit genetic expression.

Wade noted demethylation of sperm occurs shortly after fertilization of the egg with extensive re-addition of methyl groups during early embryonic development. Wade referred to these as "natural chemical modifications that occur in a person's genome shorty after conception, and that act on a gene like a gas pedal or brake, marking it for higher or lower activity." Then, over time, and as demonstrated in the study, the epigenetic marks in twins grow increasingly different and the longer the separation, the greater the change. Some marks are randomly lost as we age. But personal experiences and environmental conditions, such as tobacco smoke, can also induce changes.

The story also pointed out that epigenetic changes provide a response to the environment without causing a mutation of the genome itself. Nonetheless, the epigenetic changes (with genetic expression turned on or off) can affect behavior, development, disease, and life experience, just as if the gene was there or not there. The growing understanding of epigenetic change was increasingly seen as an important avenue for research, as it became clear that the original assumptions about the straightforward effects of genes were much too simplistic.

64. "All Cultures Are Not Equal" – David Brooks
On August 5, 2005, David Brooks wrote a column in *The New York*

Times titled "All Cultures Are Not Equal." He began by suggesting a bright young student might want to consider specializing in cultural geography that would study "why and how people cluster, why certain national traits endure over centuries, why certain cultures embrace technology and economic growth and others resist them." He said this is a line of inquiry that is now "impolite to pursue." He referred to "closed minded" academic "thugs" whose theological faith in the gospel of multiculturalism (that all cultures are equally wonderful) can make genuine academic inquiry the basis for charges of racism or sexism.

Brooks worried that this sociological fawning and lack of intellectual honesty was reinforcing tendencies to drive people into ever-smaller self-reinforcing aggregations and away from cultural unifiers who helped keep us on common ground. He saw it in politics and religion, in socio-economic classes, and in ethnic groups. He thought we needed more people like Samuel Huntington, Thomas Sowell, Lawrence Harrison, Edward Banfield, and Max Weber, who seek (or sought) to understand how cultures affect traits that, among other things, allow some to prosper and others to stagnate.

65. Adverse Effects of Low Cultural Capital – David Brooks

On October 6, 2005, Brooks wrote about cultural capital in *The New York Times*. He discussed the disparity between students of educated parents versus those of the less educated. He said getting into college was not the issue, nor was cost, given the then readily available financial aid for the disadvantaged. Instead, once in college, dropout rates tell the story. Brooks said an *Atlantic Monthly* report by Ross Douthat indicated that a child whose family earned $90,000 had a 50 percent chance of getting a college degree by age twenty-four. Family income of $35,000 to $61,000 dropped those odds to 10 percent, and family income of less than $35,000 meant the odds were 6 percent.

The students from lower income families don't do well in college, and they tend to drop out. Students from wealthier families out-compete them. They bring more cultural capital to the campus. Their academic competence is higher and they are more practical.

Some of those from low-income families adopt a "magical worldview, somehow expecting success to come to them out of the blue. They register for SAT tests and then don't show up. They don't fill out college applications because they don't feel like writing the essays. The poorer kids are also more risk averse, unwilling to borrow to go to school and instead, they leave school to take a job. And last, they lack social confidence. Poorer kids feel like they won't or don't fit in. The culture of these kids is causing them to fall behind. This is a dramatic change from the '60s through the '80s when so many, whose parents hadn't gone to college and whose family income was low, entered and graduated from college, and sometimes went on to earn advanced degrees."

66. "Benefits of Diaspora" – Eric Hobsbawm

On October 20, 2005, Eric Hobsbawm's essay, "Benefits of Diaspora," was published in the *London Review of Books*. Hobsbawm was fascinating and controversial. Born in 1917 to Jewish parents in Alexandria, Egypt, he grew up in Vienna, Berlin, and London. Orphaned at fourteen, he was adopted by his maternal aunt and paternal uncle, who had married. In 1933, the three of them moved from Berlin to London.

Hobsbawm graduated from Cambridge and later became a highly respected historian. Honored with the Balzan Prize for European history, he was also appointed Companion of Honour in 1998, a personal gift from the Queen for his outstanding achievements. Hobsbawm, who died in October 2012 was a Marxist, which was not all that unusual, particularly for a Cambridge alumnus. But what was unusual was that he remained a devoted Marxist and Communist despite the Ribbentrop Pact, Stalin's Doctors Plot, and the invasions of Czechoslovakia and Hungary (which he did criticize). In 1994, when asked about the deaths of millions under Stalin, he said it would have been worth it had a genuine Communist society been the result. Nonetheless, even the right-leaning magazine, *The Spectator*, referred to him as "arguably our greatest living historian."

"Benefits of Diaspora" is an eloquent piece. He began by noting the "impact of Jews on the rest of humanity ... in the nineteenth and twentieth centuries: that is to say, since the emancipation and self-emancipation of the Jews began in the late eighteenth century." He then wrote about the impact of the time between the "expulsion from Palestine in the first century CE and the nineteenth century (during which time) Jews lived within the wider society ... whose languages they adopted as their own and whose cuisine they adapted to their ritual requirements." But because Jews were not active in that wider society, he said the first time Jews could contribute to it was after the Jewish Emancipation, and since then, their contributions "were enormous."

Most of the article described the emergence of Jews into the secular societies in what he said, began as a trickle and emerged as a river of achievements and contributions. Unlike some who insisted that Jews benefited by their exposure to many cultures, the positive byproducts of experiencing hardship, and knowledge gained from their roles as middlemen, financiers, and professionals, Hobsbawm focused instead on tension. He said that despite emancipation, Jews felt estranged in nearly all of the countries where they achieved legal equality but were still distanced from the populace. He noted, "...given equal rights, at least in theory, a certain degree of unease in relations between Jews and gentiles proved historically useful." Later in the piece he added, "The times of maximum stimulus for Jewish talent may have been those when the Jews became conscious of the limits of assimilation." See also item 155, The Best Little Boy in the World.

67. The Haplotype Map: A "Silver Bullet" Or Not? – Sharon Begley

A November 4, 2005 Begley column in *The Wall Street Journal* took note of a conference the week before marking completion of the first phase of Haplotype Map project, a three-year $138 million effort involving 200 scientists in six countries. She described the so-called "HapMap" project as seeking to identify the differences in our genes that may be tied to various diseases. Two unrelated humans are known to be 99.9 percent identical in their DNA; it is thought that the 0.1 percent that is different must therefore account for the causes of diseases that are partially or wholly genetic. Thus the pragmatic approach is to map only the haplotype sections ("groups of genetic rarities that sit on the same chromosome and tend to be inherited together from parent to child as a chunk"). Look at haplotypes of those with a particular disease and compare it with those from people who don't have it. The hope is these comparisons can provide a powerful new diagnostic aide, a predictor of certain diseases, and hopefully a tool to assist prevention or cure.

Stepping away from role of reporter and into the role of analyst, Begley expressed some skepticism that the HapMap would prove to be a silver bullet. She noted the differences in the incidences of disease among identical twins (50 percent for schizophrenia, 40 percent for hypertension, 30 percent for diabetes, 20 percent for breast cancer, etc.). She did not opine on the HapMap applications for other purposes, such as tracing genetic heritage, but she did imply that a Duke University conference focused on epigenetics might prove a more useful venue for exploration.

68. Race, Genetic Variance and Medicine (again) – Nicholas Wade

On November 11, 2005, Wade reported in *The New York Times* that Iceland-based Decode Genetics Company reported discovering a variant gene in 6 percent of African-Americans that raises the risk of heart attack by more than 250 percent. For Americans of European ancestry, the variant is common, but it raises the risk by only 16 percent. In reporting on the finding, Decode's chief executive officer, Dr. Kari Stephansson, said the version of this gene may have become prominent in Europeans and Asians because it conferred extra protection against infectious disease. In any case, if the discovery is confirmed, it represents another point, albeit a controversial one, in the ongoing debate over the usefulness of race and ethnic genetic information in predicting and treating ailments, while also demonstrating that such differences between races and ethnicities do exist.

69. Self-Discipline, IQ, and Academic Performance – Angela Duckworth

On December 16, 2005, a paper by Dr. Angela L. Duckworth and Dr. Martin E. P. Seligman, both of the University of Pennsylvania, was published in the journal *Psychological Science*. Titled, "Self Discipline Outdoes IQ in Predicting Academic Performance of Adolescents," it was a longitudinal study of 140 eighth grade students from an ethnically diverse magnet school in the Northeast (55 percent Caucasian, 32.1 percent Black, 8.6 percent Asian, 3.6 percent Latino, and 0.7 percent American Indian).

The students' IQs were tested and self-discipline was measured by teacher reporting, self-reporting, parent reporting, monetary choice questionnaires, standardized achievement tests, and admission into a competitive high school program the following spring. The work was replicated in a study of 164 eighth graders.

In both studies, self-discipline proved a better predictor of academic performance than IQ. Duckworth, a Harvard graduate in neurobiology, with a masters degree in neuroscience from Oxford University, spent seven years teaching middle school math and science before getting her doctorate from the University of Pennsylvania. Her work in the years since has led to the emergence of the term "grit" as having psychological importance. In one online reference, grit is suggested as a synonym for chutzpah.

70. Mandatory Jewish Education/Literacy – Maristella Botticini and Zvi Eckstein[9]

In December 2005, only six months after the Cochran paper, Botticini and Eckstein's paper, "Jewish Occupational Selection: Education, Restrictions, or Minorities," was published in the Journal of Economic History. In it they argued, and leading Talmudic scholars later agreed, that disproportionate Jewish literacy was the result of "Implementation of a religious and educational reform within Judaism that had started in the second and first centuries B.C.E., and underwent a big push after the destruction of the Second Temple in 70 C.E., the most powerful denomination of Judaism shifted from the Sadducees to the Pharisees." The new religious leadership transformed Judaism from a religion based on sacrifices in the Temple in Jerusalem to a religion whose main rule required each male Jewish individual to read and teach his sons the Torah in the synagogue." ("Jewish Occupational..." p. 2-3)

Jews thus became the first tribe in history to make literacy and education mandatory. As mentioned earlier, this took place when most Jews were farmers. But literacy and education equipped them not only to study Torah and other sacred tracts, it also equipped them to perform much more complex work than most others could handle. Over time, Jews became an urban people, particularly when they were constrained from owning land. And when restrictions kept them from certain industries or jobs, education gave them options to do something else. Jews were creating their own "human capital." Education was an investment in themselves, and it provided Jews with a comparative advantage. The resulting skills allowed Jews to pursue opportunities across the Muslim world, Europe, Asia, Africa, and later the Americas, when perceived opportunities or threats encouraged relocation.

But some think that the cost and time required to pursue education resulted in many Jews opting out of the religion. It may well have been a significant factor in the decline of the world's Jewish population from ~4.5 million to ~1.25 million between the first and early eighth centuries.

Like the Cochran paper six months earlier, the Botticini-Eckstein paper received significant coverage.

---

9. A further comment about this paper may be useful. I've chosen to draw on the December 2005 version of the paper here because it was issued without reference to the Cochran paper referenced earlier. In fact, Botticini and Eckstein had been working on this paper for some time and had issued versions as early January 2003. Later versions also appeared in other journals in February 2006 and September 2007. In each succeeding version, they fleshed out their research and analysis as they responded to new papers.

Through all of the versions, the essence remained unchanged. Jews were the first to make education mandatory. They did it for religious and cultural reasons (as Rabbinic Judaism superseded the priestly religion of the Sadducees). Though it is not in the Botticini-Eckstein paper, Talmudic scholars have asserted that literacy helped keep the religion, culture and tribe alive across the thousands of miles and years of the Diaspora. It was costly, and many Jews opted out, but it helped equip Jews to operate in sophisticated professions and jobs that required much higher levels of intelligence than did farming, and those careers were more lucrative. In the process, literacy also transformed Jews from a farming to an urban people.

CHAPTER 12

2006 to 2010: Genetics and Culture—New Insights and More Data

71. Genes, the Environment, Shyness, Violence, and Intelligence – Sharon Begley

A January 13, 2006 Begley column in *The Wall Street Journal* was titled "How Nurture Overrides Kids' Nature—or Why Succotash Model Fails." It reported on a study by Nathan Fox of the University of Maryland at College Park that was published in the journal *Psychological Science*. Fox had looked at toddlers whose DNA contained the "shy gene" 5HTT. But when he revisited the same children at age seven, he discovered that not all of them were shy. As he explored differences, he concluded that the environment in which a child grows up makes a big difference.

The 5HTT gene comes in two forms. For adults, the short version is associated with anxiety and increased brain activity in the amygdala, which is linked to the generation of fear. In children, the picture is less clear. Fox found that children with the short form of the gene whose mothers "had little social support and poor social networks—which increases stress—were shy as seven-year-olds. Fox noted that there had been hints children with the gene grow up shy if their parents are very protective, but a conscious effort to get them to play with others leads away from "innate" introversion. Shy children in day care became less shy at school age than those who spent their days with mom. Different conditions appear to silence the gene.

After summarizing her own 2002 paper on the violence gene and the effect of a loving non-abusive family in silencing the MAOA gene associated with violence, aggression, and criminality, Begley went on to write about a Chicago study of 547 second- and third-graders.

166

That study explored the supposed innate male superiority in dealing with spatial problems: a concept thought at the time to be beyond question. Susan Levine, who led the study, found that results depended on socio-economics more than gender. Namely, boys and girls from the poorest families showed no differences based on gender. It was among the middle and upper class subjects that the gender differences were most evident. Levine suggested that access to toys, and the freedom to explore the neighborhoods around their homes, offered more opportunities for middle and upper class boys to develop skills earlier than those with less opportunity, and who lived in more dangerous neighborhoods.

In the end, Begley said the unfolding data suggested the notion that a clear quantifiable measure of nature (genes) or nurture (environment) e.g., that intelligence is 55 percent genes and 45 percent environment—is becoming suspect. The "innate potential we call nature perhaps becomes reality only when exposed to a certain kind of nurture. A gene contributes 0 percent of what you become if you don't grow up in an environment that turns it on." But when turned on by the right environment it can "contribute 100 percent."

72. Ashkenazi Genetics: Middle Eastern Mitochondrial DNA Is Found – Nicholas Wade

A January 14, 2006 story by Nicholas Wade in *The New York Times* reported on a further twist in the findings regarding the origins of Ashkenazim in Europe. *The American Journal of Human Genetics* published a study by Doron Behar and Karl Skorecki of Technion and Rambam Medical Center in Haifa, Israel, and others. It challenged the then prevailing view that Ashkenazi males (perhaps traders) had generally married local women who converted to Judaism and from them arose the Ashkenazi population.

Instead, using the mitochondrial DNA, the researchers concluded that just four female ancestors "who may have lived 2,000 to 3,000 years ago—probably in the Middle East—are ancestors to 40 percent of Ashkenazis alive today." Their probable Middle Eastern—rather than local origins—suggests they would have migrated with their husbands.

While Dr. Michael Hammer (see item 21 above) was generally positive about the new study, Dr. David Goldstein (see item 26 above), who had advanced the notion of single Jewish traders marrying locals, remained skeptical.

Surprisingly unmentioned in the piece was the possibility that both things may have occurred. Some Jewish men may have migrated while single and married locals, while others migrated with their families.

73. Parental Behavior May Alter Genetic Expression in Adoptees – Sharon Begley

On February 24, 2006, Begley's column in *The Wall Street Journal* reported on a paper presented by David Reiss, director of psychiatric research at George Washington University Medical Center, at the January annual meeting of the American Psychoanalytic Association. It described a study of 310 adopted children, looking first at personality types (e.g. bubbly with smiles versus solemn and dour). Then the researchers observed how the parents related to the adopted children who had, in essence, brought their own personalities to the relationship. Researchers were interested in what kinds of environments were created by the parents' reactions. That was the environment. Parents reacted so the subject of the study was what happens next. In other words, do differences in parental responses alter the expression of the traits?

Some of the preliminary findings were said to support the belief of many parents that children are born with personalities: some jolly and others cranky no matter how hard parents work to elicit a smile. Reis and others opined that "because solemn babies aren't as much fun as giggly ones, many parents respond...more impatiently, coldly and impartially, particularly if the parents are under stress." In short, the children's genes are driving the environmental circumstance—solemn babies grow up at greater risk for conduct disorders, oppositional behavior, anxiety disorders, depression, and substance abuse.

But the research also suggested that any one outcome was not inevitable. Parents who resisted responding to cranky children in kind, but instead were warm and loving, appeared to increase the likelihood that oppositional behavior would quiet down in the infant's teenage years. Coaching aided the parents, as did videos where they could see themselves, and that led to improvement. Reiss said, "If these findings hold up, it would provide an opportunity to forestall genetically linked adverse outcomes...these genes might never express themselves."

74. Brain Development and IQ – Nicholas Wade

A March 30, 2006 story in *The New York Times* by Wade reported that researchers found the brains of highly intelligent children develop differently than those of average children. Based on regular brain scans of 307 Bethesda, Maryland children, starting in 1989, the subjects were followed (and rescanned) over a seventeen-year period. Those with IQs in the 121 to 149 range showed more variations in cerebral cortex thickness and a longer period of evolution. The cortex reached maximum thickness at age 13 versus age 7 or 8 for children with IQs of 83 to 108 and then, like their less gifted peers, the cortex of the more gifted children thinned as seemingly redundant connections were pared.

The researchers were looking for DNA correlations, and noted the changes may also be related to diet, hours spent in school, number of siblings and other factors still to be studied. This research was triggered by 2001 reports from Dr. Paul M. Thompson at UCLA who, in imaging the brains of twins, reported a correlation between IQ and gray matter in frontal lobes, which he said was heavily influenced by genetics. At the same time, he said that experience could change the brain. "Unless you have a strong natural potential," Thompson said, "you won't become a world-class marathon runner. But disillusionment is rapidly replaced by the notion that you can, nonetheless, improve your own performance."

75. Asian Academic Motivation – Nicholas Kristof

A May 14, 2006 Kristof column in *The New York Times* focused on Asian-American academics. He first described Xuan-Trang Ho, a Vietnamese girl who arrived in the United States at age eleven without speaking English. Her parents, with perhaps high school educations, accepted work as manual laborers in Nebraska. The youngest of eight, Trang-Ho graduated as valedictorian from her high school, and at the time of Kristof's column, she was a senior at Nebraska Wesleyan with a 3.99 grade point average and a Rhodes Scholarship. According to Kristof, in 2005 the combined math-verbal SAT scores were 1091 for Asian-Americans, 1068 for Whites, 982 for American Indians, 922 for Hispanics, and 864 for Blacks.

Asked about Asian-American success, Trang-Ho demurred in talking about others but said of herself and her friends, "It was because of the sacrifices our parents made. It's so difficult to see my parents get up at five each morning to go to factories to earn $6.30 an hour. I see that there is so much that I can do in America that my parents couldn't."

Kristof indicated, "Success goes particularly to those whose ancestors came from the Confucian belt from Japan through Korea and China to Vietnam. Japanese-Americans still excel after four or five generations in the United States. Chinese-Americans of peasant farming parents gradate *summa cum laude*." It is much the same for Koreans, he said, but they do not do as well in Japan, where they are still looked down on. He suggests that self-doubt in that environment may be self-sustaining.

In exploring why, Kristof concludes that filial piety encouraged by Confucianism, intact families, and parents who are "focused on their children getting ahead" all matter. In addition, there is a Confucian reverence for education. "Glory and success" is achieved by "working hard and getting A's." And finally, Asians believe A grades go to students who work hard. "Anybody can be smart, can do great on standardized tests," Trans says, "But unless you work hard you are not going to do well." Kristof, whose wife is Asian-American, concludes, "the success of Asian-Americans is mostly about culture...maybe the easiest (lesson) is that respect for education pays dividends.... We would be fools not to try to learn some Asian lessons."

76. Environmental Influence On Genetic Expression of Aggression – Sharon Begley

A July 7, 2006 Begley column in *The Wall Street Journal* column reported on talks by Professors Darlene Francis of University of California, Berkeley, Stephen Manuck of the University of Pittsburgh, and Stephen Suomi of the National Institutes of Health at the International Congress of Neuroendocrinology. The three reported on environmental circumstances ("this intervening variable called life," said Francis). The aggressiveness gene MAOA that comes in two forms, long and short, was early on thought to trigger an inevitable behavioral outcome, and for a time, "there was talk of screening everyone to identify carriers." This is because the short form appeared more likely to result in adverse behavior. But Professor Manuck reported that a study of 531 U.S. men showed only those with the shortened MAOA version "who held anti-social attitudes, who received little parental affection as kids, and whose fathers had low levels of education, also had a history of aggression. Without those risk factors, those who had the short form MAOA had no history of lifetime aggression."

Since two thirds of Japanese have the short form MAOA, clearly there is more than genetics alone behind its expression. And since tests to see whether different parental styles matter were not feasible with humans, Stephen Suomi used Rhesus monkeys with the short form MAOA instead. He found those monkeys raised by their mother had no heightened aggression. The monkeys responded negatively only if there was a history of abuse or neglect. "Good mothering acts as a buffer," and in this context, Francis noted, "experience and social factors are transduced into biology."

77. Nucleosomes: Another Regulator of Gene Expression – Nicholas Wade

In *The New York Times*, on July 25, 2006, Wade drew attention to a possible "code beyond genetics in DNA." It was the subject of a *Nature* article by Eran Segal of the Weizmann Institute in Israel and Jonathan Widom of Northwestern University. Segal and Widom said they had been able to predict roughly half the locations of nucleosomes around which strands of DNA are looped. Previously, no one had seen a pattern to explain nucleosome placements. Segal and Widom concluded that it has to do with particular DNA sequences that enable DNA to bend itself to wrap tightly around the nucleosome.

Because transcription of genes to RNA (and from that, on to proteins) occurs only at the unbent strands between the nucleosome-wrapped DNA, the DNA wrapped around the nucleosome is protected but not available to be transcribed. This positioning may allow only the right genes to be transcribed for the cells in which they reside, reducing or eliminating genetic mistakes because the "wrong" genes are inaccessible. But the nucleosomes do move around, letting a wrapped gene become unwrapped and transcribed when needed. Several experts opined that if Segal and Widom's theory is true, their work offered a profound insight into the control of DNA in a way not previously known—and another avenue for regulation, variations, mutations, and mistakes.

78. *The Central Liberal Truth* – David Brooks Writes of Lawrence Harrison

On August 13, 2006, a Brooks column in *The New York Times* noted that despite diplomatic immunity, diplomats from different countries had wildly different rates of unpaid parking tickets. Kuwait, for example, had 246 tickets per diplomat. Also notably high were Egypt, Chad, Sudan, Mozambique, Pakistan, Ethiopia, and Syria. Sweden had none. The same was true for Demark, Japan, Israel, Norway, and Canada.

"Human beings," Brooks said, are not merely products of economics, but are also shaped by cultural and moral norms. He quoted Walter Lippmann (1940) by saying, "People don't become happy by satisfying their desires. They become happy by living within a belief system that restrains and gives coherence to their desires."

Brooks went on to talk of the work of Lawrence E. Harrison, and his new book *The Central Liberal Truth*. Explaining Harrison's history at USAID, Brooks said Harrison concluded that "cultural differences mostly explain why some nations develop quickly while others do not. All cultures have value because they provide coherence, but some cultures foster development while others retard it. Some cultures check corruption, while others permit it. Some cultures focus on the future, while others focus on the past. Some cultures encourage the belief that individuals can control their own destiny while others encourage fatalism."

After studying cultural transformations in Ireland, China, Latin America, and elsewhere, Harrison and a team of global academics concluded that, except in rare circumstances, cultural changes cannot be imposed from the outside—they have to be led from the inside. Values that bring results include investments in education, female literacy, economic liberalization, and other enhancements that rarely effect rapid cultural change.

79. A Genetically Demonstrable Jew that Israel Says Is Not

A December 8, 2006 item in *The Wall Street Journal*, written by Evan R. Goldstein, added an ironic and interesting twist to the Jewish DNA discussion. While wandering through Auschwitz, John Haedrich, who was raised Christian, had something of an epiphany that he might be Jewish. Sure enough, a DNA test showed he had a "rather populous pedigree of Ashkenazi Polish Jews." Knowing this, he petitioned the Israeli government for citizenship under the Law of Return. The petition was denied on the grounds that DNA does not prove Jewish identity. "As a matter of principle, Mr. Haedrich refuses to convert to Judaism because he says he is already Jewish."

Goldstein summed up by saying, "But there is a great peril in such a desire. If we accept that Jewishness can be transmitted by DNA, it would impose on us a reductive, rather clinical Judaism of molecules and genes rather than texts and arguments."

Perhaps, but if mitochondrial DNA were to establish a maternal linkage, Mr. Haedrich would have an even stronger claim than indicated in Goldstein's column. And how is Haedrich different from the hundreds of thousands of secular Jews from other countries, including Russia and the Maghreb accepted as Right of Return citizens of Israel since 1948? During mass immigrations, most were likely not screened for religious credentials or a commitment to Jewish cultural values. Some from Russia are even thought to have faked being Jewish to get out of Russia. Were they all screened? And if an Israeli converts, say to Roman Catholicism, is his or her citizenship revoked?

80. "Jewish Genius" – Charles Murray on Botticini and Cochran, et al

In April 2007, Charles Murray weighed in on the Cochran paper (see item 62 above) and the Botticini-Eckstein paper (see item 70 above). Murray's article in *Commentary* was titled simply "Jewish Genius."

After surveying the Jewish record of disproportionate achievement, drawing partly on his book *Human Accomplishment* and noting the importance of the Jewish Emancipation, Murray made a genetic case for high Jewish IQs as the "center of the answer" for their disproportionate accomplishments.

He said that while sample sizes of IQ testing of Jews have typically been small, in looking at all the testing done over the decades, "it is currently accepted that the mean IQ is somewhere in the range of 107 to 115, with 110 being a plausible compromise." In accounting for elevated IQs, Murray said, "winnowing by persecution" and "marrying for brains" were two ways in which genetic natural selection may have delivered that result, but he discounted both theories before reviewing arguments raised in the Cochran paper.

Murray agreed in part with Cochran, but made the case that early adoption of mandatory education (the Botticini and Eckstein paper) provides a better explanation and one that also helps resolve the relative IQs and performance of Sephardics. He added that the demands of mandatory education helped cull the Jewish population for those with the most intelligence because the less motivated or less talented Jews opted out.

Murray further pointed out that this approach explains Sephardic achievements during Spain's Golden Age, which the Cochran theory did not. And he added his speculation that the culling of the Babylonian captivity and the Mosaic intellectual demands of Torah and the Oral Law may also have driven intelligence higher among Jews, even before education became mandatory.

As with *The Bell Curve* and the Cochran paper, reactions to Murray's *Commentary* article were voluminous and often quite critical. One notable critic was Professor Robert Pollack, cited for his "Some Genetics for Some Jews" paper (see item 31 above). Pollack sounded angry as he argued over points Murray had failed to make. But the heart of Pollack's argument seemed to be his disdain for genetic theory and his sympathies for culture and free will.

Another critic was Cochran. He discounted mandatory education, saying that some literature suggests it wasn't widely implemented (which defies the Botticini evidence). He linked the presumed failure of mandatory Jewish education to "no child left behind," demeaned literacy, gave little importance to Torah and Talmudic study/literacy, minimized Sephardic achievement, and was skeptical of Murray's point that many Jews had opted out due to the imposition of mandatory education.

Murray responded to every critic (and every compliment). Five years later, responses were still flowing in to the *Commentary* web site. Prominent critics continued to challenge Murray, and he challenged them right back. If anything, he made the better arguments.

81. Skeptical Catholics And Protestants Do Well – David Brooks

A May 25, 2007 column by Brooks in *The New York Times* column described the evolution of what he termed "quasi-religious Catholics." Over the preceding generation, he said, Catholics have gone from an era of low college completion rates (versus Protestants), and low income and low prosperity (versus national averages), to matching or surpassing Protestant results and national averages. He cited the work of Lisa Keister at Duke University, whose research noted that "in the 1950s and early '60s," the traditional Catholic cultural base placed a strong emphasis on neighborhood cohesion and family, and a strong preference for obedience and solidarity over autonomy and rebellion."

Since then, Keister said, young Catholics have started to act and think more like Protestants. They are more likely to use contraceptives, fertility rates have dropped, and their children have been raised to value autonomy more and obedience less. They retain high marriage rates, high family stability and low divorce rates. They are conservative with their investments, but at the same time better educated than ever before, more assimilated, more future-oriented, and less bound by their neighborhoods. They still go to Mass, but are more skeptical than their parents were.

Brooks said Margarita Mooney, a Princeton sociologist, appears to endorse these observations. She demonstrated that students who attend religious services regularly do better than those who don't. They work harder and are more engaged in campus life. Moreover, those from denominations that encourage dissent are more successful.

82. Racial Genetics of Medicine, Perhaps IQ, and Fears of Misuse

A November 11, 2007 story by *New York Times* reporter, Amy Harmon, once again raised the risk of racial genetic information being misused. After noting that recently identified small changes in DNA may account for the "pale skin of Europeans, the tendency of Asians to sweat less, and West African resistance to certain diseases," she brought up concerns about "genetic information slipping out of the laboratory and into everyday life, carrying with it the inescapable message that people of different races have different DNA."

While the heart disease drug BiDil is marketed only to African-Americans, and while Jews are tested for certain genetic disorders rarely found in other ethnic groups, she raised concerns that the notion race is more than skin deep could "undermine principles of equal treatment and opportunity that have relied on the presumption that *we are all fundamentally equal*" (emphasis added). The article then moved on to conjectures about IQ and DNA with the possible spillover to race.

Harmon quoted Dr. Marcus W. Feldman, a professor of biological sciences at Stanford University, saying, "It's not there yet for things like IQ, but I can see it coming. And it has the potential to spark a new era of racism if we do not start explaining it better." She also cited a health-care consultant who indicated that she and other African-Americans had been "discussing opting out of genetic research until it's clear we're not going to use science to validate prejudices."

While the benefits of genetic information are increasingly clear and realized as such, the fear of misuse continues to be a significant issue for some people. Others worry about the willingness of some to simply dismiss or wish away facts as if they do not exist, and encourage others to do the same.

83. Jewish Achievement: The Role of Intelligence and Values – Richard Lynn

On December 3, 2007, *Science Direct* published a paper co-authored by Richard Lynn and Satoshi Kanazawa titled "How To Explain High Jewish Achievement: The Role of Intelligence and Values." Lynn, emeritus professor of psychology at the University of Ulster at Coleraine, Northern Ireland, has long been a leading proponent of the importance of intelligence in success. In this paper, he and Kanazawa drew on the General Social Surveys (GSS) performed by the American National Opinion Research Center (NORC) between 1972 and 2004.

The paper begins: "Throughout the 20th Century, Jews have been greatly overrepresented in western nations among intellectual elites, in the universities, and among the higher socio-economic classes. The two principal theories have been advanced to explain this are that Jews have high intelligence and, alternatively, that they have cultural values that promote success. We review the evidence and present new data suggesting high intelligence is the more important of the two factors."

Because the GSS data captures both intelligence, using a ten-word vocabulary test, and values, using thirteen values ranked by parents as aspired-to for their children, Lynn said one can look at both the intelligence and the values data to compare results between different groups.

The thirteen words used to define values are: 1) success—tries hard to succeed; 2) studiousness—is a good student; 3) amicability—gets along well with other children; 4) cleanliness—is neat and clean; 5) considerateness—is considerate of others; 6) control—has self-control; 7) honesty—is honest; 8) interest—is interested in how and why things happen; 9) judgment—has good sense and sound judgment; 10) manners—has good manners; 11) obedience—obeys parents well; 12) responsibility—is responsible; and 13) sex role—acts like his/her gender.

Lynn said that on the vocabulary test, the average score for the 228 Jews tested was .6 of one standard deviation higher than the average for non-Jews. This standard deviation difference is roughly the same as that found in more rigorous tests of IQ.

On the question of the values Jews most want their kids to have, Lynn found only two significant differences between Jews and non-Jews. Jews placed a higher value on judgment and a lower value on honesty. Of the three values ranked most important, the only significant differences were that Jews placed less importance on cleanliness, honesty, manners, and obedience, and more importance on considerateness, interest in how and why things happen, judgment, and responsibility.

Lynn and Kanazawa concluded: 1) the word test is essentially an IQ test, and the .6 of one standard deviation advantage was sufficient to explain most or all of the high Jewish achievement."

As for cultural values, they concluded: 1) The results provided no evidence Jews attached more importance to success or studiousness than non-Jews; 2) they doubted considerateness, interest in how and why things happen, judgment, and responsibility would contribute to Jewish success in all walks of life; 3) Jews differ little from others in values they want their children to have; 4) and in conclusion, "The results clearly support the high intelligence theory of Jewish achievement...(and) no support for the cultural values theory to explain Jewish success. Thus, "It would appear that high intelligence is the most promising explanation of Jewish achievement."

Missing was any awareness that two thousand years of anti-Semitism might cause Jews, consciously or unconsciously, to be reticent to respond to a survey suggesting they somehow place great value on achievement and success. Moreover I am skeptical of making such judgments based solely on a rather superficial 13 item ranking technique.

As will be seen in the later item (110), Lynn's own 2011 book, *The Chosen People* began to undermine most of what is said above as he came to grips with the fact his IQ math could not explain the magnitude of disproportionate Jewish success in winning Nobel Prizes.

84. Genetic Differences in Identical Twins – (again!)

A March 11, 2008 article in *The New York Times* by Anahad

O'Connor reported on an *American Journal of Human Genetics* study by scientists at the University of Alabama at Birmingham. The study, authored by Professor Jan Dumanski and geneticists at universities in Sweden and the Netherlands focused on whether the DNA of identical twins is, in fact, identical. It said the early view that genes begin identical and stay that way, unchanged for life, is proving wrong. More recently, it has become clear that environmental conditions and other epigenetic events can modify the expression of selected genes. For example, diet and tobacco smoke, the study said, can cause epigenetic changes that "have been implicated in the development of cancer and behavioral traits like fearfulness and reduced confidence, among other things." The researchers had expected to confirm this, and they did, but they also found other sources of contradiction.

Professor Dumanski said that after studying ten pairs of identical twins, in which nine showed signs of dementia or Parkinson's disease in one twin but not the other, the researchers were surprised to find differences in the twin's DNA sequences; they were not 100 percent identical after all. The specific changes were what are known as "copy number variations," in which a gene exists in more or fewer numbers or copies, and in some cases, a set of coding letters in the DNA is missing. "When we started this study, people were expecting that only epigenetics would differ greatly between twins," said Dumanski, "but what we found is that there are changes at the genetic level, (in) the DNA sequence itself...not known, however is whether these changes...occur at the embryonic level, as the twins age, or both."

A second member of the study team, Dr. Carl Bruder, said copy number variations had only recently been discovered but are thought to be important. Some "confer protection against diseases such as AIDS, while others are believed to contribute to autism, lupus and other conditions." Studying them, where one twin has the disease and the other doesn't, may help identify genes involved in disease."

And Professor John Witte, a genetic epidemiologist at the University of California, San Francisco, said their efforts were "part of a growing focus on genetic changes after the parents' template had been laid... you've got a bit more genetic variation than previously thought." O'Connor wrote, "In the meantime, a lot of biology textbooks may need updating."

85. Differences in Genetic Variances in Different Populations – Robert Lee Hotz

On March 21, 2008, Robert Lee Hotz, who took over for Sharon

Begley at *The Wall Street Journal*, reported on a number of studies under-way that focused on genetic variation and the huge number of minor vari-ations being revealed. Some were said to make humans more vulnerable to different diseases and/or resistant to treatments. A January report in *Neuron* by researchers at Munich's Max Planck Institute of Psychiatry noted that "any one of eleven variations of a single gene can make it harder for a commonly prescribed antidepressant to temper our moods," while "any of nine variations of another gene may double the lupus risk."

Different populations show more or fewer variations, with Ameri-cans of European descent carrying more potentially harmful variations than African-Americans. A story in *Nature* reported on a University of Michigan analysis of 500,000 DNA markers across twenty-nine popu-lation groups on five continents. *Science* reported on Stanford Medical School scientists looking at 650,000 markers across fifty-one popula-tions. Cornell researchers were looking at the genetic effects of migra-tion from Africa to Europe. The University of Chicago was exploring the differences between European and African responses to medications and infections. Scientists in England, China and the U.S. intended to seek more detailed information on human genetic variations by sequencing genomes of 1,000 people around the globe.

At the end of the report, Hotz noted, "Human variations may be more than medicine can easily master. Researchers at Brigham and Women's Hospital reported last month in the *Proceedings of the National Academy of Sciences* that even crucial genetic mutations in cancer cells, for example, may be different in every patient." Proven true, this would have major consequences for understanding diseases and developing and testing prospective cures.

86. Malcolm Gladwell's *Outliers*

In November 2008, Malcolm Gladwell's book *Outliers* was pub-lished. As with his earlier works, *The Tipping Point* and *Blink*, it quickly became a bestseller. The title telegraphed his notion: outliers are those few among us who are unusually successful. Gladwell's theory is that brains and drive are vital, but they aren't enough. In addition to hard work (his benchmark for the required investment of time to master a domain is 10,000 hours, essentially five man- or woman-years of effort), the stars must be properly aligned. Circumstances must offer up the third necessary ingredient in the form of an opportunity

Most reviewers of *Outliers* picked up on that idea. In David A. Shaywitz's review in *The Wall Street Journal*, he said, "Intrinsic ability appears to be a necessary, but not sufficient condition for exceptional achievement...hard work is essential too.... Intrinsic qualities are required, but a lot of things also need to break just right, and a prodigious amount of good luck is necessary."

Despite including stories of a number of entrepreneurial Jews, *Outliers* seems to have missed an essential point about Jewish achievement. One cannot reasonably look at what Jews have done in the Golden Age and conclude they were all in the right place at the right time.

87. Jewish and Moorish DNA in the Spanish and Portuguese– Nicholas Wade

On December 5, 2008, Wade reported in *The New York Times* on studies of the Y chromosome (male) DNA in Spanish and Portuguese populations. Two biologists, one Spanish and the other British, led the study that found 20 percent of the Iberian population has Sephardic Jewish ancestry and 11 percent has Moorish ancestry.

Despite some who theorized that few Jews or Muslims had ever converted, the DNA appeared to reflect the reality of historic pressures. First was the pressure on the Jews when the hostile Muslim Berbers displaced the tolerant Umayyad Muslim Dynasty. They expelled Christians and Jews who did not convert to Islam. Later, when the Catholics assumed control, they did much the same to Muslims and Jews. The urban character of the Jews suggests that significant numbers must have converted in order for their minority population in fifteenth century Spain to now be represented in 20 percent of the Spanish and Portuguese populations.

88. Lawrence E. Harrison's *Jews, Confucians and Protestants*

In April 2009, Lawrence E. Harrison participated in a Moscow seminar on culture and cultural values. A video of his speech, available online, previewed his book *Jews, Confucians and Protestants: Cultural Capital, and the End of Multiculturalism* (issued in late 2012). Harrison, who kindly provided a positive blurb for the back cover of *The Golden Age*, has written extensively on culture and its role in economic advancement.

Jews, Confucians and Protestants makes the point that the values, beliefs and attitudes of some groups represent invaluable cultural capital. That capital is fundamental in helping them realize their full potential, both individually and collectively. Among groups he singles out for discussion, in addition to Jews, Confucians and Protestants, are Ismaili Muslims, Basque Catholics, Sikhs, and Mormons.

Harrison lays out common elements of the core values most of these groups share (also see Part 1, "Culture Matters"). He describes the history and basis for each group's values. As an example for Confucian values, he draws on the work of Edwin Reischauer, a noted scholar of the history and culture of Japan and East Asia, and a former American Ambassador to Japan.

Among key tenets, Reischauer and Harrison say, Confucianism assumes:

"Human nature is basically good, and the good, ethical life can be assured by order, harmony, moderation, good manners, and the Confucian formulation of the Golden Rule, 'Do not do to others what you would not have others do to you.'

"The Confucian system is built of five relationships: father/teacher and son (filial piety is the most important virtue), ruler and subject, husband and wife, older and younger brother, and friend to friend. Three of the five concern the family, society's building block, and it is organized on authoritarian principles. The authoritarian family pattern was applied to the whole of society. The role of the emperor and his officials was that of the father writ large.

"While the first four relationships are those of superior to subordinate, the responsibilities run in both directions for all five. Both the superior and the subordinate must respect their responsibilities to assure peace and harmony.

"Confucius placed heavy emphasis on education as the engine of progress. Merit formed the basis for selecting those who would govern and merit was determined by testing the scholarly achievements of those who aspired to govern.

"Chinese kinship ... (reaches) out in each direction to the fifth generation ... to one's ancestors back to great-great-grandparents, and descendants down to great-great-grandchildren, and also to one's contemporaries—to one's third cousins (descendants of one's great-great grandparents). This tradition is the root of the clan. Ancestor worship (and desire to never displease ancestors or descendants) is a spur to achievement and the accumulation of wealth.

"With respect to economic development, the Confucian emphasis on education, merit, hard work and discipline, combined with achievement-motivating tradition of ancestor worship and Tao emphasis on frugality, constitutes a potent, albeit largely latent formula for growth comparable to (Max) Weber's view of Calvinism. (It) was, however, suppressed by the low prestige Confucianists attached to economic activity."

Many know of Imperial China's early prominence as a nation, even before the time of Christ, and later as gunpowder's inventor, the originator of printing, and producer of cast iron well before Europe. China was a world power that sailed to Africa before Columbus landed in America. But it all came undone following a change of leadership.

For hundreds of years, authoritarian culture in Japan and China placed the greatest emphasis on governance. They created administrations with a "literati" upper class, which presumably could be attained based on merit. But everyone else was subordinate to the upper class. Merchants depended on officials for protection. Stability more than economic growth was promoted, and those in charge—the literati—looked down upon making money. For hundreds of years, the literati held Japan and China back. They were closed societies.

But the offshore Chinese (those who lived outside China) were not constrained by the literati. There were no literati in the countries to which they migrated, and no stultifying bureaucracy holding them back. They retained their positive Confucian values without the constraining influence of authoritarianism.

And thus, well before the Asian Tigers emerged as successful economies late in the 20th Century, and before Deng Xiaoping transformed Mainland China in the 1980s, the offshore Chinese" were high achievers.

Nearly everywhere they settled, they had more education and greater success than most locals among whom they lived. In his book *Migrations and Cultures*, Thomas Sowell reported:

— Although the Chinese minority was less than five percent of the Indonesian population, they controlled an estimated 70 percent of the country's private domestic capital and ran three-fourths of its 200 largest businesses.

— In Thailand, the Chinese were 10 percent of the population but they controlled all four of the largest banks. (p 176)

— In Vietnam, on the eve of World War II, the Chinese owned twenty-three of the twenty-seven large mechanized rice-processing mills.

— The first president of Guyana was Chinese, as was the first governor-general of Trinidad. (p. 219) Less than 1 percent of the Jamaican population, the Chinese were nonetheless dominant in the country's retail trade. (p 218)

— In the United States, by the 1990s, the median income of native born Chinese-Americans was 60 percent higher than the U.S. average. (p 226). In American schools, Chinese students consistently bested the graduation rates of Whites.

— Singapore, possibly carved from Malaysia because of Chinese success, was and still is an astonishing tiny country. With no natural resources, a population of 5.2 million, a total land area of just 274 square miles, it has the world's thirty-eighth largest economy (13th based on per capita income). Literacy is more than 92 percent, unemployment is 2.2 percent, and Singapore is ranked as the easiest country in the world in which to do business.

Drawing on its own largely Confucian value system, Japan became the first country to rebel against the authoritarian system. Fifteen years after Commodore Matthew Perry opened up Japan in July of 1853, several young Samurai overthrew the Tokugawa shogunate and brought about the Meiji Restoration. Three years later, two of them led a delegation to the United States and Western Europe. What they found was so revolutionary, that they immediately launched the wholesale adoption of "Western technology, public and business administration, and education in Japan.

Between 1871 and 1905, Japanese male school-age enrollment went from 40 percent to 98 percent. For females, it jumped from 15 percent to 93 percent. By 1905, the Japanese were able to defeat the Russian Navy in the Battle of Tsushima, having earlier defeated the Chinese and taken Taiwan as a colony.

We revile the Japanese attack on Pearl Harbor and much of their World War II behavior, but the incredible advance of Japan from a small, feudal island nation in the 1850s to a world power in just fifty years is astonishing. After the near-total destruction of Japan in World War II, the country completely rebuilt itself to become the world's second largest economy, despite its population of only 150 million people. Now they are third, behind China and the United States. The Meiji restoration removed the constraining authoritarian impulse half a century earlier leaving in place positive Confucian influences on education, merit, responsibility, family, and all the rest.

As suggested above, a similar transformation of culture took place after China's failed Cultural Revolution and Mao's death in 1976. Deng Xiaoping took over and engineered the transformation we see today. "It doesn't matter whether a cat is white or black," he said, "as long as it catches mice." His aphorism captured the point that Mao's authoritarian style of Communism and class warfare had left China in a mess. The "red" cat simply could not catch mice, nor, for more than 500 years, had the Imperial cat of China's dynasties been able to either.

While Deng kept tight control on the power of the Party, the military, and thus the government, he unleashed the individual power of "getting rich." "To get rich is glorious," was Deng's 1978 pronouncement. Entrepreneurs were no longer looked down upon. No bullet in the back of the head for personal success. No long prison sentence. Deng's was a revolution of pragmatism all its own.

Today, China is the world's second largest economy and still growing. It has its share of problems, but its literacy is beginning to match that of offshore Chinese and its academic, science, and technology performance have become world class.

Space does not permit additional examples here, but Harrison covers them all, explaining their histories and the role of values in realizing success in each case.

89. Effort May Trump IQ in Predicting Success – David Brooks

An April 30, 2009 Brooks column in *The New York Times* featured two recent books: Daniel Coyle's *The Talent Code* and Geoff Colvin's *Talent Is Overrated*. Both reported on recent research suggesting IQ is generally a bad predictor of success. One noted that young Mozart was not so much a genius prodigy as a copier of pieces from others. But he put in countless hours learning and building skills that later flowered in *The Marriage of Figaro* and other works. Tiger Woods was the same with his early work ethic as a golfer.

Top performers often demonstrate "slightly above average ability" and then find themselves with a mentor or a circumstance that lets them visualize how far they can go. That bent toward achievement might, in turn, be enhanced by insecurity from something like a family tragedy, or an outsized commitment to practice and hone the necessary skills.

Brooks' synopsis is that "public discussion is smitten by genetics and what we are hard-wired" to do. And it is true that genes can place a leash on our capacity. But the brain is also phenomenally plastic. We construct ourselves through our behavior. As Coyle observes, it's not who you are, it's what you do."

90. *The Israel Test* – George Gilder

In July 2009, George Gilder's *The Israel Test* was published. A non-Jew, Gilder argues the case for Israel. He begins by explaining that while preserving Israel is vital, it is not so much the geography or country he is writing about. Nor is it the war with radical Islam or even the split between Arabs and Jews. The real issue, he said is between the "rule of law and the rule of leveler egalitarianism, between creative excellence and covetous 'fairness,' between admiration of achievement versus envy and resentment of it."

Early in the book, Gilder discusses anti-Semitism, which he loathes. And he challenges the view that anti-Semitism is complex and arises from numerous causes. Though he respects those arguments, he draws on the academic work of Benzion Netanyahu (a noted scholar and the recently deceased father of Benjamin Netanyahu). Benzion Netanyahu delved back 1,500 years before the Inquisition to find the first recorded anti-Jewish pogroms in Alexandria, Egypt, when Hellenistic Egyptians simply resented the secular power of Jews. Later, during the Spanish Inquisition, Netanyahu finds evidence it was spurred by Spanish envy of the success of Jews who, as new Christian clerics, "were taking over the Spanish church by being more learned, eloquent, devout, resourceful, and charismatic than Christian leaders of Spanish ancestry." He concludes it was simple envy of Jewish social and economic success, not religious resentment. "The source of anti-Semitism was Jewish superiority and excellence."

Gilder traces Charles Murray's arguments in his book *The Bell Curve* (see item 20 above) and the "Jewish Genius" *Commentary* article (see item 80 above). He politely challenges the notion that Jewish IQ is 110 and thus 10 points above the norm. Instead, he says "as recently as 1999, Israelis of all races had failed, on average, to outperform Americans in international tests of eighth-grade math and science skills." Gilder does, however, draw on Murray's notion that perhaps there are a disproportionate number of Jews with "exceptional intelligence" (particularly in America.) He quotes Murray, "The proportion of Jews with IQs of 140 or higher is...around six times the proportion of everyone else."

But Gilder does not push the point (p 33). Instead, he shifts to say envy of Jewish success reflects a cultural collapse of those who demean Jews for their spirit of enterprise, their premium on education—particularly science education that elevates intellectual achievement—and their strong work ethic. In short, they demonstrate David McClelland's "Need for Achievement." Others, he says, can do just as well. He is scathing in challenging a Marxist "zero-sum" mentality that posits whatever Jews have must have been taken from others. Instead, he believes, Jewish performance can and should be emulated to everyone's benefit.

91. Ashkenazim Are Khazars – Shlomo Sand

An October 2009 opinion piece in *The Wall Street Journal* by Evan Goldstein, and a November 2009 story in *The New York Times* by Patricia Cohen, both raised the Khazar/Ashkenazi issue again. Tel Aviv University professor Shlomo Sand had just published a book that "undercut the Jewish claims to the land of Israel by demonstrating Ashkenazis do not constitute a people with a shared racial or biological past." In addition to alleging that Palestinian Arab villagers are descended from the original Jewish farmers, he raises the Khazar theory, which Cohen says goes back to the early nineteenth century (making Arthur Koestler's 1976 book, *The Thirteenth Tribe*, a bit of a latecomer to the theory).

In his piece, Goldstein notes the Khazars dissolved at the beginning of the second millennium, leaving the mystery of what happened to them. Did they migrate west as Jews?

Both Cohen and Goldstein suggest that "self-described post-Zionist" Sand's true motive was to discredit the Jewish claim to Israel. Cohen noted Sands is a scholar of modern France, not Jewish history (and apparently not genetics either). Goldstein, who spoke to Sand and challenged him regarding the possible effect on heightened anti-Semitism, citing an Arab translation of his work, elicited the comment, "If I were to write it today, I would be much more careful."

92. *Start Up Nation* – Dan Senor and Saul Singer

In November 2009, Dan Senor and Saul Singer's book, *Start Up Nation,* was published. It chronicles the explosive recent growth of high technology start-ups in Israel—now the world's first or second most prolific creator of new high technology companies. Apart from the recent arrival of many Russian scientists, Senor and Singer attribute much of this to the unique culture of Israel.

Quoting from the book's flyleaf, "Israel's adversity-driven culture fosters a unique combination of innovative and entrepreneurial intensity ... Israel is not just a country, but a comprehensive state of mind ... Israelis put chutzpah first. 'When an Israeli entrepreneur has a business idea, he will start it that week ... Israel's policies on immigration, R&D, and military service have been key."

Senor and Singer give particular credit to the Israeli Defense Force

(IDF) as a shaper of character for Israel's young adults. For most young Jews, military service is mandatory. The IDF is an extreme meritocracy where the best excel and then exercise remarkable levels of autonomy and responsibility at a young age. Technology-driven, with Israel's existence always at risk, these young Israelis learn early to take charge and that, together with their knowledge of technology, makes them ripe for entrepreneurship.

93. *The Golden Age of Jewish Achievement* – Steven Pease

In December 2009, *The Golden Age of Jewish Achievement* was published.

CHAPTER 13

2010 to 2012: Culture, Genomics, and Epigenetics

94. Mapping IQ in the Brain

On February 22, 2010, *Science Daily* reported on a study slated for publication later that week in *Proceedings of the National Academy of Science*. The researchers were neuroscientists at Caltech, the University of Iowa, the University of Southern California, and the Autonomous University of Madrid. The study focused on mapping the locations of lesions in the brains of 241 subjects, all of whom had taken IQ tests.

Lesion locations were correlated with IQ scores to build a map of the brain's regions associated with general intelligence ("g"). The study found that "rather than residing in a particular part of the brain, general intelligence is "determined by a network of regions across both sides of the brain…(in)…a distributed system…(which) depends on the brain's ability to integrate—to pull together—several different kinds of processing, such as working memory." While this finding does not directly relate to the development of intelligence in any one group, it shows how little we understand about brain function and the nature and nurture of complex thought processes.

95. Human Culture as an Evolutionary Force – Nicholas Wade

On March 1, 2010, Wade wrote a column in *The New York Times* article titled, "Human Culture, An Evolutionary Force." He began by saying, "As with any other species, human populations are shaped by the unusual forces of natural selection, like famine, disease or climate. A new force is now coming into focus. It is one with a surprising implication—that for the last 20,000 years or so, people have inadvertently been shaping their own evolution. The force is human culture, broadly defined as any learned behavior, including technology." Previously, biologists thought culture retarded change from "the full force of... selective pressures."

As an example of culture shaping evolution, Wade wrote of the example of genetic change caused by diet. Namely, the increased lactose tolerance of Northern Europeans who raised cows, drank milk, and received greater nutrition from it. It is seen to have conferred a selective advantage in Northern Europeans over those who did not drink milk. All of this is detected by looking at the recent increases in the commonness of the genetic variation associated with lactose tolerance.

Scientists are identifying more commonalities in genetic variations they believe are associated with dietary changes as humans evolved from hunter-gatherers to an agriculturally-based society some 10,000 years ago. Those who live in societies based on agriculture, where starches are part of the diet, are found to have genetic variations resulting in more copies of the amylase gene. In saliva, amylase breaks down starch. The change is not seen in societies that depended on hunting and fishing for food.

Historically, going back more than a million years, genetic changes occurred very slowly. But in recent years that pace appears to be increasing. "This raises the possibility that human evolution has been accelerating in the recent past under the impact of rapid shifts in culture." In short, nurture appears to be shaping nature.

96. The Genetics of Low IQ in Williams Syndrome Patients

On April 22, 2010, *Science Daily* reported on a research study of sixty-five Williams Syndrome patients. The study sought to determine which genes and gene expressions affected their reduced intelligence level (typically, their IQs were around 60). The report by teams from UCLA, Cedars-Sinai Medical Center, Salk Institute, and the University of Utah had published their joint report the day before in the scientific journal *PLoS ONE*.

Williams Syndrome is caused by the deletion of two-dozen genes on chromosome 7. It leaves patients with one less copy of each gene. In the 2010 study, the researchers found that the STX1A gene plays a significant role (accounting for 15.6 percent of the cognitive variation). The STX1A variation in question apparently hampers neurotransmission of electrical signals from one neuron to the next (synaptic function).

This study is one of several that appear to show the genetics of intellectual deficits are easier to identify than those for intellectual giftedness.

97. "Limits of Policy": Culture, Ethnicity, Group Psychology and Behavior – David Brooks

On May 4, 2010, Brooks began his column in *The New York Times* by noting that more than a century ago, Swedes immigrated to the United States. They prospered, with only 6.7 percent currently living in poverty despite the recent economic downturn. The curious thing was that of those who stayed in Sweden, there too, 6.7 percent were living in poverty. Life expectancies in both countries were much the same. In 1950, the average Swedes lived 2.6 years longer than the average American. But fifty years later, despite dramatically different political systems and adoption of a welfare state, Swedes lived 2.7 years longer than the average American.

Brooks went on to talk about other groups of people. Fifty percent of Asians are college graduates, versus 31 percent of Whites, 17 percent of African Americans, and 13 percent of Hispanics. Similar stratifications occur among them for life expectancy. He also talked about similar distinctions between populations from different regions of the United States.

With the influence of these cultures, ethnicity, group psychology, and regional differences, he said, we see major influences that shape and make enormous differences in individual lives. "All we can say for sure," he says, "is that different psychological and social factors combine in a myriad of ways to produce different viewpoints. As a result of their different viewpoints, the average behavior is different between different ethnic and geographic groups, leading to different life outcomes."

98. "Leading With Two Minds": Petraeus and the Army – David Brooks

On May 6, 2010, a Brooks' piece in *The New York Times* described how a culture can be transformed, sometimes rather quickly. He focused on General David Petraeus, who had recently received the Irving Kristol Award. That Award is given to individuals who have made exceptional intellectual or practical contributions to improving government policy.

Five years earlier, the U.S. Army in Iraq—a huge organization—had an entrenched way of thinking. Particularly following Vietnam, the Army was trained to use overwhelming force. But by 2004 and 2005, it simply wasn't working in Iraq. Despite the intent to eradicate the villains and disrupt the hubs and networks of terrorists, the Army seemed to be creating Iraqi enemies as fast as it was dispatching them, perhaps even faster.

Petraeus left Iraq to write a counterinsurgency field manual at Fort Leavenworth, Kansas. What he and his colleagues devised went against the status quo, and that status quo was endorsed at high levels in the Pentagon. The new paradigm had to be sold; Petraeus and his team did just that. They institutionalized their view of a "light footprint"—soldiers living among the people they were trying to protect—rather than search and destroy operations followed by a retreat to a home base. The locals were to become friends and sources of information. Soldiers would help the community more than fight the bad guys. Petraeus and his team convinced General Ray Odierno, who was then leading the operations in Iraq, and together they used the strategy in the successful Iraq Surge.

As Brooks acknowledged, there were still gaps, but the new counterinsurgency has been "bred into their bones." And they need sufficient forces on the ground to carry it off. Brooks thought more institutions should be set up to encourage such changes. "Most institutions are hindered by guild customs, by tenure rules, and by the tyranny of people who can only think in one way."

More than two years later, on December 27, 2012, Janet Maslin, a leading book reviewer for *The New York Times,* wrote about Fred Kaplan's book, *The Insurgents: David Petraeus and the Plot to Change the American Way of War,* on the same subject. Kaplan traces the evolution of the Army's doctrine about how to fight an insurgency, starting with Petraeus and others who found U.S. Army doctrines outdated in the First Iraq War and led the effort to change the doctrines and culture of how the Army combats insurgencies.

Though we often think of culture as a complex milieu of factors, it is also true that at times, a single element or event can significantly alter or shape a culture. Mandatory education did that for Jews. So did Andrew Grove's corporate cultural value of "constructive confrontation" at Intel Corporation during its Halcyon years. Petraeus' counterinsurgency doctrine was such an element. It led to Sunni support for American forces, battlefield success, and relative peace in Iraq until American forces were withdrawn and failed Shiite leadership ended that peace.

99. Culture and Crime: Richard Cohen Changes His Mind

On June 1, 2010, the *Washington Post* ran a column by Cohen titled "Acknowledging the Cultural Roots of Crime." It described a phenomenon many liberals found astonishing—namely, that crime rates were declining as the economy worsened. This completely undermined the notion that crime is driven by hard times, something anyone familiar with the Depression could have already confirmed.

Cohen said, "Surprisingly, this has happened in the teeth of the Great Recession, meaning that those disposed to attribute criminality to poverty—my view at one time—have some strenuous rethinking to do. It could be, as conservatives have insisted all along, that crime is committed by criminals. For liberals this is bad news indeed." "Whatever the reasons, it now seems fairly clear that something akin to culture and not economics is the root cause of crime."

With this understood, criminals risk losing the caché of victimhood. Cohen mentioned the woman who told him a necklace had been ripped from her neck. She said, "He probably needed it more than I did." Cohen calls this "liberal guilt at its apogee. Recalling "I'm just misunderstood" lines from "Gee Officer Krumpke" in West Side Story, Cohen ended the column with, "the latest crime statistics strongly suggest that bad times do not necessarily make bad people, bad character does."

100. Jewish Genome Wide Scanning Links Jews, Discredits Khazar Theory – Nicholas Wade and Sharon Begley

A June 9, 2010, Wade piece in *The New York Times* reported on two studies comparing genetic origins of "many Jewish communities around the world. Both went beyond the earlier studies based only on the Y chromosome. These drew on "genome-wide scanning." The first, by Gil Atzmon of Albert Einstein College of Medicine and Harry Ostrer of New York University, appeared in the *American Journal of Human Genetics*. The other, by Doron Behar of Rambam Health Care Campus in Haifa and Richard Villems of the Estonian University of Tartu, was in the journal *Nature*.

Wade reported that the two studies showed genetic linkages between most of the world's Jewish communities. "Jewish communities from Europe, the Middle East and the Caucasus all have genetic histories tracing back to the Levant." Atzmon and Ostrer's analysis shows Iraqi and Iranian Jews separated from the other Jewish communities 2,500 years ago, suggesting they arose around the time of the destruction of the First Temple and the ~587 B.C. Babylonian exile. Excepting Ethiopian Jews and two Judaic communities in India (both much closer to their host populations), the genetic ties between the other Jewish populations were clear.

Atzmon also noted, "members of any Jewish community are related to one another as closely as fourth or fifth cousins ... about ten times higher (than the relationship) between any two people chosen at random off the streets of New York."

Covering the same studies for *Newsweek*, science reporter Sharon Begley reported that European Jews (Sephardics and Ashkenazis) separated from Middle Eastern Jews 100 to 150 generations ago, sometime during the first millennium BCE. "Sephardic groups," Begley noted, "share genetic markers with North Africans, probably as a result of marriages between Moors and Jews in Spain from 711 to 1492." Wade said the surprise for some was the close genetic linkage between Sephardics and Ashkenazis. Both studies reported about 30 percent European ancestry for Sephardics and for Ashkenazis, with the rest coming from Middle Eastern ancestry. And Begley noted that the Jewish Roman historian, Josephus, reported mass conversions to Judaism between Hellenic times and the height of the Roman Empire. Furthermore, the genetic material from each was similar to the other. That closeness was, she said, surprising given they had been separated for so long.

Additionally, the Atzmon-Ostrer study indicated that Sephardic and Ashkenazi genetic signatures are both similar to that of Italian Jews. One possible explanation is that an ancient population of Jews in Northern Italy may have married Italians, giving rise to both communities. Aaron Rodrigue, a Stanford Historian of Sephardic and Ottoman history, suggested to Wade that there was more interaction between Sephardic and Ashkenazi populations in Italy than most experts previously thought. Wade also reported (as had others) that the Ashkenazim first appeared in Northern Europe around 800 CE.

Finally, Wade cited the two studies (and confirmed by earlier Y chromosome analysis), in refuting Professor Shlomo Sand's 2009 assertions that Khazars who converted to Judaism and later intermarried with other Asians and Europeans were the genesis of Ashkenazi Jews. That same week, Begley wrote in her *Newsweek* article that, as regards the Khazar theory, "The DNA has spoken: No."

101. "What? Not All Jews Are Geniuses?" – Jews and MacArthur Fellowships

On October 6, 2010, *Forward* ran a story by Joy Resmovits about MacArthur Fellowship winners. It was titled "What? Not All Jews Are Geniuses?" By *Forward*'s conservative analysis, 13.5 percent of MacArthur "genius" grant recipients over the past decade had been Jewish. This was among Americans where Jews are 2.2 percent of the population. Resmovits indicated that Arthur Hu, a long time explorer of ethnic group overachieving, used a less cautious method and came up with 15 percent.

The story mentioned Jewish success in winning Nobel Prizes, and indicated that while MacArthur Fellowships focus on creativity and promise in science and work outside academia, many are still focused on the arts and sciences. Daniel Socolow, the Jewish director of the Mac-Arthur program, noted Jews won 30 percent of the Fellowships in 1987 when the focus was oriented more toward science and academics, but they continue to receive Fellowships in other domains as well.

Asked why she thought Jewish scientists do so well, 2010 winner Michal Lipson, an Israeli physicist at Cornell, said she thought it came from the cultural emphasis on education. She noted that when her family lived in Sao Paulo, Brazil, she attended religious school even though she does not consider herself observant. "It brought rigor," she said, which she continues to apply to her work. "I got that emphasis on education from my father and tried to give it to my kids."

Other Jewish MacArthur winners also said their Jewish upbringing affected their careers. Joan Abrahamson, who had been Assistant Chief of Staff to U.S. President George H.W. Bush, attended Sunday Hebrew School in San Francisco. She said, "Part of my cultural heritage is trying to make the world better." Fellowship winner Leonard Zeskind, author of *Blood and Politics,* remembers reading *Black Like Me* at bar mitzvah class and said, "I was brought up in a world in which civil rights issues were at the forefront of the Jewish community's agenda. That showed up a lot in my work."

102. "Sins of the Grandfathers": Trans-Generational Epigenetic Effects – Sharon Begley

A November 8, 2010 Begley article for *Newsweek* was titled, "Sins of the Grandfathers." She began with a quote from Michael Skinner, a Washington State University molecular biologist who said, "We just published a paper last month confirming epigenetic changes in sperm." Most of us, Begley said, would have no idea of the importance of Skinner's utterance. He had exposed rats to a fungicide vinclozolin. That had changed genetic switches controlling DNA in their sperm and eggs. Prevailing wisdom had said these changed switches would automatically get reset back to their genetic "default positions" whenever new embryos were created from eggs and sperm. Skinner's experiment showed that not every change is "reset to the default position in embryos. This was groundbreaking.

The environmentally triggered changes affecting Skinner's lab rats were being carried over in succeeding generations, just as though they were part of the rat's original DNA. In fact, the default positions were changed for sixteen genetic switches in the pups' DNA. Later tests showed those changes in genetic expression not only affected a rat's offspring, but also its grandchildren and great-grandchildren. The term for this is "trans-generational epigenetic inheritance."

The sixteen altered switches included some normally set to the "on" position that were turned "off," and vice versa. The pups ended up with abnormalities in their testes, prostates and kidneys. The point of the experiment was not to harm the rats, Begley said, but that "life experiences of grandparents and even great-grandparents can alter eggs and sperm so indelibly that the changes are passed along to children, grandchildren, and beyond." And, it has nothing to do with the traditional sense of "genetic inheritance." And again, any deterministic notion of genetics stability was undermined by the new epigenetic evidence. And if that is so, perhaps traits like IQ are similarly malleable?

In like fashion, Tufts professor, Larry Feig showed multigenerational epigenetic changes in which a healthy diet and an enriched environment stimulates enhanced memory in mice and improved performance traversing mazes. Feig's 2009 *Journal of Neuroscience* report said that the neuronal effect showed up in offspring even if the offspring did not live in the same enriched environment. As Begley says, the pup was not even a gleam in the mother's eye when both she and the pup benefitted from the enriched environment.

Begley cited two other studies that explored inherited effects of diet and smoking.

103. Family Medical History Matters – Sharon Begley

Begley's Nov. 14, 2010 *Newsweek* column foreshadowed the arrival of the $1,000 genome scan (see item 136 below). Her take was that for many diseases, family history is a much better predictor than genetic testing. She noted that surprisingly, the American Society of Human Genetics has declared family history to be the gold standard for assessing disease risk. In short, the tests cost money, but many of them are simply wrong—in part because "genes do not operate in a vacuum."

In noting that two-thirds of the early studies and linkages have proven wrong, Begley highlighted a link between KIF6 and cardiovascular disease, where a study of 57,000 people found that a linkage identified by the $100 tests had no predictive power for the disease as was claimed. The same was true for four gene variants linked to Alzheimer's, certain cancers, type 2 diabetes, and other ailments. Her take was that genes don't operate in isolation, but depend on some of the more than 20,000 genes and environmental conditions. Family history is more likely to be meaningful than the existence of a single gene variant.

104. "The Costly Neglect of Child Rearing Practices" – Jerome Kagan

On February 16, 2011, Jerome Kagan, professor emeritus of psychology at Harvard University, was featured in a *Christian Science Monitor* story. It focused on the importance of early support for parents of infants two years old or younger, when the parents have little formal education.

Kagan's position was that changing the attitudes and behaviors of such parents when the infants are very young is critical. He noted numerous studies in Soviet Poland, Washington DC, Boston, and other locales where data indicated that later interventions, while much more expensive, still resulted in dropout rates of 50 percent or more for children who did not have warm, supportive parents while young.

Kagan said that early pre-school intervention with parents—as little as ten sessions of two hours each—can lead to improvements for at least one-third of the mothers and children. He urged easy, low-cost intervention as being much less expensive and wiser than more expensive, later interventions that rarely work after age five. Kagan and others feel that without such intervention, many children who lack a warm, supportive environment in their early years are "programmed for academic failure."

105. "The Jewish Bias of the Nobel Prize": The Deck Is Stacked in their Favor

In March 2011, Jan C. Biro, whose online resume lists a medical degree from an unnamed school and a doctorate from the Karolinska Institute in Stockholm, released his paper titled, "The Jewish Bias of the Nobel Prize." He wrote it in the form of a serious research paper with forty-seven endnotes. After starting out with pages of statistics demonstrating the astonishing number of Nobel Prizes Jews have earned, he made the case for bias.

Biro's explanation of the disproportionate number of Jewish Nobel Prize winners is that the outcome defies stipulations of Alfred Nobel's will (which established the Nobel Prizes). The will said, "No consideration should be given to the nationality of the candidates." Biro says Swedes "have recognized the enormous PR value of this prize for their country ... and it (Sweden) would probably remain largely unnoticed by the 'big' world without its annual Nobel ceremony." Further, he says, "Swedes are rather sensitive to corruption...but (they) can be moved by a nominee with many weighty supporters...with a talent for networking…(the Swedes are) very responsive to all kinds of often stupid egalitarian argument (such as) the idea of giving one prize to a Jew and one to a Gentile."

Biro goes on to say, "That Swedes are still entrusted to provide a prestigious prize is almost a joke," and then surprisingly that "Swedes do not care who the recipients are...and do not care about the gender or ethnicity of a laureate." He avoids the demagoguery of many rants attributing Jewish success and disproportionate achievement to cheating, fraud, conspiracies, and other nefarious behavior. But in every case where I have explored the arguments, they are superficial, factually wrong, and foolish. Instead, Biro's paper at first appears professional, polite, and serious. It acknowledges Ashkenazi IQs and successful collaborations between "brilliant Jews and Gentiles." But in the end Biro is simply biased and wrong.

Longer than it deserves, the commentary on Biro in this book hopefully provides a sense of the pseudo-scientific form of anti-Semitic bias that is all too common. For more on Biro, see "Anti-Semitism—They Cheat, Or, The Deck Is Stacked in Their Favor" in Part 1.

106. Correlating Religion, Education, and Income – Pew Charitable Trust

On May 15, 2011, *The New York Times Sunday Magazine* published a brief article with a chart similar to the one shown below that summarized a study by the Pew Charitable Trust Forum on Religion and Public Life. It correlated the percentages of the members of various religious denominations in terms of the percent who are college graduates and those whose family income exceeds $75,000 per year.

It showed a clear, near-linear relationship between education and family income. It surprised some that Indian-American Hindus showed the highest education level and second highest income level, until it was revealed that the subjects were immigrants or progeny of immigrants who came from India for the educational and economic opportunities available in the United States. Certainly, this is a smart and motivated group of people.

Notable as well were data for Reform and Conservative Jews—in second and third place respectively for educational attainment, and first and third for family income.

The comparison of various denominations was also interesting. One had to wonder how much the cultural values of each denomination contribute to where they ended up on the chart.

107. *Epigenetics: The Ultimate Mystery of Inheritance* – Richard Francis

On June 13, 2011, Richard Francis' book *Epigenetics: The Ultimate Mystery of Inheritance,* was published. Though epigenetics was the sub-

Correlating Religion, Education and Income

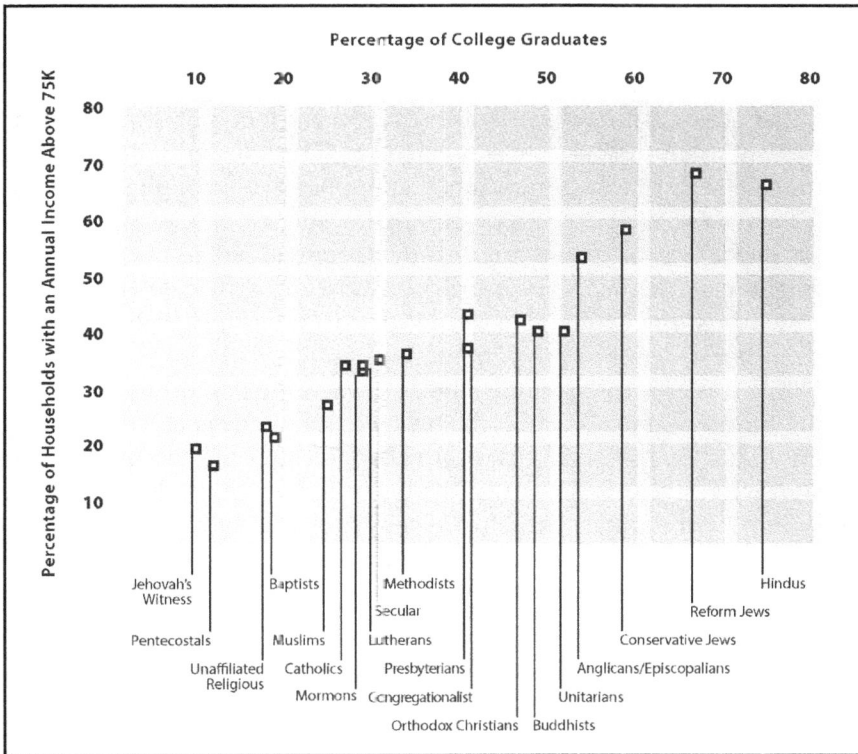

Percentage of College Graduates

Percentage of Households with an Annual Income Above 75K

10 20 30 40 50 60 70 80

80
70
60
50
40
30
20
10

Jehovah's Witness
Pentecostals
Unaffiliated Religious
Baptists
Muslims
Catholics
Mormons
Methodists
Secular
Lutherans
Presbyterians
Congregationalist
Orthodox Christians
Buddhists
Unitarians
Anglicans/Episcopalians
Conservative Jews
Reform Jews
Hindus

ject of earlier books, such as *Epigenetics* by Reinberg and Jenuwein, *Evolution in Four Dimensions* by Jablonka and Lamb, and others, the Francis book was the first addressed to a general audience.

He began with a report on identical twins. It is an interesting choice, since much of heritability theory has drawn heavily on studies of identical twins, especially twins reared apart. In this case Francis reported on a twenty-year-old monozygotic (identical) twin who developed poorly, compared to his normal appearing brother. The underdeveloped twin looked preadolescent, had no facial hair, and his voice was childlike. Examined by a physician, he was found to have genitals that appeared vestigial. He was diagnosed with Kallmann syndrome and faced significant, long-term risks for Alzheimer's disease, lupus, cancer, and other ailments. The healthier twin also had Kallmann's, but in much less severe form.

Francis said the difference was likely epigenetic. While a mutation in a twin after the zygote has split is not impossible, it is highly unlikely. In this case, the change may have been a random epigenetically induced chemical attachment to one or more of his genes that adversely altered its/their expression and with that the severity of his Kallmann syndrome.

He also reported on a Nazi-induced World War II famine in Holland that was an immense hardship for everyone. But for pregnant women and their offspring, it was a disaster. The affected Dutch infants were smaller than those of mothers that did not live through the famine and the infants ballooned in size later in life. And as they aged, they had higher incidences of behavioral disorders, depression, substance abuse, schizophrenia, high blood pressure, heart disease, and Type-II diabetes. In some cases, the ailments varied by the trimester in which the pregnant mother experienced the famine.

While it is easy to conclude a link between the famine and its effect on the mothers and offspring, in this case, the truth is it is not simply genetic. The DNA of the fetus was unchanged after the sperm fertilized the mother's egg. Instead, it was the environment (food deprivation in the womb) that permanently altered the regulation of the fetus' cells to its detriment. Those same disabilities were passed forward to the next generation of the damaged kids.

Rats that frequently lick their offspring have been found to affect their pup's gene expression through demethylation of their genes. The consequence is a decrease of the stress response and with that reduced fearfulness and less anxiety over a lifetime for the pups. Conversely, the offspring of less affectionate rat mothers were methylated leading to the opposite effect. In other rat experiments, the epigenetic chemistry of offspring was changed for better or worse simply by placing offspring rats with "foster" mothers whose licking behavior was the reverse of their natural mother's. And in still other cases, stressed young rats raised with well-adjusted peers later changed their genetic expression and their stress response for the better.

Among other stories, Francis also told of experiments with sea urchin zygotes in which the cells were rearranged. Cells that typically would have become "spines, were moved to a position appropriate for mouth parts." Surprisingly, the cells adapted to their new roles. In other words, the genetic roles of individual cells were not pre-ordained. The environment of the cells ultimately determined their role in the organism.

The prospective consequence of epigenetics is not that a change of diet will improve one's IQ, or make a Jew or non-Jew into a high achiever. Instead, epigenetics significantly alters our understanding of the relationship between genes and the environment, including culture. We had long thought that genetics is akin to "unalterable destiny". We had long believed genes did not change, except over very long periods of time, and that nature and nurture were bifurcated forces that did not directly and immediately change or effect each other. We thought many diseases we experience, such as cancer, and most of our traits were in effect, largely preordained in our DNA. Epigenetics alters that simplistic and deterministic notion. It is something of a throwback to the long-discredited notion of Lamarckism (see item 2 above) in which experience and environment were thought to change our genes. Epigenetics says environmental conditions, some as simple as a mother's warmth towards an infant, can change that infants response to stress and turn on and off our genes, effectively altering the trait, making the infant warmer, more confident and outgoing. Further, it says that trait may be passed to an unknown number of succeeding generations.

If we can alter that trait, many others may also be found to be influenced by "nurture." And if we can induce a predisposition for diabetes in succeeding generations (we now know we can), perhaps we can also do the reverse and induce a predisposition to avoid diabetes. Since World War II we have seen the influence of diet on the height of northern Europeans. For now we know that inside a cell, long-lasting gene-regulating chemicals such as methyl and acetyl are being attached to and removed from genes. With that, the expression of those genes is changed to magnify or reduce their expression, for good or for ill.

108. God's MBAs – The Mormons

On June 19, 2011, *Business Week* featured a story by Caroline Winter and Brandon Bird titled, "God's MBAs: Does the Mormon Faith Build Better Leaders?" It was followed on May 5, 2012 by an article in *The Economist* titled, "The Mormon Way of Business," and on July 13, 2012 by another *Business Week* story, "How the Mormon Church Makes Its Billions." In late 2012, Lawrence Harrison's book *Jews, Confucians, and Protestants* was released. Half of one chapter was devoted to the Mormons and their culture of achievement.

The first *Business Week* story pointed out that the 182-year-old Mormon religion, whose adherents are only 1.4 percent of the U.S. population, has members who disproportionately occupy the corner offices of major U.S. corporations. More recently, Mormons were two of nine Republicans competing in the U.S. presidential primary, from which Mitt Romney emerged as the nominee.

Both *Business Week* and *The Economist* had the same take—it's the culture. In no small measure, both credited the mission experience of the one million Mormon youth who have served as missionaries worldwide, plus the values espoused by the church and lived by its followers.

The articles described the life of the 20,000 nineteen- and twenty-

year-old Mormons who sign up annually for the two-year mission commitment. They spend three months, six days a week, learning a foreign
language and being trained from 6:30 AM to 10:30 PM. They wear
shirts and ties through ten hours of daily classes to prepare them for
their mission as part of a two-person team in any of 150 countries. They
use the native language in the assigned country to talk to the locals
seeking converts—and they get "No" for an answer nearly all of the
time. No dating, only two calls home a year, a firm set of rules covering what they can and cannot do, all while their family and friends are
thousands of miles away. It is a life-changing experience. And they do it
while paying for much if not most of their own expenses. "What happens is you grow up pretty fast," said Dave Checketts, Chairman of SCP
Worldwide, owner of the St Louis Blues, and a Mormon.

Among the dozens of prominent Mormon business and government leaders who were described and counted as former Mormon missionaries were:

— Mitt Romney—CEO of Bain Capital, former governor of Massachusetts, former head of the Salt Lake Olympics, and 2012
  Republican presidential nominee.

— Jon Huntsman, Jr.—U.S. Ambassador to China, U.S. Trade Representative under President George W. Bush.

— J.W. "Bill" Marriott Jr.—Chairman of Marriott International,
  which was founded by his father;

— Stephen Covey—international self-help mogul.

— Kim Clark—former Harvard Business School dean, and

— Clayton Christensen—Harvard Business School professor

The Mormons that *Business Week* interviewed spoke of the confidence gained from their mission, and the value of learning what leadership is all about from living among other cultures ("If they don't have
plumbing, you don't have plumbing").

Mormon clergy are unpaid laymen. All are expected to tithe. Nearly
everyone volunteers for various roles in the local congregation. Children are taught early and expected to speak in two-minute presentations at the age of three. Adolescents, age twelve through eighteen,
benefit from youth groups, at which they lead meetings and take
responsibility. And as employees, Mormons are generally serious, sober,
hard-working and usually faithfully married—all desirable traits.

As a relatively young denomination still actively recruiting large numbers of converts, with many coming from among the middle class and lower middle class, the disproportionate executive skill (and attendant intelligence) of Mormons is highly unlikely to have arisen as a genetic inheritance.

109. Sad Moms and Stressed Parents Can Scar Kids – Sharon Begley

In 2011, three columns by Sharon Begley reported on studies focused on how stress and depression that effect mothers and fathers can leave lasting marks on children.

On August 22 in *Newsweek*, Begley's article "How Sad Mom's Change a Child's Brain" discussed a study by Sonia Lupien of the University of Montreal published in the *Proceedings of the National Academy of Sciences*. It reported on research of seventeen children whose mothers had been depressed since their births. Those infants were compared with twenty-one others whose mothers had no history of depression. The research focus was the size of the amygdalas in both groups. Those results showed the amygdalas of infants whose mothers were depressed averaged 1085 cubic centimeters, versus 879 for offspring of mothers with no history of depression.

She said those results are in line with results from studies of orphans and lab animals that had similar experiences. The working assumption for all three groups was the view that one job of the amygdala is "to scan the environment for threats and with that to learn what to be afraid of and assign emotional significance to the experiences." In short, said Lupien, "the amygdala is highly sensitive to the quality of maternal care. If you grow up in an environment in which you don't have all the support you need, you may become a super-detector of threats."

Begley explained that, "one way this might occur is by flooding the brain with stress hormones (glucocorticoids) whose production is triggered by the amygdala. Levels of these hormones in children of depressed mothers soared when put in an unfamiliar situation. Their stress-response goes into overdrive at the slightest provocation."

She noted the data are not yet available on whether the amygdala enlargement is permanent or not. The hope is that with a better understanding of "neuroplasticity that has swept through neurobiology over the last decade," enlargement may be reversed with a change to a healthier environment.

Begley's September 12 column in *The Daily Beast*, "How Stressed Parents Scar Their Kids," reported on a 15-year longitudinal study focused on the effects of parental stress on the epigenetics of infants as they mature. Begley felt that this was of a piece with earlier research reports (items 37 and 54 above) from the journal *Nature Neuroscience.* In one, the grooming by a rat mother activated a gene resulting in fewer stress hormones coursing through the pup. As a result, it was much more relaxed, curious and well adjusted.

110. *The Chosen People:* Jews Intelligence and Achievement – Richard Lynn

On September 5, 2011, Richard Lynn's book, *The Chosen People— A Study of Jewish Intelligence and Achievement,* was published. A retired psychology professor emeritus at the University of Ulster and a Cambridge Ph.D. in psychology, Lynn has authored more than 200 scholarly articles and books on achievement, IQ, and IQ variations between various groups since the 1980s. Two earlier items (52 and 83) feature Lynn's writings and they are discussed in Part 1.

He begins the book with a history of disproportionate Ashkenazi achievement, and he argues it began with the Jewish Emancipation. He then identifies those who first recognized the emergence of Jews as high achievers, what they said and when they said it. He concludes his introductory material with a review of the timing and results of tests of Jewish IQ since such testing began early in the 20th Century.

He briefly summarizes what he sees as the major theories intended to explain the disproportionate performance, and describes what he sees as the four major groups of Jews: the Mizrahim, the Sephardim, the Ashkenazim, and the Ethiopian Jews. He covers their respective histories, genetic differences since the Diaspora, and the present-day IQ differences between them.

Lynn says the average IQs of the four groups are: Ashkenazim ~ 110; Sephardim ~ 98; Mizrahim ~ 91; and Ethiopian Jews ~ 68. Furthermore, he says that those figures must be considered in the context of the dominant populations among which each group lived during the Diaspora. European and American Gentiles, among whom most Ashkenazim lived, have average IQs of ~100. The Balkan Gentiles, among whom most Sephardim lived, have average IQs of ~92.5. Arabs, neighbors to the Mizrahim, average ~84. And finally, Ethiopian Negroids have average IQs of ~67. Except for the Ethiopian Jews whose IQs are essentially on par with their neighbors, the other three groups of Jews have higher IQs than the surrounding populations.

In comparing the relative achievements of the four groups, Lynn says, the results tend to correlate with IQ. Generally, there are outstanding individuals in each group, but the standout group is the Ashkenazim. (He notes, incorrectly, that, "very few distinguished painters have been Jews." See Chapter 12 of *The Golden Age*.)

Lynn's discussion of alternative theories begins with the one he likes best—namely, that Ashkenazi Jews have higher IQs. He says this is genetic, and that is the main factor behind their disproportionate achievement. He feels the reason this is not universally accepted as fact is because it is "politically incorrect." (In other words, how can all cultures be equal, and the disadvantaged be held back by an unfair world, if somehow Jews have overcome far worse hardships over two thousand years, seen six million fellow Jews murdered, experienced vile anti-Semitism, and yet have recorded phenomenal achievements absent any discernable entitlements?)

Lynn doubts any environmental influence, such as culture, explains the phenomenon. Regarding education, he notes Ashkenazi infants score high on IQ tests even before they enter preschool, something formal education could not have influenced. He talks about better infant care and stimulation, but says high IQ is independent of that as well. Better nutrition, greater attention and more cognitive stimulation provide "for the optimum development of intelligence, but not the intelligence itself"—a "double advantage" is what he calls them.

Lynn also takes issue with "pushy Jewish mothers" as an explanation. He says the "press for achievement" (a nice way of saying pushy Jewish mother) has been established as true by a Canadian experiment, but then he dismisses the idea saying, "There is no general acceptance of the thesis that pushy mothers can raise the IQs of their children. Indeed, the contemporary consensus is that family environmental factors have no long-term effect on the intelligence of children." He ends the section with commentary on the correlation between IQ and myopia (near-sightedness). Lynn says both phenomena are largely genetic, raising the possibility that the genes for both are shared. He says two British studies have shown Ashkenazi's have a higher incidence of near-sightedness than Gentiles.

Lynn writes about the "Eugenic Hypothesis." Perhaps an unwise choice of words, this is not the kind of eugenics practiced in the early 20th Century, but instead is an unconscious process of natural selection in which the best, brightest, and most successful marry and have larger families than their less successful compatriots. It is a variation on the theory that Rabbis had large families, while bright Catholics joined the priesthood and were celibate. He also picks up on the Cochran theory: namely, that the few careers open to Ashkenazim from late Medieval times were those in banking, tax farming, trade, and similar work, all of which were intellectually demanding. And again, Jews who didn't do well generally didn't prosper, didn't have large families, and many of them left Judaism. But he ends by noting it remains unclear how the "Eugenic Hypothesis" explains the differences between Ashkenazis, Sephardics, Mizrahim, and Ethiopian Jews.

Lynn describes the "Persecution Hypothesis," detailing the length and depths of the mistreatment Jews suffered for 2,000 years. He says that, "While it is difficult to show conclusively that the more intelligent Jews have tended to survive these persecutions, it is reasonable to conjecture that this is likely to have been the case." (The poor and less able were unlikely to flee while the smart and wealthy left early, etc.) And, he says, the Ashkenazis suffered the most because they were largely in Europe where the treatment of Jews by Christians was the worst.

The "Discrimination Hypothesis" is attributed to Cochran, Hardy and Harpending. Lynn says their thesis relies on the fact that Ashkenazi Jews could not own land, be farmers, or work in craft trades such as blacksmiths, but were allowed to work in more intellectually demanding jobs such as money-lenders, tax collectors, merchants, import-exporters, and peddlers of secondhand goods. Lynn says that while difficult to prove, the Cochran thesis is plausible. He adds that Cochran et al also argued that Christians were harder on Ashkenazis than Muslims were on the Sephardim and Mizrahim, who at least were allowed to do menial work—work that made lower demands on intelligence.

The "Miscegenation Hypothesis" posits that no matter where Jews lived, there was always some intermarriage with surrounding populations, thus explaining the blond hair and blue eyes of some Jews. All four of Lynn's groups began with Semitic IQs. The European Gentile interplay (including the cultural interplay) may have helped raise Ashkenazi IQs to 100. And it may have nudged the Sephardim when they lived among Moors and European Gentiles. Later, because of the Inquisition, Sephardic IQs may have declined when many left Spain and Portugal to return primarily to the Middle East. Lynn ends by saying that miscegenation does not explain Ashkenazim IQs of 110, but it is a start.

He attributes his "Apostasy Hypothesis" to Charles Murray. Since it was described in conjunction with Murray's *Commentary* article (see item 80 above), it is only summarized here. The theory is that education became mandatory for Jews after ~70 CE, but was too expensive and time consuming for many Jews who were farmers at the time. Their "opt-out" accounted for the sharp drop in the number of Jews from 4.5 million to 1.5 million by the sixth century.

Late in his book, Lynn appears to buy into a synthesis of several of these hypotheses. He sees eugenic, discrimination, miscegenation, and apostasy hypotheses all playing roles, and he supports Cochran, et al in how the genetics of higher IQ and risk of genetic disease may be linked—namely, the alleles that confer higher risk of ailments may also positively affect IQ.

But then Lynn takes a turn that is surprising for those who have followed his earlier work. First, he does the calculations anyone challenging his IQ hypothesis would do. He gets the same answer I did. Namely, even if Ashkenazis have average IQs of 110, and that leads to a greater percent of Jews with IQs of 130 to 145 (levels thought necessary to win a Nobel Prize), the math doesn't yield enough brilliant Jews. That is, the absolute number of Ashkenazi Jews in the world, generously estimated at ten to twelve million, is too small to yield enough brilliant Jews to explain why Jews have won one hundred times more Nobel Prizes than should rightfully be expected. High IQs alone cannot account for the outcome.

Lynn's 2007 paper with Kanazawa (item 83 above) must also be dealt with, since it said culture could not account for the high rate of Jewish achievement. He reiterates that study, saying there is "no support for the theory that Jews attach more importance to success or studiousness than non-Jews ... Jews do not differ much from Gentiles in the values they would most like their children to have."

But then, Lynn cites various studies showing stronger motivation to achieve among Jews, and adds that some have likened this to the "Protestant work ethic." He says studies indicate Jews place greater importance on high incomes, prestige, advanced education, and reduced interest in watching television, and they spend more time on pursuits such as homework. He concludes that "the high Jewish motivation for achievement, together with high intelligence, most likely have a genetic basis, brought about by eugenic customs plus persecution and discrimination."

In short, Lynn says it's genetic but it is also culture. He seems not to recognize that he has just reversed his earlier writings that said it was all genetic (higher IQ) and not cultural. Now he has made it both genetic and cultural. In part this is because he used one notion of culture in the prior article and a different one in the book (see the prior paragraph). He seems to have missed the contradiction.

111. The Malleability of IQ In Teens

An October 19, 2011, *BBC News* ran a story by David Shukman titled, "IQ Can Change in Teenage Years." Shukman described the findings of Professor Cathy Price of Wellcome Trust Centre for Neuroimaging at University College, London, whose research was published in the journal *Nature*. Nineteen boys and fourteen girls were tested for verbal and non-verbal IQ, and given brain scans at age fourteen and again at eighteen. The initial IQs of the thirty-three teenagers ranged from 80 to 140. One girl's verbal score increased from 120 to 138 while her non-verbal score dropped from 103 to 85. Another's verbal score jumped from 104 to 127. While it has generally been thought that IQ is very stable over a lifetime, the new research showed surprising changes. Price reported that 39 percent of verbal IQ scores altered over the four-year period, and 21 percent of spatial reasoning scores altered. Scores increased for some subjects and decreased for others.

Lee Hotz, reporting in *The Wall Street Journal* on October 20, 2011, included images of the brain scans from this same study. The scans showed the changes in gray matter density in the areas of the brain having to do with speech (the left motor cortex for verbal IQ) and motor control and hand movements (the anterior cerebellum for spatial ability). The research said the images correlated with the increases and decreases in the children's IQ scores.

Later, Begley reported on these results in a January 1, 2012 *Newsweek/The Daily Beast* column. In one case IQ rose by twenty-one points (the standard deviation for IQ scores is fifteen). In another, it fell by eighteen points. Begley and Hotz both noted that the Price study did not attempt to explain the cause for the changes, and given the small sample size, some experts were skeptical of the results while others were "confident the IQ variations were evidence of the neural impact of experience for better or worse." At the end of his story, Hotz quoted Robert Sternberg, a past president of the American Psychological Association, who was not part of the study, saying, "Those who are mentally active will likely benefit. The couch potatoes among us who do not exercise themselves intellectually will pay a price."

For most, the message from the study was simply that IQ can go up or down significantly, at least among some children in this age range. A second takeaway was that those who don't show early promise might later perform much better (or even worse). One of the students in which the positive change was most dramatic was Sebastian Friston, who was 23 when the BBC story was issued. He told Shukman of struggling in his early years, taking remedial classes, but now planning a doctorate in computer engineering. He attributed the change to finding subjects that really interested him. Once engaged by those courses, he found them "easier and far more interesting."

When the study first came out, a common reaction was that it reflected changes that can occur only in those who are not yet adults. But Cathy Price of Wellcome Trust believes it may also hold true for adults as well. "The same degree of plasticity may be present throughout life." Begley went further in talking with Irving Kandel of Columbia University, a Nobel Laureate in Medicine, who opined, "if you really work on memory (training)…it probably improves some aspects of cognitive function…. The key to (significant improvement) is intensive training."

112. Nobel Prizes (again) and the Debate over Jewish IQ – Lazar Berman

On October 19, 2011, shortly after the 2011 Nobel Prize announcements, the American Enterprise Institute journal, *The American*, published an essay by Lazar Berman. He used the piece to survey various theories purported to explain why five of the thirteen 2011 Nobel winners (38.5 percent) were Jewish and why the rate has been 32 percent since 2000 (a number higher than I come up with). He says it is up from 29 percent in the second half of the 20th Century, and 14 percent in the first half of the century, quite an accomplishment in a world where Jews are just 0.2 percent of the population.

After talking about the sensitivities and somewhat "schizophrenic" attitude of many Jews on this topic (mostly for fear of accusations of "scientific racism"), Berman surveyed the theories. He described Charles Murrays' evidence and his 2007 *Commentary* essay "Jewish Genius" that pointed to IQ as the main answer, and therefore most likely genetically inherited. Berman contrasted that with the Cochran, Hardy and Harpending genetic theory describing Ashkenazi achievements in Central and Eastern Europe. But in his comments, Berman did not touch on the idea that Ashkenazi genes for IQ had also raised the risk for genetic diseases. Berman appeared to disfavor the Cochran theory, because of the substantial earlier achievements of Sephardics.

Berman raised, but generally discounted the arguments favoring culture. That brought him to the Botticini and Eckstein studies linking mandatory education and Jewish education, and the possible opting out of less capable Jews because of the mandate. The Babylon exile also came into the story. And Berman raised the celibacy of the Catholic meritocracy theory as well.

In the end, however, he demurred, saying that it is "likely a combination of factors," and further, that "the debate will go on." Finally, he raised the question of "whether we as a society are mature enough to debate these questions honestly."

113. Genetics of Brain Development From Fetus To Age 82

On October 26, 2011, *Science Daily* reported on a large study slated for publication in the journal *Nature*. It was titled, "Found in the Developing Brain: Mental Health Risk Genes and Gender Differences." Led by a Yale University team, the study looked at 1,340 tissue samples of brain cells taken from fifty-seven subjects of different ages: from as early as forty days after conception, to age eighty-two. Because the brain is said to contain a hundred billion brain cells linked through billions of connections, the scientists said that roughly 15,000 genes (of a total 20,000 to 25,000) are involved in the brain's development. The researchers analyzed 1.9 billion data points, yielding a data map of genetic activity at various stages of development—in particular, how much development occurs before birth.

So much for the notion that a limited number of genes shape human intelligence. Fifteen thousand genes represent 60 to 80 percent of all human genes.

114. Perhaps Not All Superior Mathematicians Are Male – Sharon Begley

A December 26, 2011 Begley column in *Scientific American* was titled, "Anything Boys Can Do …" In it, she reported on what she said is the "greater male variability hypothesis." This is the issue that got Larry Summers into so much trouble at Harvard University, and ultimately led to his to stepping down as president. The hypothesis says that the wider range of math ability in men is inherent in the way the male brain develops. That is, while the average ability of men and women (the arithmetic mean) is the same, the greater range (a higher top end and lower bottom end) of the male distribution (a "long tail" in the parlance of statisticians) means there are more men at the upper reaches of math ability. They consistently outperform women in math competitions and become math's high achievers. As a consequence, they far outnumber women on the faculties of elite college math departments.

Begley then reported on the results of "the most ambitious study so far" by Jonathan Kane of the University of Wisconsin, Whitewater, and oncology professor Janet Mertz of the University of Wisconsin, Madison. Kane and Mertz looked at math performance data from 52 countries, including elite competitions, examined the variances, and discovered two patterns. They found the variances between men and women to be equal in some countries, but the variance ratio of males to females was very different from country to country.

In some countries, the male variance is greater. In others it isn't. And while it is possible that human genetics is somehow different from country to country, more likely it is not simply a sexual difference, but the result of social and cultural factors as well. One clue is that in the United States, the ratio of men scoring over 700 on math SAT tests has fallen from 13 to 1 in the 1970s to 3 to 1 in the 1990s. Genes do not change that quickly. So the hypothesis of greater male variability looks to have holes, and "nature" is not looking quite as determinative as before.

It should be noted that the theory that women are genetically less suited for math, science and engineering has more recently come into question. And as mentioned above for men, the recent improvement in female results cannot be genetics (it takes too long) and the differences between countries also suggest the same thing. Culture (the environment) may be more important than was ever realized. See also items 140 and 146 below.

115. Expectations For $1,000 Human Genome Scanning Tests

On January 10 and April 3, 2012, news stories in Reuters, *The Wall Street Journal* and *The New York Times* reported on the arrival of a new gene sequencing machine expected to bring the cost per human genome scan down to $1,000 per test. The first human gene sequenced, in April 2003, was estimated to have cost $500 million. A few years later the cost was down to about $10,000 per test. At $1,000 per test, all three articles said the new machine would usher in significant volumes of "whole gene sequencing" of a person's DNA.

Equally as remarkable, however, was the muted response and skeptical commentary about how useful it is to have one's three billion base pairs of DNA sequenced. Despite all the early optimism about personalized medicine and the diagnostic potential, one thing we have learned in the ensuing years is how much more complex it is to understand and apply the genetic information. Many early predictions about what the data mean were wrong. The idea of one mutation, one disease (as is the case for Tay-Sachs and cystic fibrosis) died early. Many, including medical professionals, believed that at this point, family history is still a more reliable disease predictor than results from DNA sequencing.

We are just learning how the various genetic regulatory mechanisms (epigenetics, nucleosome wrapping, copy number variations, and others) work to turn genes on or off, and up or down. And increasingly we find many traits and perhaps some diseases involve many more genes than expected. It is all simply much more complex than was expected.

Nonetheless, the research value of lower cost faster scans is enormous and in particular cases (see item 131 below), test results have already saved lives.

116. IQ Decline in Older Scots Is Only 24 Percent Genetic

On January 19, 2012, *The Wall Street Journal* ran a story by Gautam Naik reporting on a new study published in *Nature* magazine. Scientists had found IQ tests for 1,940 Scots sixty-five years old or older that were taken when they were age eleven. Seeing an opportunity to explore the effects of aging on IQ, and the possible causes of changes, Ian Deary of the University of Edinburgh led a study to retest IQs and draw blood samples (for DNA analysis) from all 1,940 participants in the earlier tests. Using a technique called genome-wide complex-trait analysis, the scientists looked at half a million single nucleotide polymorphisms (SNPs) genetic markers in which alleles differ within populations. The differences allow comparisons.

Among the findings from this research was that genes play a role in intelligence changes (24 percent) over a lifetime, but "environmental factors likely play a greater role." Also interesting was that, while there were exceptions, people tended to retain a similar rank order in their intelligence levels over the years. When asked which genes may account for the changes, Deary said, "Most of us think that we shall be looking for many genes, each contributing very small effects."

Naik's story then referenced the prior study in England that measured significant IQ changes in teens (see item 111 above), results of cognitive training (see items 124 and 171, below), and a three-decade U.S. National Institute of Mental Health study, which found "people whose jobs involved setting up elaborate systems or dealing with tough and complex relationships tended to do better over time on cognitive tests." He further noted, "Schooling also has been shown to boost IQ, while music lessons have also been associated with higher IQ throughout life. And brain imaging studies have found circus jugglers and London cab drivers who use maps can show positive brain changes linked to practice." In short, IQ malleability is proving to be a more open question than we thought just a few years ago.

117. *A German Generation* – Thomas Kohut

In February 2012,Thomas Kohut published *A German Generation: an Experiential History of the Twentieth Century*. Its subject is the generation of Germans born between 1900 and 1915, chronicling the numerous traumas of their lives and the conscious and unconscious culture that shaped them.

As infants and early teens, this generation lived through the deaths of millions of Germans killed in World War I, as their country went down to humiliating defeat and then faced impossible reparations. That was followed by the degenerate Weimar Republic, runaway inflation, political crisis leading to the Nazi era, and more war. Over the six years between 1939 and 1945, they watched unbelievable victories, concentration camps, the Holocaust, humiliating losses, night bombings, and again ignominious defeat. When it was over, the generation of Germans born between 1900 to 1915 was seen as the goat—reproached by their children and the world for having supported the Nazis.

In the 1990s, the German government interviewed sixty-two of these surviving Germans at length. Kohut gained access to the transcripts and used them to frame six composite interviews, painting a picture of the circumstances and culture that shaped them.

He says the thread that ran through their lives was their serial membership in ultra-nationalist associations. These included the Youth Movement of World War I, the Bunds of the Weimar era, and the 1933 beginnings of the Hitler Youth and Reich Labor, both designed to integrate Germans into a national community. Camping, bonfires, celebrations, group retreats, hiking, and songfests: all were group bonding experiences designed to build a collective solidarity, class leveling and shared sense of euphoria en route to becoming Nazis. "One People, One Nation, One Fuhrer," was their anthem.

Shaped in this way, and given Hitler's early success, they were not dragged into the horrors of Nazi Germany against their will. Hitler established concentration camps within two years of coming to power. They were not secret. One composite witness is quoted as saying, "we had only experienced the helplessness of the previous bourgeois government, and we yearned for something completely different." These Germans went through Kristallnacht and later the "Night of the Long Knives." When 200 supporters were made into political enemies and liquidated on Hitler's orders, his young German supporters did not turn on him. Their enthusiasm remained.

In a few years, it was genocide, night bombing of Berlin, Russian, American, British, and French invasion and defeat. An incredible sense of waste and guilt ensued, but not for most of these Germans. Of them, Kohut says, they "cannot face the losses they suffered and they cannot face the crimes against humanity that were associated with these losses." With their "inability to mourn…they are chronically repressed."

One is hard-pressed to find such a clear, if tragic, depiction of what culture can do to a group and to individuals. The Nazis inflicted this on a generation of Germans whose experiences helped shape their vulnerability, then their participation in crime, and finally their subsequent inability to come to terms with it.

118. Genes and Intelligence Links Remain Elusive – David Laibson and Christopher Chabris

On February 24, 2012, *Science Daily* covered a forthcoming article in *Psychological Science* that explored the link between genes and intelligence. Led by Harvard professors David I. Laibson and Christopher F. Chabris, the research looked at dozens of genes suggested by ten to fifteen years of research and testing aimed at identifying the genes associated with intelligence.

Laibson and Chabris found that "in nearly every case, the hypothesized genetic pathway linking genes to intelligence failed to replicate. In other words, intelligence could not be linked to the specific genes that were tested." Chabris was quoted as saying, "In all of our tests, we only found one gene that appeared to be associated with intelligence, and it was a very small effect…. This does not mean intelligence does not have a genetic component. It means it's a lot harder to find the particular genes or gene variants that influence the differences in intelligence."

The *Science Daily* story commented, "…identifying intelligence's specific genetic roots may still be a long way off…. There are probably thousands of genes and their variants that are associated with intelligence. And, there may be other genetic effects beyond the single gene effects—there could be interactions between genes, there could be interactions between genes and the environment. What our results show is that the way researchers have been looking for genes that may be related to intelligence—the candidate gene method—is fairly likely to result in false positives, so other methods should be used."

119. Experience Affects the Brain –Eric Kandel

On March 6, 2012, *The New York Times* ran an interview with Nobel laureate and neuroscientist Eric R. Kandel. His new book, *The Age of Insight*, was due for release shortly. The interviewer noted Kandel had received his Nobel Prize for research on the biology of memory. He had shown that "long-term memory involves enduring changes that result from the growth of new synaptic connections."

Asked if this surprised him. Kandel said, "It is astonishing! You could double the number of synaptic connections in a very simple neurocircuit as a result of experience and learning. The reason for that was that long-term memory alters the expression of genes in nerve cells and that causes the growth of new synaptic connections. When you see that at the cellular level, you realize the brain can change because of experience. It gives you a different feeling about how nature and nurture interact. They are not separate processes."

120. Multiple Language Skills Might Make You Smarter

On March 18, 2012, Yudhijit Bhattacharjee wrote a piece in *The New York Times* on the positive cognitive benefits of knowing two languages. He began by saying the benefits of bilingualism might extend well beyond the practical benefits in a globalized world. Scientists, he said, have begun to show it "makes you smarter. It can have a profound effect on your brain, improving cognitive skills."

Instead of being a source of interference in the brain (with both languages and their vocabularies constantly present), Bhattacharjee said bilingualism forces the brain to work harder to resolve the conflict. The workout strengthens the "cognitive muscles." In the same vein, in 2004, two psychologists, Ellen Bialystok and Michelle Martin-Rhee, showed that bilingual preschoolers were better at solving more challenging puzzles than monolinguals.

Scans of brains also suggest that the brain of a bilingual person not only performs better, it does so more efficiently, with less activity. Seven-month-old bilingual infants were better at anticipating changes in the activities going on around them. Bhattacharjee concluded by discussing the work of neurophysicist Tamer Gollan at the University of California, San Diego. Gollan, who found individuals with higher degrees of bilingualism were more resistant to the onset of dementia and Alzheimer's disease, and the higher the skill, the later the age of onset.

One wonders about the ramifications for a Diaspora-based culture, where capabilities in multiple languages were an inherent part of life for so many Jews.

121. Epigenetics and Cancer

An April 7, 2012, an article in *The Economist*'s Science and Technology section titled "Cancer's Epicenter" began saying that "the biggest conceptual breakthrough in the war on cancer was the realization by the 1980s that it is always a genetic disease." Sometimes cancer is caused by an outside agent such as tobacco smoke, other times it is a random piece of bad luck in miscopying DNA during cell division, and in some cases it is an inherited flaw. But this "genetic cause" insight has not yet led to cures because we don't yet know how to repair the DNA.

The article goes on to briefly describe epigenetics and say that some cancerous genes are involved in epigenetic regulatory processes. Those processes, it said, are amenable to "chemical intervention in a way that genetic mutations are not." As an example, it described the work of GlaxoSmithKline to inhibit an enzyme (EZH2) that attaches methyl groups to histone proteins. The overactive EZH2 is said to silence tumor suppressor genes, leading to some lymphomas. Early tests of one drug candidate are quite promising in restoring the tumor suppression while "having no apparent effect on nearby normal cells."

A second substance, developed by the Dana-Farber Cancer Institute in Boston, is being tested for a different epigenetically implicated cancer. And two epigenetic drugs are already on the market: one to treat the precursor of acute myelogenous leukemia and the other to treat cutaneous T-cell lymphoma. These are just four of a number of similar efforts to develop epigenetic-based drugs to treat cancers by permanently eliminating their underlying causes, with minimum damage to healthy cells. The story ends with the statement, "epigenetics might justly take its place alongside genetics in the analysis and treatment of cancer."

122. Rhesus Macaques and the Epigenetics of Induced Stress

On April 15, 2012, and article in *The Economist* reported on research using rhesus macaques monkeys. It noted that status among macaques appears to be governed by the sequence in which they join groups of other macaques (the last macaque introduced tends to have the lowest status), and that status affects their stress response.

The researchers then created new groups, and set up their own sequence for introducing the macaques into each group. As before, those introduced later had lower status. Then, looking at the blood chemistry of the macaques, they found that the relative status had triggered methylation changes that altered genetic expression for inflammation and other immune responses. Over time, lower status and greater stress response (more inflammation) can be a risk factor for a long list of ailments. And unless the methylation effect is reversed later, the epigenetically influenced gene expression can last a lifetime.

After the experiment concluded, the researchers found some macaques changed their own status within the group. That, in turn, further altered the methylation and genetic expression arising from the earlier experiment.

Once more the gene expression is seen to be altered by the environment. Nurture is changing nature.

123. Pooled Brain Scan Research Explores Disease and IQ

Another April 15, 2012 *Science Daily* story reported on results published in *Nature Genetics*. More than 200 scientists from 100 international institutions pooled the brain scans and genomic data from 21,151 presumably healthy people, which they said was sufficient to help them to map "human genes that boost or sabotage the brain's resistance to a variety of mental illnesses and Alzheimer's."

Written by UCLA neurology and psychiatry professor Paul Thompson, the study looked for genes that increase risk of a single disease inheritable by offspring, as well as factors that contribute to tissue atrophy and reduced brain size. These may be biological markers for heredity disorders such as schizophrenia, bipolar disorder, depression, Alzheimer's, and dementia. The scientists were looking for clear patterns in genetic variations, to see how those variations physically altered the brain. They were able to zero in on the DNA of those with smaller brains where they found subtle shifts in the genetic code and diminished memory centers.

The researchers believed they also found "genes that explain differences in intelligence." These involved a variation in the gene HMGA2 that they say affects brain size and intelligence. Thompson's final quote says it all—"This is a really exciting discovery: that a single letter change leads to a bigger brain. We found fairly unequivocal proof supporting a genetic link to brain function and intelligence. For the first time, we have watertight evidence of how these genes affect the brain. It supplies us with new leads on how to mediate their impact."

124. Building a Smarter Brain: Jaeggi and the "N-back" Exercise – Dan Hurley

An April 22, 2012, a story in *The New York Times Sunday Magazine* by Dan Hurley was titled, "Can You Build a (Better Brain?)" and subtitled, "A New Working-memory Game Has Revived the Tantalizing Notion That People Can Make Themselves Smarter." Hurley reported that in a 2008 study, Susanne Jaeggi and Martin Buschkuehl, now at the University of Maryland, found that young adults who "practiced a...(computer) game...showed improvement in a fundamental cognitive ability known as "fluid intelligence." This is the capacity to solve novel problems, learn, reason, see connections, and get to the bottom of things."

The implication was that playing the game literally made people smarter. Fluid intelligence has long been thought to peak early, remain stable and later slowly decline. It was considered to be largely genetic, and impervious to training. Jaeggi's work suggests that fluid intelligence might not be quite so fixed after all. But as with physical exercise, you have to keep exercising fluid memory. The effect seems to wane as practice ceases. If this is true, some basic assumptions about IQ and IQ tests will be less "right" than was previously thought. And it is possible to imagine how fluid memory training could be adopted as an exercise regime akin to jogging.

Impressive and controversial as these results were, the story said others have achieved similar results in preschoolers, elementary school children, college students and the elderly. For example, Jaeggi and

Buschkuehl say their interest was triggered by the work of Swedish neuroscientist Torkel Klingberg, who began working with fourteen children afflicted with ADHD. Five weeks after starting the experiment, Klingberg reported early success with less fidgeting and improved measures of fluid intelligence. Three years later, he replicated the results with a different group of fifty children.

One skeptic, Randall Engle at Georgia Tech School of Psychiatry, views all this as something akin to cold fusion—the much-hyped but failed claim that nuclear fusion could be achieved at room temperature on a desktop. Engle said, "Fluid intelligence is not culturally derived. It is almost certainly the biologically driven part of intelligence.... Do I think you can change fluid intelligence? No."

Others described in Hurley's article were also skeptical, although more qualified in their response. Nonetheless, numerous supporters are pursuing the lines of research stimulated by Jaeggi and Buschkuehl. They counter the skeptics with their own positive results. Hurley's article included descriptions of several of them.

The impression left is one of "early times." A May 6, 2012 opinion piece in *The New York Times* by David Z. Hambrick was quite skeptical of the studies. Hambrick called for more replication, different fluid intelligence tests of the subjects, and longer periods of study, noting the prior history of such claims for cognitive improvement have consistently been wrong. And, he said, if achieved, would it be worth all the time it takes?

But if the positive results are replicated over and over by credible experts, and the benefits "stick" over time, will something new and important have been uncovered? If so, it will refute a long-held belief that cognitive ability is unchangeable.

All of us might benefit if this proved true.

125. "How Dickensonian Childhoods Leave Genetic Scars" – Matt Ridley

Ridley's May 12, 2012 column in *The Wall Street Journal*, "How Dickensonian Childhoods Leave Genetic Scars," has to do with epigenetic effects on genes brought on by the environment of our upbringing. His new wrinkle was not just the methylation angle, but also the telomeres (the DNA sequences at the ends of chromosomes which are not thought of as genes per se). Early on, telomeres were considered "junk" DNA, but more recently they have come to be thought of as being related to aging. The idea is, the longer they are, the better.

Ridley mentioned the work of Stacy Drury from Tulane University, who found shortened telomeres in children at Bucharest orphanages, as compared with those in foster families. It suggested the stress of life in those bleak environments had negative consequences for the orphans.

More recently, Avshalom Caspi, Terri Moffit and others at Duke and at Kings College, London, examined telomeres of 2,200 Britons born in 1994 and 1995. Blood samples were taken from these late teens beginning when they were five to ten years old. It was a good source of telomere data of kids from homes where there was bullying, beating, or domestic violence. In many cases, the telomeres shrank faster where there was more violence. And yet in some individuals, the telomeres lengthened.

Ridley also reported on research involving children who lost a parent or were maltreated. They found greater methylation and the continuing consequences of stress and anxiety. In discussing the considerable unknowns of epigenetics, Ridley opined:

> "But supposing it becomes possible to link bad early experience with bad later health, what then? Epigenetics demolishes the old—and always misleading—distinction between deterministic genes and environmental manipulations. To have your fate determined by your early experiences is not much different from having it determined by your genes, and when experience acts by changing genes, the distinction vanishes.
>
> Yet fortunately, given the medical advances, genetic determinism is not necessarily a life sentence, as those who wear glasses for short-sightedness or take growth hormone for growth problems can attest. The same will almost certainly be true for epigenetic determinism: Understanding the mechanism should bring forward possible cures."

Perhaps we will have ever more tools to shape our own lives for the better.

126. A Case for Genetic Jewishness and "Is There a Jewish Gene?" – Harry Ostrer

Ivan Oransky's review of geneticist Harry Ostrer's book, *Legacy: A Genetic History of the Jewish People*, appeared in *Tablet* magazine on May 15, 2012.

Oransky began with the Khazari controversy and the indictment of Ostrer by Israeli historian Shlomo Sand in 2010. Sand has long championed the theory that Ashkenazis are not genetically Jews of Mid-Eastern origin, but instead descendants of Khazaris, a Central Asian tribe who converted to Judaism more than 1,000 years ago. Ostrer's work establishes, even more clearly the legitimacy of Ashkenazi claims to a Middle Eastern and Palestinian heritage on a par with their Sephardic and Mizrahim brethren.

Sand reportedly said of Ostrer, "Hitler would have been very pleased by your work." That spoke both to Sand's theory being completely discredited by the work of Ostrer and others and to the fears of many Jews that proof of a Jewish genetic legacy could bring back the horrors of Nazism. Ostrer and others have countered saying genetic facts are important for medical reasons, particularly in assessing risks. Moreover, many Jews and non-Jews are interested in knowing more about their genetic ancestry. Shutting one's eyes and arguing against demonstrable facts is seen to be a foolishly Luddite proposition.

Later, on December 6, 2012, *The New York Times Book Review* section included Richard Lewontin's combined review of Harry Ostrer's book, Nadia Abu El-Haj's *The Genealogical Science: The Search for Jewish Origins and the Politics of Epistemology*, and Raphael Falk's book, *Zionism and the Biology of Jews*.

Lewontin's comments were something of an extended essay on why some people might care about their genetic legacy. He added his own ideas about Ostrer, Falk and Abu El-Haj's motivations, and his ruminations about the difficulties surrounding words like race, which he called "loaded." Clearly, he was uncomfortable with the term race, but even more so with anyone saying Jews have higher IQs traceable to a genetic heritage.

127. Rare Genetic Mutations: More Complex Than Was Expected – Nicholas Wade

Wade's May 18, 2012 column in *The New York Times* story was titled, "Rare Genetic Mutations May Underpin Diseases." He reported on the continuing discovery of complexities in finding genetic variances/mutations linked to common diseases. Early hope had it that common mutations would account for many if not most such diseases, and we would soon be able to predict, diagnose, and cure them.

Wade reported, "It now appears that large numbers of so called 'rare' genetic mutations may underlie common human diseases like schizophrenia and cancer. But because the mutations are rare, costly studies involving large numbers of patients will be needed to identify the genes and their role(s) in each disease."

Jacob A. Tennessen and Joshua M. Akey of the University of Washington (U of W), and Matthew R. Nelson and Vincent Mooser of GlaxoSmithKline, also indicated this will be very difficult because significantly more rare mutations lie behind many diseases than were expected. The U of W team indicated 313 of 25,000 genes in each person carry rare mutations, and the Glaxo team said that one of every seventeen base pairs is likely to be a rare variant. Thus, "many different genetic variants may contribute risks too small to have shown up in current medical surveys," said Jonathan Pritchard, a University of Chicago geneticist.

Once more, the benefit of less-expensive decoding of our genome is mixed. Tests are less immediately useful for individual predictions than originally expected because of genetic complexity. Yet, the ever-lower cost for testing means that we can accomplish more with fewer dollars when unraveling that complexity. Ultimately, low-cost genome scans will be highly useful, but sometimes it seems the goalposts get moved out with each advance. And, if this is the case for common diseases, how much harder will it be for traits such as intelligence?

128. The Haredim (Ultra-Orthodox) Aid Jewish Population Growth

Joseph Berger's June 12, 2012 article in *The New York Times* story led off with reporting on the return to growth for New York City's Jewish population. The UJA-Federation study said that from the 1950s' peak of two million Jews, the city's Jewish population dipped below one million in 2002, then rebounded to nearly 1.1 million in 2011. With 316,000 Jews on Long Island, plus 136,000 in Westchester County, the total Jewish population in the eight surrounding counties was 1.54 million, of which 220,000 were Russian immigrants since the 1970s. The eight-county total represents 20 to 25 percent of America's six to seven million Jews.

Among the study's highlights were increases, since 2002, in the Haredim population by 115,000 and in nondenominational Jews by 127,000. Offsetting those gains were declines in the membership of the Reform (42,000) and Conservative (38,000) denominations. The study counted the Orthodox total at 493,000, roughly 32 percent of the 1.54 million Jews.

The rate of intermarriage among all Jews was said to be about 22 percent, but it was higher at 40 percent and growing among the non-Orthodox Jews. Half of non-Orthodox spouses were reported to not be converting.

Surprising for some was the study's finding that 25 percent of the Jews qualified as being poor, up from 20 percent in 2002. Among the "Hasidic population in Brooklyn where college degrees are rare," it said, "poverty rates have reached 43 percent." Finally, because of high fertility rates among Orthodox Jews (40 percent of New York City's Jews), their Orthodox Jewish children are now 74 percent of New York's Jewish youth.

These trends are worrisome for one whose efforts have long focused on the importance of human achievement and the role and lessons to be learned from Jewish high achievers. Perhaps the Golden Age is on the wane as the numbers of Jews motivated towards secular achievement declines and is replaced by those who disdain such aspirations.

129. Asian Immigration Exceeds Hispanic Immigration – A First

On June 18, 2012, *The Wall Street Journal* and *The New York Times* reported on a Pew Research Center study, "The Rise of Asian Americans." Though some knowledgeable critics dispute the Pew numbers, the lead in the *Times* was that Asians have surpassed Hispanics as the largest wave of new immigrants—430,000 immigrants in 2010—bringing their Asian total to 18.2 million (6 percent of the U.S. population) and growing faster than any other group. They are expected to total 40 million by 2050. Of Asian Americans, 23.2 percent are Chinese, 19.7 percent Filipino, 18.4 percent Indian, 10 percent Vietnamese, 9.9 percent Korean, and 7.5 percent Japanese.

The shift from mostly Hispanic immigrants to a plurality (36 percent) of Asians was partially driven by declines in blue collar work, including U.S. construction jobs in recent years and the fact that 45 percent of Hispanics are in the country illegally and have been pressured by stepped-up enforcement measures.

But in addition, a greater number of Asians are emigrating to the United States. Equally as startling as the shift from Hispanic to Asian were the demographics and the values expressed by the Asians. They are more likely to hold a college degree (49 percent) than U.S. adults (28 percent), and have higher household income ($66,000) versus Whites ($49,800).

Asians place a strong emphasis on family (59 percent are married versus 51 percent for American adults). Their children are less likely to be born to a single mother (16 percent versus 41 percent), and more likely to be raised in two-parent households (80 percent versus 63 percent). Of Asians, 67 percent say being a good parent is one of the most important things in life versus 50 percent for American adults. With that, they are more likely to be satisfied than the general public (82 percent versus 75 percent).

The Asian-Americans believe strongly that rewards come from hard work, with 69 percent of those surveyed saying that people can get ahead if they are willing to work hard. For all Americans, the comparable figure was 58 percent. And 93 percent of Asians believe their fellow Asians are "very hardworking," while only 57 percent of Americans say the same about their fellow Americans.

Finally, while 39 percent say Asian-American parents put too much pressure on their children to do well in school, 62 percent feel American parents put too little pressure on their offspring.

130. Identical Twins: *Born Together – Reared Apart* – A Fresh Look

In June 2012, thirty-three years after two identical twins ("the Jims") were reunited following their thirty-nine year separation, Dr. Nancy Segal's book, *Born Together—Reared Apart* was released. (Also see item 16 above.) Segal joined the Minnesota Identical Twins Reared Apart (MISTRA) study team in 1982 as a post-doctoral fellow. Three years later she became the Assistant Director, a post she held for six more years. Now a distinguished professor of humanities and social sciences, and director of the Twin Studies Center at Cal State Fullerton, Segal was in a unique position to trace the history of the Jims and write about the significance of the MISTRA work.

Though still subject to some dispute, the passage of time, the rigor of the research, advances from the Human Genome project, and growing acceptance of genetics have made the project less controversial than it was during the '80s and '90s, when discussions of race, IQ, heritability and cultural differences were subject to waves of attack.

Because of the importance of the MISTRA project, much of what was learned is extensively described in Chapter 1 of this book. Rather than repeat that test, we encourage readers to return to pages 29 to 32 for that discussion.

Many stories of identical twins raised apart are compelling in terms of how alike they become despite being raised in completely different environments. A 1995 *New Yorker* article told of Beth and Amy, a very sad story of identical infant twins adopted into radically different family circumstances. Amy was placed into a troubled and in many ways depressing family circumstance while Beth landed with a family that cherished her, was warm and caring, and gave her every advantage. Despite the differences, both twins ultimately turned out to be quite troubled in nearly identical ways.

131. Breakthrough in Treating Adult Acute Lymphoblastic Leukemia – Gina Kolata

On July 7, 2012, *The New York Times* carried a story by Gina Kolata titled, "In Leukemia Treatment, Glimpses of the Future." The article focused on Dr. Lukas Wartman, a Washington University research physician who had adult acute lymphoblastic leukemia. This is the same cancer he was researching, and he had survived several prior bouts of the disease. This time it came back with a vengeance, and no significant progress had been made in understanding its causes and treatments.

Wartman's colleagues responded with a full-blown effort to try to save him. They used their twenty-six DNA sequencing machines and their supercomputer to fully sequence all three billion base pairs of his DNA, including a sample of cancer cells from him, a sample of healthy cells, and a sample of his RNA. All of this in a frantic effort to figure out exactly what it was that was killing him. Their work revealed the culprit in a genetic mutation working overtime making proteins that spurred the cancer's growth. They also determined that a new kidney cancer drug might shut down the mutant gene even though the drug had never been tried on leukemia before.

While it is too early to say a permanent cure has resulted, Wartman is alive, his cancer is in remission, and has been for about a year. Full genome sequencing tests may not yet have proven their predictive worth, but they certainly might provide a huge breakthrough in diagnosing and treating specific genetic ailments.

And this success may portend uniquely-designed treatments to meet the individual needs of single patients. If so, the ramifications are momentous—not only in treatment, but also in testing and drug approval processes. These processes have historically have been based on broad assumptions about common causes of particular diseases, rather than unique mutations that effect multiple organs to varying degrees.

132. *The Chosen Few:* How Education Shaped Jewish History – Maristella Botticini and Zvi Eckstein

In July 2012, Botticini and Eckstein's *The Chosen Few* was published. It culminated a dozen years of research (and various publications) by the two scholars. Having highlighted their research in *The Golden Age of Jewish Achievement*, their book and this one updates that material, providing a much more complete description of their work. *The Chosen Few* covers Jewish history from the Roman destruction of the Second Temple in 70 CE to the Spanish expulsion of Jews in 1492.

Botticini and Eckstein challenge a great deal of conventional wisdom about Jewish history over that era, offering credible insights with major ramifications for anyone interested in why Jews became disproportionate high achievers. Their work points to what others can learn from Jewish history.

Judaism has always been intellectually demanding, and its Torah emphasizes the importance of study and educating one's children. Though scholars disagree on the exact timing, parts of the Written Torah (the first five books of the Jewish Bible) may have been put into written form as early as the eighth century BCE (Deuteronomy), with the bulk of the five books codified during the Babylonian exile and canonized sometime between the seventh and fifth centuries BCE. Later, around 450 BCE, the entire Tanakh (Jewish Bible) was compiled and canonized between 200 BCE and 200 CE. Over the Second Temple Period, particularly from the fifth to first centuries BCE, the Oral Torah (Oral Law)—encompassing religious judgments, debates, and rulings of thousands of Jewish sages and leaders—was studied, organized and clarified, particularly in later centuries. It would become the written Mishnah, canonized around 200 CE, and was later augmented with the Gemara to form the written Talmud of the Land of Israel in roughly 368 CE, and the Babylonian Talmud around 425 CE. Collectively, all of these written volumes, Torah, Tanakh, and Talmud(s), gave rise to the expression, "People of the Book."

Before the destruction of the Second Temple, there were a number of Jewish denominations or sects in Palestine. These included the Essenes, Zealots, Samaritans, Sicarii, Sadducees, and Pharisees. Of them, the Sadducees and Pharisees were the most important. The Sadducees represented a wealthy elite of merchants, aristocrats, and priests focused on Temple worship and sacrifices. They believed in The Written Torah but not in the Oral Law, and they controlled the Temple. The Pharisees emphasized that all Jewish men must read and study the Torah in Hebrew, and send their sons to primary school or synagogues to learn how to read and study it. They also believed in the Oral Law. Both the Sadducees and Pharisees treasured education and set up academies, but the Sadducees focused theirs on training the priestly Jewish elite, while Pharisees promoted education for all Jewish men and boys from the age of sixteen or seventeen. Later this was broadened to encompass all boys from the age of six or seven.

Because the Zealots and Sicariis strongly supported the Jewish revolt against the Romans, they were obliterated by war. At the same time, the Sadducees may also have supported revolution. If so, the destruction of the Second Temple removed their source of wealth and importance. The Pharisees did not support revolution, and they were left as Judaism's principle denomination. That allowed them to go far beyond the simple promoting of education. Rabbinic leaders made the synagogue a center of study, as well as worship and prayer. Literacy was made mandatory for the first time in history, and with that, and the end of the Sadducees and Temple, Rabbinic Judaism took over and revolutionized Jewish life. In succeeding centuries, universal literacy became ever more stringently demanded, while Jewish leaders disdained those who failed to comply.

Mandated for religious rather than economic reasons, literacy was expensive and time-consuming. As discussed elsewhere in this book, literacy was a hardship for a people composed mostly of generally poor farmers. Over the ensuing centuries, from the time of Christ, when the world's population of Jews was 5.0 to 5.5 million, Jewish numbers crumbled until, by the early seventh century, the Jewish population was down to 1.0 to 1.2 million. This decline of roughly four million Jews far exceeded losses explainable by the Roman slaughter, disease, or other causes. Botticini and Eckstein make a compelling case (as did Charles Murray in his 2007 *Commentary* essay, "Jewish Genius") that in the years before the rise of Islam, large numbers of Jews converted to Christianity. Like Judaism, it was monotheistic, it used the Jewish Bible as a principle text, and it made fewer demands on its people.

Later, from the 632 CE death of Muhammad until the thirteenth-century Mongol era, the ascendency of Islam led to a long period of economic development, growth, and prosperity across the huge geographic expanse controlled by the Umayyad and later Abbasid caliphates. It reached from the Maghreb and Iberia in the west to India and China in the east. The Caliphate geography shared a common religion for nearly all its peoples, as well as common laws, a common principle language (Arabic), and with that, commercial opportunities. Literate Jews were often in a unique position to pursue these opportunities.

Before Muhammad, during the fourth and fifth centuries, literate Jews began leaving farming to become ever more urban. *The Chosen Few* says that, "between 750 and 900 CE almost all Jews in Mesopotamia and Persia—nearly 75 percent of the world's Jewry—had left agriculture." Jews had become an urban people pursing "a myriad of skilled occupations."

Botticini and Eckstein argue that the ensuing Jewish Diaspora was not so much driven by persecution as by the pursuit of opportunities (though they also recognize there were eras of harsh persecution of Jews, particularly in Christian Europe). As Caliphate communities grew and prospered, they needed merchants, traders, bankers, physicians, and other professionals. These professions and trades demanded literacy few others could provide.

And such skills could not be concentrated in just a few places, where many Jews might live in close proximity to fellow Jews—demand for certain skills in a particular place were limited. Thus Jews moved apart into many communities across the globe. They benefited from the comparative advantage of the common laws, norms, and languages of the Caliphates, and their own common language, literacy, culture, Jewish Law (with its commercial applications), and the ability to partner with

Jews they knew they could trust to carry out complex international trading and transport. Jewish numbers and wealth grew in the Caliphates and later in Christian Europe.

It all ended with the thirteenth century Mongol attacks that eclipsed Islamic dominance and threatened Christian Europe where half the world's Jews then lived. The effect was to dramatically damage world commerce, and with that, substantially reduce the value of the skills Jews possessed. As demand for their skills declined, so too did the numbers of Jews. Once again, education was expensive relative to its benefits. Christianity and Islam demanded less of its people than Judaism in terms of education and literacy, and with that, many Jews converted. This may help explain, at least in part, the substantial decline in Ashkenazi numbers reported by Robert Pollack in his 2002 essay, "Some Genetics for Jews" (see item 31 above).

The Chosen Few ends in 1492 with the Spanish expulsion. Botticini and Eckstein have plans for a second book to focus on Jewish history from 1492 to the present. Certain to be a worthwhile read, its later chapters will likely cover the *The Golden Age* period—roughly 1800 CE to now—as disproportionate Jewish secular achievements grew to astonishing levels.

133. ENCODE: Much Junk DNA Is Found Not To Be Junk After All

On September 5, 6, and 8, 2012, David Brown and Hristio Boytchev of the *Washington Post*, Gina Kolata of *The New York Times*, *The Economist*, and others all reported on early results from the Encyclopedia of DNA Elements project (ENCODE).

This nine-year effort by 440 scientists at thirty-two institutions dramatically altered the notion of "junk DNA" prevalent from the late 1980s. Junk DNA presumed that since only about 1 to 3 percent of the human genome is coded (meaning responsible for producing proteins), the remaining 97 percent was presumably vestigial or its equivalent. In short, it was "junk DNA." The ENCODE research, published in thirty-seven reports, said "at least 80 percent of the genome appears to be active at least some time in our lives.

ENCODE discovered that much of that DNA had to do with regulating genes (turning them on or off or up or down), thus controlling a gene's output and coordinating its activities with other genes. This is akin to the environmental effects that do much the same thing. One ENCODE participant said, "researchers suspect that ten times as many risk variants occur in the regulatory switches as in the genes themselves."

Another discovery was that in looking at the three-dimensional structure of DNA, researchers could see how the tightly-wrapped chromosomes can place a previously called "junk" sequence close to a particular gene it regulates, even if the sequence is at a substantial distance from the gene on an unwrapped chromosome—another indication that gene regulations are much more complex than was earlier thought.

Again we learn genetics is enormously more complex than we thought as new regulatory mechanisms are found. It helps us to understand why finding genes for intelligence and other traits has proven so very difficult.

134. "Why Fathers Really Matter" – Epigenetic Effects

On September 9, 2012, *They New York Times* published a major opinion piece by Judith Shulevitz, the science editor of *The New Republic*. The subject was the epigenetics of fatherhood, and it provided new confirmation that the demarcation between nature and nurture is not as stark as was thought just a few years ago, when conventional thinking was that embryo DNA was reset to the default position at conception.

In a brief summary, Shulevitz said: "Mothers have long been scrutinized. But through epigenetics, the male also molds his children. What he eats, his age, his income—it can all affect the health of the baby." To that end, she was succinct in naming three things that she said really matter in the epigenetics of offspring. They are that genes can be turned on and off by: 1) environmental factors such as what we ingest (e.g., food drink air, toxins, etc.); 2) experiences such as stress and trauma; and 3) the age of the parents—for pregnancies, generally younger is better.

Researchers are now beginning to explore whether or not the incidence of Down syndrome and schizophrenia may have a something to do with older fathers as more adult men remain sexually active and have children late in life with premenopausal partners.

In short, as Shulevitz notes, "our physical and mental tendencies were not set in stone during the Pleistocene age as evolutionary psychology had sometimes seemed to claim. She went on to provide numerous examples from diet, exercise, stress, age, and more to show how culture and other environmental phenomena effect the genetic regulatory mechanisms in men and then through sperm, their offspring.

The above paragraphs are of a piece with a November 3, 2012 article in *The Economist* titled, "Grandma's Curse." It described a study done by Virender Rehan of the Los Angeles Biomedical Research Institute and reported in the journal, *Biomed Central Medicine*. The study looked at epigenetic intergenerational transfer of asthma in rats arising from nicotine injections when the female rats were six days pregnant. The rat pups developed asthmatic lungs and had defective sex cells. So too did the next generation of pups. Part of the significance was the appearance of those same symptoms in third-generation pups though they were never directly exposed to nicotine, even in the womb.

135. Lung Cancer Genetics Point To Tailored Solutions – Gina Kolata

Kolata's article, "Study of Lung Cancer's Genetics Suggests a More Tailored Treatment," ran in *The New York Times* on September 10, 2012. It reported on the first major study of squamous cell lung cancer, a disease that kills 400,000 people worldwide each year. The research on the 178 squamous cell lung cancer patients would have been impossible until very recently, when whole genome scanning made it possible to look at all three billion base pairs of DNA. The study added further insight into cancer as a genetic disease, "defined by DNA alterations that drive that cancer's cell growth." And further, "no one mutation of squamous cell lung cancer stood out—different patients had different mutations."

Part of the National Institutes of Health's Cancer Genome Atlas, the study said the majority of squamous cell tumors involve mutations that may be treatable with new drugs already in the pipeline, or ones that could be developed easily—but the drugs must be tailored to each patient's major genetic abnormality. The critical thing is not the organ, but the mutation (or mutations) involved. And researchers say new tests are being developed to match each patient's abnormality with a drug designed to attack it.

Dr. William Pao, a researcher at Vanderbilt-Ingram Cancer Center, noted, "The field is really moving toward personalized medicine." However, the study also emphasized the difficulty of performing research, testing new drugs, and obtaining FDA approvals when so many different mutations are involved and relatively few patients in a particular area have that mutation.

Again, breakthroughs in medical genetics, but no counterparts in our understanding of traits.

136. Catching Infant Genetic Defects Within Days of Birth. – Gina Kolata

On October 4, 2012, Gina Kolata's article, "Rapid Analysis of Infant's DNA Aids Diagnosis of Rare Disease," appeared in *The New York Times*. It explained how recent advances in whole genome scanning, particularly the reduction in cost and the gains in speed, now permit many newborn infants to be quickly tested for suspected genetic ailments in a matter of days, using blood samples. This capability can save lives through early intervention, and help parents avert futile and often painful treatments in the event of a fatal prognosis. It is an example of another breakthrough after years of stagnation.

137. Genetic Testing Helps Samaritans

A December 9, 2012 article in the *Los Angeles Times* by Edmund Sanders told the little-known story of Israeli Samaritan resurgence arising from advances in genetic science. Samaritans, like Jews, draw on the Torah, but do not revere the Talmud, and they honor their own Temple at Mt. Gerizim, a remote West Bank site. They believe they are descendants of the northern Israeli tribes conquered by the Assyrians (genetic tests suggest Samaritan men carry the Cohen gene). Though their roots date back 2,700 years, the world's Samaritan population declined to just 146 individuals by 1917 because of persecution and forced conversion to Islam.

Rebuilding their numbers has meant marrying relatives, including first cousins, with all the genetic risks inherent in that practice. Today, genetic tests are required before marriage, and a test failure means the marriage is off. Samaritans have now rebuilt their numbers to 750, They are split between Kiryat Luza village near Nablus, and Holon, a city south of Tel Aviv.

138. "The Origin of Species" – Perhaps It's Not All Junk DNA After All

A December 1, 2012 article in *The Economist* described a new class of recently-discovered genes that may regulate embryonic development and perhaps drive evolution. That was *The Economist's* take on the further results from the ENCODE project, completed in September 2012, which contradicted the idea of "junk DNA" (see item 133 above).

Meanwhile, David Kelly and John Rinn of Harvard authored a study in *Genome Biology*. It said some of the former junk DNA may be copied to a new genetic element called lincRNA. It does not encode proteins but appears to be involved with gene regulation. Nine thousand lincRNA are now known, and there is speculation perhaps some of them are also involved in a process by which species separate from one another. As a further oddity, some of the lincRNA appears to contain transposable elements (sometimes called "jumping genes") that move DNA from place to place along the genome. (Also see item 164 below.)

Again it seems the goalposts of genetic understanding move further out with each new discovery.

139. "Asians: Too Smart for Their Own Good?"

On December 20, 2012, Professor Carolyn Chen's opinion piece with the above title appeared in *The New York Times*. It was one of the first articles alleging academic bias against Asians in college admissions.

Chen focused on the high school academic grades and test scores of Asians in the U.S., noting that despite being 5.6 percent of the population, and 12 to 18 percent of Ivy League students, qualified Asians were still being passed over for admission—this despite their superior academic records, top SAT scores, and other proofs of high achievement. Chen likened it to discrimination against Jews that commenced in the 1920s and may have lasted until the 1960s. Chen said that while she was sympathetic to Blacks and Latinos, the discrimination against Asians was still unfair. She suggested that perhaps Blacks and Latinos should be a privileged class for admission despite fewer qualifications, but the playing field should be leveled for White and Asian middle- and upper-income kids.

This piece should be read in conjunction with item 142 below in which ironically, the Ivy League schools appear to be admitting a disproportionate number of Jews despite their poorer academic records and test scores. Asians and others may soon challenge this seeming bias.

The tensions between merit, "fairness," and political correctness are rising.

140. Cleverer Still – High-scoring Women's and Men's Math Scores and the Flynn Effect

The Economist's December 22, 2012 issue reported on a study by Jonathan Wai, Martha Putallaz, and Matthew Makel at Duke University. They looked at variations between female and male standardized math test scores of 1.7 million high school students over a 30-year period. In addition, they analyzed the data to see if they could discern a Flynn effect (meaning a substantial continuing increase in average test scores) over those years.

Variation in male and female math test scores is the issue that caused Larry Summers to step down as Harvard's president in 2005. He attributed higher male enrollment in physics, engineering and math to greater aptitude, as evidenced by their superior math test scores at the "tails" of test score distributions relative to women. It created a firestorm.

Wai, Putallaz, and Makel looked at three decades of standardized SAT, EXPLORE, and ACT scores between 1980 and 2010. Their findings were something of a surprise. They found that the gap between the ratio of men to women who scored in the upper 0.01 percent of those tested had narrowed from a ratio of 13 to 1 in 1980 to about 4 to 1 in

1995. Clearly, this drop was much too fast to be genetic. Equally interesting, the decline came to an end and stabilized at 4 to 1 after 1995. No one yet has a good explanation for either the drop or the fact that the gap has not budged over the 20 years since 1995.

They also looked for the Flynn effect and found it. Years earlier, Professor James Flynn of the University of Otago in New Zealand had reported that average IQ scores worldwide have been rising at the rate of about 0.3 points per year over the last eight decades (see item 47 above). The aggregate gain has been a 24-point increase in average IQ since 1930. Wai, Putallz, and Makel saw the same kind of gain in their bright, high-scoring youngsters over the three decades of data they studied.

Like the rapid decline an then subsequent stability in the ratio of male and female math test scores, no one has yet come up with a definitive cause for the Flynn effect. Among the seemingly reasonable theories are better nutrition or a more stimulating environment. But whatever is going on, it is happening too quickly to be traceable to traditional genetics. Another long standing notion of stable genetic determinism is dying as we learn female achievements in math and science and that IQ test scores may be altered by cultural and environmental changes.

141. How Much Are 30,000 Human Genomes Worth?

A December 24, 2012 *Business Week* story by Ryan Flinn and Ashless Vance described the competition to acquire what was thought to be an ailing company, Complete Genomics that had reported a quarterly loss of $18 million on sales of $7.3 million.

It had been for sale for about six months, but now, the Chinese company BGI and the San Diego based-company Illumina were head to head in a bidding war. While some expressed concern about the Chinese getting their hands on the world's most accurate gene-sequencing technology, it turned out the real value was in the 30,000 human genomes in the Complete Genome database. This arose from its history of sequencing client genomes.

It is interesting that at a time when an individual whole genome test can be bought for $1,000, a database containing 30,000 of them is worth $4,000 per test result. Perhaps the test subjects deserve a piece of that action?

But it also shows the immense value (the whole is worth more than the sum of its parts) of a reference database from which new insights can be gleaned. Exploration of correlations and variances in the genes of the 30,000 tests may yield many valuable insights. Perhaps from analysis of large data bases such as this one, we will learn useful knowledge about the genetic basis for traits as well as for disease. It may also tell us where those correlations and variances are limited. Time will tell.

142. The Collapse of Jewish Academic Achievement – The Ron Unz Essay

On December 25, 2012, David Brooks began his annual Sydney Awards column (his picks for the year's best essays) by describing an essay titled "The Myth of the American Meritocracy" by Ron Unz, a Jew. Brooks said, "You're going to want to argue with the Unz article all along the way, especially for its narrow math-test driven view of merit. But it's potentially ground-shifting."

Unz, a Harvard graduate with a dual major in physics and ancient history, also attended Stanford. He never completed his doctorate in theoretical physics, but he later created a successful financial software business that he sold to Moody's, and in 1994 he ran unsuccessfully for the California Republican gubernatorial nomination against incumbent Pete Wilson. Unz is now a major donor to *Wikipedia*, and in March 2007 he became publisher of *The American Conservative*.

His essay's main point is that the supposed meritocratic selection process of Ivy League schools is a myth. Instead, he says, selecting incoming students has become a "politically correct" process administered by an underqualified admissions staff. That staff essentially follows guidelines that favor groups such as Blacks, Hispanics, and Jews at the expense of Asians and non-Jewish Whites. In his view, rather than objectively admitting the top academic performers from among America's high school graduates, consciously or unconsciously, the Ivy League confers its present and future prestige to select individuals from groups it wishes to assist, and who represent values it generally encourages.

Central to the debate over Jewish achievement is Unz's other big conclusion—namely, that over the last generation, Jewish academic performance has plummeted. The context for his comments is his observation that college-age Jews are now roughly 1.8 percent of all college-age Americans. But, drawing on Hillel data, he says they are 27 percent of the students at Penn, 26 percent at Harvard and Yale, 25 percent at Columbia, 24 percent at Brown, 23 percent at Cornell, 13 percent at Princeton, and 11 percent at Dartmouth. This would not be surprising if Jewish academic results were ten to fifteen times better than those of others—as they were in earlier eras. The more recent academic declines chronicled in Unz's essay are startling. Based on identifying Jews by their Jewish-sounding names (see more on this aspect of selection criteria below), Unz says:

— In the U.S. Math Olympiad of the 1970s, more than 40 percent of those selected were Jewish. Over the next two decades, the numbers remained strong (roughly 33 percent). Since 2000, however, the figure has dropped to 2.5 percent.

— From the 1950s through the 1990s, Jews were 22 to 33 percent of the winners of the prestigious Putnam Exam (also math[10]). Since 2000, they have fallen to less than 10 percent, and there has not been a Jewish winner in the last seven years.

— Since 1942, the prestigious America's Science Talent Search has selected just forty high school students each year. From the 1950s through the 1980s, Jews were 22 to 23 percent of that elite group. In the 1990s, the figure declined to a still respectable 17 percent, and declined further to 15 percent in the 2000s. And since 2010, it has dropped to only 7 percent. Of the top thirty students over the last three years, only one was Jewish.

— In the Physics Olympiad, Unz says, from 1986 to 1997, Jews were more than 25 percent of the top students. That number has fallen to 5 percent over the last ten years.

— In the Biology Olympiad, only 8 percent of the top students in the last twelve years have been Jewish, and in the last three years there has not been a single Jew selected.

— In the Computing Olympiad, Unz says, only 11 percent of the top students between 1992 and 2012 were Jews, and in the Chemistry Olympiad, for which he only had the names of winners over the last two years, none were Jews.

— Looking at National Merit semifinalists (America's top 0.5 percent in academic results), Unz says the 8 percent figure for Jews in 1987 is 35 percent higher than today's equivalent number. Moreover, since 1997, when verbal skills became more heavily weighted than math and science in the judging (historically Jews have

---

10. Unz also notes that many recent Jewish math standouts have names suggesting they are the offspring of recent Soviet emigrant families. As such, their exemplary performance masks an even greater decline among third, fourth, and fifth generation Jewish-American immigrants.

demonstrated stronger verbal skills than math and science), Jewish numbers have, nonetheless, declined. His analysis of the extensive database of semifinalists indicates Jews are now just 6 percent of National Merit semifinalists.

— When Unz looks at schools such as Caltech, the top five University of California campuses, and MIT, all of which he says select students on a more meritocratic basis, he finds results that accord with his overall analysis. Namely, Jews are 5.5 percent of the Caltech population (versus 39 percent Asians). At the five most selective University of California schools, Jews are 8 percent of the students, and at MIT, Jews are 9 percent. These percentages are in the same ballpark as the National Merit data, but are significantly lower than Jewish Ivy League enrollment levels.

It appears that Unz' analysis (and that of others on whose data he draws) should be qualified by his use of "Jewish names" as the principal identifier of Jews on these lists. As a Jew, Unz probably has a very good instinct for this, but as one with a good bit of experience, I reviewed my own list of *Forbes 400* Jews to test the reliability of "Jewish names" as an indicator of being Jewish. Roughly 60 percent of the Jews on the *Forbes 400* list have names one would consider "Jewish" (e.g. Rubenstein, Bluhm, Greenberg, etc.), but roughly 40 percent of the names are not (Roberts, Lauren, Wynn, Cuban, Balmer, Dell, etc.). Using Jewish-sounding names as the indicator can easily understate or overstate actual Jewish performance.

Nonetheless, that does not even begin to explain the dramatic recent declines in the academic performance of Jews. Nor does it explain the comparative National Merit data and the contrast between the student populations in Ivy League schools versus those at schools such as Caltech, which select on a more meritocratic basis.

In the end, there is clear reason for concern. Recent declines in academic performance, coupled with the ever-growing proportion of high school and college age Jews that are Haredim (ultra-Orthodox) rather than traditional Orthodox, Conservative, Reform, or Secular, raises fears that the Jewish Golden Age may be at risk.

And since DNA cannot possibly change so quickly, nor can IQ scores fall so fast, these results reinforce the argument that culture is likely the principle driver of disproportionate Jewish achievement. It may also be the driver of the behavior of young Jews to place their attention elsewhere.

In America, Jewish culture is evolving. Eric Hobsbawm's 2005 essay (item 66 above) pointed to the importance of anti-Semitism as a driving force behind historic disproportionate Jewish achievement. My earlier book chronicled thousands of years of hardship and the struggles of Jews to survive and thrive despite those hardships. In the United States, anti-Semitism has substantially diminished since World War II. (Edgar Bronfman reportedly said he knew anti-Semitism was mostly dead in the United States when Al Gore lost the 2000 election and no one blamed his vice presidential pick, Joe Lieberman.)

Meanwhile, the post-war economic affluence and philanthropy of Jews has been astonishing. Perhaps one consequence of these trends is that these days, a semester spent studying art and culture in Florence may be more appealing than remaining on campus to study math, science, pre-med, pre-law, or similarly demanding subjects. My teaching physician friends and acquaintances also report dramatic declines in Jewish students in medical schools; they appear to have largely been replaced by Asians.

Additionally, there has been substantial growth in the priority of "social justice" (a term virtually unknown by most people when I was young and rarely heard even a generation ago). Today it is commonplace, and young Jews (and Gentiles) are prominent among its advocacy. These progressive efforts, and an applicant's leadership stance in them, may appeal to an Ivy League admissions staff as much or more than it does to the kids. This may contribute to disproportionate Jewish enrollment despite the downward trend in the numbers of college-age Secular, Conservative, Reform, and Orthodox Jews and their reported declines in their academic achievements.

143. Unmarried Poor: Bad Values or Bad Jobs – The Effect on The Children

On December 25, 2012, *Bloomberg News* ran an opinion piece by Andrew Cherlin, a Johns Hopkins professor of sociology and public policy.

Cherlin was reporting on the recent failure of an attempt to encourage low-income parents to marry. Though Cherlin did not favor the program (The Healthy Marriage Initiative), he found its failure simply tragic. The Initiative was part of a government-sponsored effort funded with $150 million in 2005. It brought well-known specialists together to design and implement a program to encourage marriage. The target subjects were young, unmarried couples expecting a child, or those who had just become parents. The goal was to convince them to stay together and hopefully to marry.

Five thousand couples were recruited, with half chosen at random for "special services" ($11,000 each) at eight sites around the United States. The other half served as a control group. Both groups were followed for three years. On November 30, 2012, the results were released.

It was a complete failure. The programs did not keep couples together, and the "special services" group results were no better than the control group. Only 55 percent of couples showed up for the sessions, and there was little effect on those that did. Only 57 percent of the couples remained together after the three years.

The long term consequences for their offspring are likely to be devastating and Cherlin's report and his concerns are of a piece with Charles Murray's 2012 book, *Coming Apart*. That book was said by David Brooks to perhaps be one of the most important published that year. These kids are highly unlikely to ever be high achievers. Instead they may be relegated to long term status as "underclass." It is a daunting problem crying out for attention.

There is debate over whether all of this represents an adverse shift in values among a growing number of middle and lower middle class Americans, or is it simply driven by a lack of jobs. Meanwhile, as reported elsewhere, staying together and staying married remains a priority for America's college-educated middle class. More than 90 percent of college graduates wait until after graduation to get married and start a family. Since 1980, the U.S. divorce rate has dropped, returning to the levels of the 1960s. These couples are part of the global economy, while others, for whatever reason, appear to fall by the wayside.

144. Staying Focused: Characteristics of Successful Children

A January 19, 2013 review in *The Economist* described Paul Tough's new book, *How Children Succeed: Grit, Curiosity, and the Hidden Power of Character. The Economist* called it "a fine and provocative book about the kind of work that seems to be making a difference."

Tough, a former journalist and editor of *The New York Times Magazine*, wrote of KIPP charter schools' self-perceived failures in the mid-1990s. He said KIPP delivered exceptional academic results from its high school students, but many of those students became part of a disastrously high dropout rate when they went on to college.

Tough said a growing body of data now shows "the skills that see a student through college and beyond have less to do with smarts than with more ordinary personality traits, like the ability to stay focused and control impulses." He says that KIPP has learned this, and is developing techniques to solve the focus problem that bedevils so many of America's students today, males in particular. KIPP, the Chicago program OneGoal, and a number of others are focused on shaping the culture for children who often begin life with two strikes against them. KIPP is experimenting with a "character report card" intended to track the development of important traits over time. OneGoal is stressing the link between hard work and destiny.

According to Tough's research (see item 180 below), non-cognitive skills such as curiosity and persistence predict future success, and like Professor Angela Duckworth's earlier research, "grit" is a big element.

Some data support the idea that childhood stress (perhaps from an unstable family life and poverty) can adversely affect individuals on a neurological level. Early parental nurturing is vital, Tough says. The pre-frontal cortex is responsive in children and stays malleable well into early adulthood. "Character can be taught," he says, "but still, there is much to be done to find and refine the techniques." (Also see David Brooks's comments in item 186 below.)

CHAPTER 14

2013 to Date: Medical & Cultural Advances, Traits Slower

145. Epigenetics: Gene Regulation and Disease – Gina Kolata. Why Worry: Stress, Panic, and Test-Taking – Bronson and Merryman. Orchids, Dandelions, Dopamine and DRD4 – Jonathan Rockoff. Exercise and Methylation (Epigenetic Changes) – Gretchen Reynolds. Poisoned Inheritance? – The Folate Studies - Economist

Five media stories in 2013 reported on significant epigenetic research. To avoid repetition and a possible impression that epigenetics was the area of greatest genetic advances in 2013, we have consolidated them into this single entry.

The first story was Gina Kolata's January 21, 2013 *New York Times* article describing work at Johns Hopkins School of Medicine and Sweden's Karolinska Institute. The researchers explored selected genes involved in causing rheumatoid arthritis and learning what it is that regulates those genes. She noted that rheumatoid arthritis occurs in only 12 percent of identical twins. Thus, something must cause the relevant genes to be turned on or off resulting in the disease in one twin but not the other. One study focused on 354 newly diagnosed patients and 337 healthy people (the control group). White blood cells were sampled looking for chemical "tags"—methyl groups—attached to genes that turn them on or off.

They found hundreds of tags, but only four related to rheumatoid arthritis. All four were in a cluster of genes that control immune response and known to affect rheumatoid arthritis risk. Some in the control group also had gene variations associated with the same risk,

237

but none had the four chemical tags. Susceptibility was there, but not the disease.

On February 10, 2013, Po Bronson and Ashley Merryman's article, "Why Worry", appeared in *The New York Times Magazine*. It focused on students who panic when faced with tests. They wrote about the physiological symptoms and a causative gene (COMT). COMT is thought to predispose a person to panic in response to perceived pressure. One of the kids was a fifth-grader who asked for—and received—an exemption from taking the unnerving tests. Interestingly, his eighth-grade brother was a very confident test-taker and both siblings are in gifted programs.

Critics say testing is creating a generation of miserable children, but we now know that some students love the competition and do quite well. Researchers say there may be a genetic predisposition toward anxiety but they add that those fears can be overcome. Others remind us that pressure is a fact of life, particularly if we aspire to accomplish something.

Bronson and Merryman say the COMT gene comes in two variations: one quickly clears dopamine; the other acts more slowly. The key is achieving the proper balance to regulate neural activity and mental function. And, while the research says the slow-acting version is associated with higher IQ, those with that variation are more vulnerable to stress. Their IQ advantage does not help them cope, and they may perform poorly. In one high-stakes test, children with slow-clearing dopamine (and a likely 10-point IQ advantage) scored 8 percent lower than their counterparts with fast-clearing dopamine. Those in the second group were "more laid back." For them, the test was an interesting challenge rather than a threat.

Jonathan Rockoff's September 17, 2013 *Wall Street Journal* article told a similar story about the DRD4 gene and children who panic under stress.

Like COMT, DRD4 helps regulate dopamine. In certain genetic variations, it may predispose some children to be "orchids"—meaning students who flourish in supportive environments—as opposed to "dandelions"—children that are much less affected by the world around them, whether supportive or harsh.

Individuals who produce less dopamine (the neurotransmitter that helps us experience pleasure and reward) are the so-called orchids. They do not learn well from negative feedback or distractions, but can do very well in a "warm but strict" setting. One study says perhaps 30 percent of Caucasians are orchids but that the majority of people are not at the extreme ends of orchid or dandelion. They fall somewhere in between.

Rockoff also wrote about a 2008 study at Leiden University in the

Netherlands. It examined 157 children at risk for aggression and disobedience focusing on their DRD4 variations. The researchers counseled parents of half the children on how to be warmer while also setting stricter limits. The other parents were not counseled at all.

According to Dr. Van Ijzendoorn, who led the study, the results were conclusive. Children of the parents that were counseled had fewer problems after the training. In 2011, Van Ijzendoorn published an analysis of 15 additional studies involving more than 1,500 children, which reached essentially the same conclusion.

On August 6, 2013, *The New York Times* ran a Gretchen Reynolds report on studies of how methylation caused by exercise changes the ways that cells operate. In some cases, she said, exercise seems to reduce the risk of developing diabetes, although exactly how that works is unknown. Further, she said, it is not yet clear whether exercise-induced methylation is passed along to offspring, but we do know that other studies have shown the reverse phenomenon—namely, artificially induced diabetes in rats can be passed to offspring for at least several succeeding generations. So the unanswered question is whether or not exercise can substantially reduce diabetes risk in an epigenetic way for offspring.

A study at Lund University in Sweden involved several dozen sedentary healthy adult males. Some of their fat cells were removed and examined for DNA methylation patterns in those cells. The study group was placed on a six-month exercise regime. They lost weight, built up endurance, improved their blood pressure, and improved their cholesterol levels. In follow up lab work, more than 17,000 locations on 7,663 separate genes of the fat cells showed changes in the methylation patterns. Those changes are thought to play some role in fat storage and the risks for diabetes and obesity.

In a similar study, Karolinska Institute in Stockholm looked at methylation in muscle cells of humans. After a single workout, researchers could see cellular methylation changes that had produced proteins affecting metabolism and the risks for diabetes and obesity. The more vigorous the exercise, the greater the methylation changes.

Later, in her year-end wrap-up column, Reynolds said that of all the exercise-related columns she wrote during 2013, both she and her readers thought this one was the most remarkable. She ended noting that one scientist told her that studies of exercise and genes are an important and inspirational reminder of the "robust effect exercise can have and effect on the human body, even at the level of our DNA."

On December 14, 2013, *The Economist* reported on the seriously adverse effects to the offspring of male mice whose diet lacked folate.

Specifically, the researchers observed deformities of the head, spine, and limbs. They also found clues suggesting future problems such as cancer, diabetes, autism, and schizophrenia. It was another example of epigenetic consequences previously thought impossible.

Such adverse effects might have been expected from an absence of folate in the mother's diet. In fact, pregnant women and those who plan to become pregnant are encouraged to eat plenty of green leafy vegetables, a rich source of vitamin B9 (folate). That helps encourage formation of the neural tube—a brain and spinal cord precursor. But prospective fathers had not been encouraged to "eat their greens," since the father was thought to contribute only the sperm and thus have nothing to do with the physical substance of the embryo. And, of course, it was traditionally thought that all genetic switches or marks were reset to their default positions at conception.

In the folate study, researchers raised male mice with low exposure to folate from conception on. Neither they nor their mothers were fed folate; the mice otherwise had a normal life. They proved to be less fertile than mice in the control group, and more of their resulting embryos were reabsorbed by the mothers.

Examining the sperm, researchers they found 57 places where methylation patterns of folate deficient mice were different from those fed a normal diet. When they saw similar patterns in humans, the affected genes were associated with cancer, diabetes, autism, and schizophrenia.

Though test results in mice can be different from the same tests in humans, the researchers noted the explosion of diabetes in the United States, which has grown from six million cases in 1985 to 20 million today. In short, our diet may perhaps play a role in infants "inheriting" diabetes or a diabetic predisposition because of their parents' and grandparents' eating habits. Nurture may be reshaping nature.

An undated Web page on the British Society for Cell Biology[11] tells a similar story. And rather than try to rewrite what is a very clear explanation, it is reproduced below:

> "Researchers studying the microscopic roundworm *Caenorhabditis elegans* recently discovered a set of mutations that extended the worms' normal 2–3 week lifespan by up to 30%. This was exciting, not least because discoveries in animals such as roundworms can sometimes help us understand processes like ageing in humans. This was not the end of the story though, as the researchers found that the

---

11. http://bscb.org/learning-resources/softcell-e-learning/epigenetics-its-not-just-genes-that-make-us/

descendants of the long-lived roundworms could also live longer than normal, even if they only inherited the non-mutated version of the genes from their parents. This doesn't seem to make sense at first; surely characteristics such as hair colour, height and even how long we or a microscopic worm could potentially live are carried in the DNA sequence of the genes that we inherit from our parents. So how can we solve the conundrum of how the roundworms inherited the long lived characteristic, without inheriting the DNA sequence that initially caused it? The answer is epigenetics."

These articles reinforce a point made previously. Namely, genetic predisposition need not always be destiny. Cultural influences, including the right motivating factors, diet, exercise, and other experiences can shape us—and perhaps our offspring—in ways that may override certain genetic predispositions.

146. A Visual Analysis of Science Test Scores in 65 Countries

A February 5, 2013 visual chart in *The New York Times* plotted the scores for a science test given to 470,000 boys and girls in 2009. The kids that took the two-hour exam were 15 years old and they were selected at random from 65 countries. What was striking were the variances. Asian boys and girls both got the highest scores, while the United States was ranked twenty-first overall, and was ranked third among the only five countries where the boys' average scores were at least 2 percent higher than the girls'.

In well more than half the countries tested, the girl's scores were higher than the boys', and in Finland, Japan, and Slovenia the girls' scores averaged more than 2 percent higher than the boys'—and all were well above those of the United States.

It's important to note these scores were averages, not the scores of the outliers at the high- and low-end tails of the score distributions. Nevertheless, the data imply that ability in math and science may not be genetically linked to sex.

The relevance to the debate on Jewish achievement is that genes cannot account for the fact that girls have begun doing strikingly better in recent years. Cultural influence may well be the cause.

147. A Genetic Code for Genius – Gautam Naik

On February 16, 2013, *The Wall Street Journal* ran an article by Gautam Naik about the Chinese company, BGI (see item 141 above). The story focused on Zhao Bowen, a 20-year-old "whiz kid" who had taken on the task of finding the genetic roots of intelligence in DNA. At age fourteen, Bowen signed up for an internship at the Chinese Academy of Agricultural Science, where he did menial work while studying genetics. By fifteen, he was a participant in a study of cucumbers and when published, he was listed as a co-author. He quit school to go to work for BGI, where he was soon appointed director of BGI's new genomics unit. In 2010, the unit began to study of the genetics of cognition. The kid is a hard charger.

The BGI methodology is to collect a large sample of DNA from very gifted people, and from a control group of people with average IQs. Then the company is mounting a major effort to analyze the data for variances between the DNA of the two populations, to explain the elevated levels of IQ.

After years of work and 10,000 DNA samples, BGI researchers only recently identified 1,000 different genetic variations that *partly* explain height—seemingly a much simpler task than tracking down variations that explain intelligence. Then add the environmental factors that may have contributed to recent substantial increases in the average heights in some northern European countries (genes alone cannot account for it; most think it has to do with diet and lifestyle). One senses this could all become quite daunting. Then consider traits like drive, self-control, grit, etc.

This may take a while, but whether BGI succeeds or fails, the results will be fascinating.

148. Connectomics: How Brains Are Wired

A week later, on February 23, 2013, *The Economist* ran a story about a U.S. government plan to launch a major Brain Activity Map study the following month. It would research the brain's wiring and institutionalize "what is called the emerging science of connectomics." The project was a centerpiece of a mid-February meeting of the American Association for the Advancement of Science (AAAS).

The Brain Activity Map is a huge and daunting task involving hundreds of billions of brain cells and trillions of connections. It is an effort akin to the original Human Genome Project: an enormous challenge, but one that may yield invaluable insights.

Part of project will proceed by exploring very thin slices of brain tissue from rats and cadavers to build diagrams showing the connections. It is likely to also involve other kinds of imaging, such as scans of metabolic activity in living creatures and humans. It is hoped that all of this will ultimately unravel disorders of the mind, such as schizophrenia and clinical depression that do not have anatomical evidence, as well as disorders of the brain, such as Alzheimer's disease and Parkinson's disease, that do.

149. Japan's Prisons and Their Prisoners

The Economist's February 23, 2013 issue described the behavior of prisoners in Japan's jails. Proportionately fewer Japanese are imprisoned as a percent of population, compared with the United States, and recidivism is rare.

According to the article, Japanese prisoners are housed in buildings that, while modest, look interesting, well groomed and spotless. Prisoners are uniformed and walk in lockstep behind guards, bowing before entering rooms. Talking is banned, except during breaks. Conjugal visits are banned. The prisoners work, but are not paid. Escapes are almost non-existent. There has not been a documented jailbreak since just after World War II, and no one recalls a violent attack on a staff member.

All this occurs despite some seeming injustices, with innocent people sometimes convicted in a country where the conviction rate is over 99 percent. Some incarcerated Europeans and Americans develop mental disorders in Japanese prisons. Still, it remains striking how the culture of Japan results in such a stark difference in the operation of its jails and the behavior of its prisoners, as compared with the United States.

150. "The Learning Virtues": Cultures of Learning – David Brooks

A February 28, 2013 Brooks article in *The New York Times* column focused on the differences in academic approaches and cultures of Chinese, Americans, and to some extent Jews. It began describing Jin Li, who lived through the hardships of China's failed Cultural Revolution before being recruited to learn what the West could offer her.

Li ultimately married an American and moved to the United States where, as a teacher, she was stunned by the cultural differences. Despite excellent facilities, American students seemed uninterested. After years studying at Harvard and Brown, she concluded, "Westerners tend to define learning cognitively while Asians define it morally. Westerners learn in order to understand and master the world. Asians consider learning arduous, but they do it to cultivate virtues inside themselves."

The comparisons of how the two cultures think about learning are stark, Li said. Harvard and Yale's mottos emphasize "Truth" and "Light and Truth." Chinese schools' mottos describe processes such as "Strengthen self-ceaselessly and cultivate virtue to nurture the world," and "Be sincere and hold high aspirations, learn diligently and practice earnestly."

The West appears to believe that students arrive without intelligence and curiosity. Teachers try to arouse that curiosity with field trips and projects, while also encouraging the questioning of authority and sharing of ideas. By comparison, Chinese culture does not focus on curiosity or subject matter so much as the learning process itself. The goal is to perfect the virtues of learning to become a sage—which is seen as both moral and intellectual. The Chinese culture treasures sincerity, diligence, perseverance, concentration, and respect for teachers, whereas Li felt western students work harder because of praise. Asians, on the other hand, sometimes work harder after they have been criticized.

Brooks ended by noting that cultures that fuse the moral and academic, such as Confucianism or Jewish Torah study, can produce remarkable explosions of motivation. And he spoke of possible replication of similar motivations with other moral and academic codes.

151. Tiger Students – Warren Kozak

On April 5, 2013, Walter Kozak wrote an opinion piece in *The Wall Street Journal*. He reported on the new freshman enrollees at Stuyvesant High School in New York City, widely regarded as one of America's best schools. Unlike the Ivy League where there is no clear picture of admissions criteria, Stuyvesant goes "solely on the numbers," Kozak said. He pointed to three schools: Stuyvesant, The Bronx High School of Science, and Brooklyn Technical High School as elite schools with Nobel Prize-winning alumni and graduates who go on to study at top universities.

The Stuyvesant admissions test takes two and a half hours, and it has a math section and a verbal section. Out of the 28,000 students who took the test in 2012, nine Blacks were admitted, 24 Latinos, 177 Whites and 620 Asian-Americans. Roughly the same proportions were admitted to Bronx Science and Brooklyn Tech.

The NAACP called the testing and the results racist, but some of the Asian-Americans are from immigrant homes where English is a second language. The verbal test is not based on cramming or prepping, but on cumulative knowledge built over the years. Yet minority children of immigrants can pass it with flying colors.

Kozak also covers of the work of Dr. Angela Duckworth, who became curious about the finalists of the annual National Spelling Bees. What Duckworth found were students with immense tenacity who have foregone immediate gratification. They were not spending hours texting friends, watching TV, or playing games on their electronic devices. Instead they were writing out thousands of flashcards with the words they were learning, and practicing how to spell them correctly.

Kozak also pointed to the now-prominent Dr. Benjamin Carson, who grew up impoverished in Detroit. He was the son of a black single mother who only finished a third-grade education—but she turned off the television, demanded that he study, and took no excuses. He is now a brain surgeon, an author, and a TV personality, among other accomplishments.

Kozak argued for the importance of evening out the ethnic proportions at Stuyvesant over time, but says it will not happen by spending more money on schools, teacher salaries, or Head Start. A better and much less expensive approach, he said, is to find out what Asian-American parents and families are doing and replicate it in more American homes.

As Kozak suggests, "leveling" will also not happen simply because some are admitted based mostly on race. Learning after admission that they cannot compete will demoralize and harm them. But helping them learn how to qualify based on their own academic skills will help them and provide role models (like Carson) for others.

152. Post-Human Genome Project Progress – Eric Green

On April 15, 2013, *The New York Times* Science section published an interview with Eric Green, the director of the National Human Genome Research Institute of the National Institutes of Health. The topic was the progress made in the ten years since April 15, 2003 when scientists announced they had completed the Human Genome Project.

Green made two main points. First, that the costs for whole genome tests were dropping fast; and second, he acknowledged that progress had accelerated in the last few years after a slow start.

Green wrote, "What has happened over the last three years in particular, is told in the sheer aggregate volume of success stories … we are understanding cancer and rare genetic diseases. There are incredible success stories now, such as our ability to draw blood from a pregnant woman and analyze the DNA of her unborn child … increasingly, we have more informed ways of prescribing medicine because we first do a genetic test. We can use microbial DNA to trace disease outbreaks in a matter of hours. These are game changers."

153. Tools for Finding Genetic Variations – Anne Eisenberg

Less than two weeks later, on April 28, 2013, Eisenberg wrote an article in *The New York Times* about the new tools that facilitate more rapid cancer diagnosis, sometimes leading to effective drug development in a shorter timeframe.

She noted the recent and fast-paced discoveries of genetic flaws behind individual cancers, the difficulties oncologists face in mastering them, and the limited number of drugs approved so far (700 are in testing). She described one web site, *MyCancerGenome.org*, a free resource maintained by 51 contributors from 20 institutions. The site lists the mutations identified in different kinds of cancers, and the possible drugs (some still in testing) that may or may not work for each one. In some cases, patients might be able to enroll in ongoing research tests.

Eisenberg further noted that a newly available, $5,800 test, called FoundationOne, offered by Foundation Medicine, is now in use by more than a thousand doctors and over a dozen pharmaceutical companies with drugs under development. Another company, Genomic Health, offers a $4290 test that helps a doctor and breast cancer patient decide whether chemotherapy is a viable option.

Eisenberg concluded with a quote from Dr. Razelle Kurzrock, director of the personal cancer therapy center at Moores Cancer Center at the University of California, San Diego. Kurzrock feels that tests such as FoundationOne are invaluable. "We have to know," she said, "what's inside a tumor cell that is causing it to grow and then (we may be able to) match that knowledge with the specific drug that targets the abnormality."

Again, medical genetics breakthroughs now arrive day by day; progress with traits, however, seems stalled.

154. Genetic Linkages of Cancers – Gina Kolata and Ron Winslow

On May 2, 2013, Kolata, a reporter for *The New York Times* with an interest in genetics, wrote about two recent studies of genetic linkages to different cancers in different organs. On the same day, Ron Winslow covered the same studies for *The Wall Street Journal*.

Kolata described findings of the first study, which linked uterine, ovarian, breast, colon and lung cancers. Winslow reported that from the study, scientists now know, "all of the major molecular aberrations that drive the development and growth of endometrial cancer." Both reporters indicated the new data provides a much better means for categorizing the cancers and thus the protocols for treatment. With 50,000 endometrial cancers diagnosed annually, and 8,000 deaths, that knowledge can potentially save many lives.

Winslow also reported on a second study identifying all the major molecular aberrations for acute myeloid leukemia (AML). AML strikes about 14,000 people each year and kills about 10,000. The new study of 200 cases found two patients with 260 different mutated genes, making treatment more complicated than expected. Nonetheless, the same study also found much better ways to link specific mutations with aggressive forms of AML. With that information, doctors can better evaluate the risks of treating a patient with chemotherapy versus a bone marrow transplant. It can make a big difference. Bone marrow transplants can be very successful, but they have high risk and are fatal about 10 percent of the time. So for patients with the less aggressive AML, chemotherapy is the better option. But for those with Aggressive AML, despite the risk, bone marrow transplants are wiser given the otherwise lethal prognosis .

155. The Best Little Boy in the World – Adam Chandler

The May 7, 2013 edition of *The New York Times* carried an opinion piece by Adam Chandler, a gay lawyer who works for the U.S. government. He wrote about his experiences in relation to a new study by John Pachankis and Mark Hatzenbuehler published in *Basic and Applied Social Psychology*. Chandler says the study substantiates what he called, "The Best Little Boy in the World" theory, put forth in 1973 by a well-known gay journalist and investment writer, Andrew Tobias. Chandler said that Tobias' theory suggested "young closeted men deflect attention from their sexuality by investing in recognized markers of success"—good grades, athletic achievement, elite employment, and so on. And, he said, the subtitle for the report might as well be, "The Adam Chandler story."

Chandler writes that after showing his preference for dolls when he was young, he learned to "fit in." At school, he studied and copied the behavior and dress of the straight boys, got excellent grades, petitioned for and received a higher-than-normal case load in college, and sought the presidencies of student groups. At Yale Law School he found many fellow gays, including more than half the men in his randomly assigned small group seminar.

Pachankis and Hatzenbuehler said, "the longer a young man conceals his sexual orientation, the more heavily he invests in external measures of success." Moreover, the more stigmatizing it is to be gay in a particular place, the more likely the gay man is to "seek self-worth through competition." The consequence, to some extent, is heightened stress and social isolation.

For Chandler, the key question was what happens next? What happens after gays reveal themselves and being gay is no longer stigmatizing? It is an intriguing question on several fronts, involving nature and nurture. Do gay men have a genetic predisposition for higher IQs? How about ambition? Neither Chandler nor the research raises such questions, but certainly both seem to imply that "the need to achieve" may diminish as the broader culture becomes more accepting of homosexuality.

This item is not meant to suggest a connection between being gay and being Jewish or that like gays, Jews may have been inclined to hide their Jewishness. Instead, the Chandler story contains a thread that ties it back to item 66—Eric Hobsbawm's article "Benefits of Diaspora," in which—writing about Jewish achievement— he said "given equal rights, at least in theory, a certain degree of unease in relations between Jews and gentiles has proved historically useful." Hobsbawm's view was that even after Emancipation, anti-Semitic tensions continued, and those tensions helped stir Jews to disproportionate levels of achievement.

Like Jews, gays have produced large numbers very high achievers. Perhaps reacting to a perceived hostile environment and discrimination has been a significant force contributing to disproportionate achievement in both groups.

156. Values Despite Hardships – Andrew Kohut and Michael Dimock vs. Charles Murray

On May 10, 2013, Andrew Kohut, the founding director and former president of the Pew Research Center, and Michael Dimock, director of the Pew Research Center for the People and the Press, released an opinion piece on *Bloomberg View*. It later appeared in *The Huffington Post* and other news sources.

The piece argued that the values of middle and lower income Americans (according to Pew studies) have not turned noticeably more negative over the last 25 years—this despite the inability of those in these demographics to maintain their on-par income and net worth relative to those in the upper-middle and high-income ranges. Kohut and Dimock said that data show the middle and lower income populations remain just as committed to hard work, individualism, patriotism, concerns about becoming dependent on government, work ethic, potential for personal progress, and similar values as they were 25 years ago.

Kohut and Dimock also mention Charles Murray and his book *Coming Apart* several times, giving the impression they are challenging Murray—not on his economic, demographic and lifestyle statistics, but about degradation in the basic values of those at or near the bottom. They disagree with Murray on that.

It must be noted that part of this is apples and oranges. For one thing, Murray begins with 1972 data, Pew with 1988. A lot changed over that first 16 years (think stagflation, the Reagan revival, and the end of the Cold War). Second, all of Murray's data came from credible sources, including the Census Bureau, the University of Chicago's National Opinion Research Center (NORC), the Bureau of Labor Statistics, the Federal Bureau of Investigation, the Bureau of Justice Statistics, and others of similar caliber. The values and opinions data Murray used came from the General Social Survey (GSS). The well-respected GSS has been conducted since 1972 by the NORC and those data are used by many researchers in important projects.

Given the credibility of both Murray and Pew, one wishes there could be mutually respectful dialogue to explore and explain the divergent data and conclusions.

157. *Men on Strike* by Helena Smith – Charlotte Allen

On June 26, 2013, Allen's book review in *The Wall Street Journal* looked at Smith's tome, *Men on Strike*. Allen said that she found the book interesting, but more of a polemic than a fact-filled, persuasive explanation and set of recommendations.

Allen began by noting that more men are dropping out of society, not going to college, not holding down jobs, and not getting married, although some of these men are becoming fathers. Smith's book noted that male workforce participation has dropped from 80 percent in 1970 to 66 percent today. Meanwhile, more women are getting better educations: 58 percent of bachelor's degrees now go to women.

There are many divergent opinions as to why this is happening, but Smith's view according to Allen, is that the men in question are behaving rationally. This is because the incentives are not there to be responsible providers, husbands and fathers. In other words, they are following the model of John Galt, the lead character in Ayn Rand's *Atlas Shrugged*.

Perhaps, but it seems likely that cultural values have shifted making this lifestyle change ever more acceptable to a growing number of men.

158. A Gene for Fatness? – Gina Kolata

On July 19, 2013, *The New York Times* carried another Kolata column. This one was about a possible gene for fatness. Kolata said researchers had noted that among rats on the same diet and exercise regime, some were getting fatter than others. When researchers deleted a gene that helps control metabolism (how quickly calories are burned), the subject rats gained more weight than those whose gene was functioning properly.

The researchers then contacted Dr. Sadaf Farooqui at the University of Cambridge, who was conducting research on obesity in humans. They found one obese person with the same defective gene as the rats, and three others with mutations that may also render the gene non-functional.

Though there has long been discussion of whether or not genes cause metabolism rates to differ, here was a lead on a specific candidate gene that may predispose some of us to more easily gain or lose weight.

159. Isaac ben Judah Abravanel's Speech to Ferdinand and Isabella

Abravanel was a Portuguese Jewish statesman, philosopher, bible commentator, and financier. His speech is a timeless exploration of how Jews thought of their own culture in contrast with that of Ferdinand and Isabella's Spain. He delivered it at the end of the Reconquista after the Catholic monarchs had defeated the Moors and begun burning all the books in the great Moorish libraries. Until Lawrence Harrison forwarded it to me in July, 2013, I had not read it nor anything so powerful or prescient in contrasting the two cultures.

"Yes my king and queen, hear me well; error, your error profound and uncorrectable, the likes of which Spain has never seen before. You and you alone are responsible. As arms measure the might of a nation, so arts and letters measure its finer sensibilities. Yes, you have humbled the Moslem infidel with the force of your army, proving yourselves in the art of war. But what of your inner state of mind? By what right do your Inquisitors go about the countryside burning books by the thousands in public bonfires. By what authority do churchmen now want to burn the immense Arabic library of this great Moorish palace and destroy its priceless manuscripts? By whose rights? By whose authority? Why, it is by your authority, my king and queen. In your heart of hearts, you distrust the power of knowledge, and you respect only power.

"With us Jews it is different. We Jews cherish knowledge immensely. In our homes and in our prayer houses, learning is a lifelong pursuit. Learning is our lifelong passion; it is at the core of our being; it is the reason, according to our sages, for which we were created. Our fierce love of learning could have counterbalanced your excessive love of might. We could have benefited from the protection offered by your royal arms and you could have profited more from our community's advancement and exchange of knowledge. I say to you that we could have helped each other.

"As we are reminded of our own powerlessness, so your nation will suffer from the forces of disequilibrium that you have set in motion. For centuries to come, your descendants will pay dearly for your mistake of the present. As it is might of arms you most admire, you shall verily become a nation of conquerors—lust after gold and spoils, living by the sword and ruling with a fist of mail.

"Yet you shall become a nation of illiterates; your institutions of learning, fearing the heretical contamination of alien ideas from other lands, and other peoples, will no longer be respected. In the course of time, the once great name of Spain will become a whispered byword among the nations: Spain, the poor ignorant has-been; Spain, the nation which showed so much promise and yet accomplished so little.

"And then one day Spain will ask itself: what has become of us? Why are we a laughing-stock among nations? And the Spaniards of that day will look into their past and ask themselves why this came to be. And those who are honest will point to this day and this age as the time when their fall as a nation began. And the cause of their downfall will be shown to be none other than their revered Catholic sovereigns, Ferdinand and Isabella, conquerors of the Moors, expellers of the Jews, founders of the Inquisition, and destroyers of the inquiring Spanish minds."

It is an eloquent description of Jewish cultural values and an indictment of the Spanish Inquisition. Abravanel's predictions ultimately proved prescient when the gold flows from the Americas ceased, when the Spanish Armada was defeated by the British, and when the Dutch revolted, and broke away from Spain. That tiny country (Holland, or the Netherlands) went on to eclipse both Spain and Portugal on the world stage, and it was to Holland that the family of Spinoza immigrated. It was in Holland, not Spain, that Spinoza became one of history's most prominent figures.

160. More Than One Genome Per Person? – Carl Zimmer

Many people who closely follow genetic progress were astonished by Carl Zimmer's September 17, 2013 column in *The New York Times* Science section.

Zimmer began by acknowledging that most of us think we have only a single genome, and it is the most unique thing about us. Stanford geneticist Alexander Urban said that as recently as three years ago, the idea of a person carrying more than one genome would have been greeted with huge skepticism. Nonetheless, Zimmer said, "Scientists are now finding it is quite common for an individual to have multiple genomes. Some of these arise from mutations that affect only cells in one part of the body. Others come from genomes received from other people, including occasionally one's offspring.

An early clue arose in 1953 when a woman was discovered to have two different blood types: A and O. It turned out she most likely received some blood—and that blood's genome—from her twin brother in the womb. This was considered a very rare condition in 1953, and was assigned the term "chimerism." Scientists now think it is not so uncommon for a mother to gain genomes from the developing fetus in her womb. As one doctor stated, "It's pretty likely that any woman who has been pregnant is a chimera."

Zimmer said it was when she was 52-years-old and needed a kidney transplant that a woman learned that, in a way, she was not the mother of two of her three children. She had originated from two genomes, with her own blood and some of her eggs arising from one of the genomes, and other eggs arising from the second genome.

Autopsies performed on the brains of 59 women in 2012, found neurons with Y chromosomes in 63 percent of them. Those male chromosomes are thought to have developed from their sons. Similarly, Y chromosomes were found in breast tissue of 56 percent of women tested at the Dana Farber Cancer Institute in Boston.

Like so much in recent genetics, more knowledge brings us ever more surprises. With every gain, the goalposts of complete understanding move further out and ahead of us.

161. The Malleability of IQ (again) – Alison Gopnik

On September 21, 2013, Gopnik, a science writer for *The Wall Street Journal*, wrote a column titled, "Good Genes Only Get You So Far With Intelligence." Her point was that there is no clear dichotomy between nature and nurture when it comes to the brain and IQ because they interact. As she put it, "changes in our environment can actually transform the relationship among our traits, our upbringing and our genes."

Gopnik cites the PKU gene mutation as evidence of this. Historically, individuals with the defective gene were mentally retarded with a low IQ. After scientists discovered how PKU works (it inhibits one's ability to process an amino acid), they changed the diets of those with the defective gene. Now their IQ is more determined by diet than the genetic variation they were born with.

As Gopnik says, the lesson of PKU is that if you wish to measure the influence of nature versus nurture, you have to consider not just the current environment, but all the possible environments it might be possible to create. She notes that in studies of poor subjects with low social and economic status, "IQ is hardly heritable at all." Since DNA obviously cannot be changed by availability or lack of money, the conclusion is that, "haphazard differences in educational opportunity swamp genetic differences." With greater understanding of epigenetics, perhaps we may be able to fashion greater opportunities (greater intelligence) for children and help them achieve more than was ever thought possible.

162. U.S. Jewish Identity

In late September 2013, The Pew Research: Religion and Public Life Project issued the results of its poll on Jewish identity. Pew took the survey over from the Jewish Federation, who declined to continue polling after its 2000 results led to controversy over the numbers. The 2013 data is important in reflecting both positive and negative trends, and including some surprises. Some key findings:

— There are 6.6 million American Jews (2 percent of the U.S. population), down from 4 percent in the 1950s. Jews marry later and have fewer children; it is the Ultra-Orthodox who are sustaining the 2 percent.

— Of Jews: 35 percent identify as Reform, 18 percent as Conservative, 10 percent as Orthodox, and 19 percent as "no denomination." Of the total, 25 percent of Jews do not believe in God; 26 percent of Jews say religion is very important versus 56 percent of all Americans. Two-thirds do not belong to a synagogue and 58 percent intermarry and the intermarriage statistic is 71 percent for non-Orthodox Jews.

— 62 percent of Jews define being Jewish as mainly a matter of culture or ancestry; only 15 percent think of it as a matter of religion.

— 75 percent of Jews say they have a strong sense of belonging to the Jewish people; 69 percent have an "emotional attachment" to Israel.

— In saying what is "essential to their Jewishness," 73 percent of Jews cite remembering the Holocaust, 69 percent say leading an ethical life, and 56 percent say social justice.

— And finally, 58 percent of adult Jews have a college degree and 28 percent have a graduate degree. By contrast, only 29 percent of all adult Americans have a college degree.

163. Jewish Scientists Score Nobel Prizes – An Israeli Teacher's Analysis

The October 9, 2013 issue of the *Jewish Journal* featured a brief story noting that "six of the eight 2013 Nobel Prize winners in the sciences announced that week were Jewish."

Approximately a week later, Noah Efron, a teacher in the graduate program on science, technology, and society at Bar-Ilan University in Israel, who is writing a book on Jews in science, offered his opinion on website *Haaretz.com*. Efron reiterated the "six of eight" statistic and then summarized the brains (nature) and culture (nurture) theories, quickly discounting both.

As regards brains, Efron said, Jewish involvement in science is a "new thing." He noted that Joseph Jacobs' 1886 comparative analysis of Jews versus other westerners found them mediocre except in medicine.

Efron appears to have missed the effects of the Enlightenment, the Jewish Emancipation, and the Jewish Reform movement. He also appears unaware of historian Raphael Patai's analysis (*The Jewish Mind*) regarding the prominence of Jewish scientists during the Golden Age of Spain, as well as historian George Sarton's *Introduction to the History of Science*, in which Sarton noted that 95 of the world's 626 known scientists between 1150 and 1300 CE were Jews. At 15 percent of the total, this was likely well more than 20 times the proportion of Jews in the world's population at the time.

Efron brings up the notorious early 20th Century IQ test results for illiterate Jews newly arrived from the Russian Pale. But he does not contrast them with the Sephardic and German Jews who had arrived in the United States between 1654 and the mid-to-late 1800s. Those Jews were quite literate and often very successful. Ultimately, the credibility of the initial IQ test results on Jewish immigrants was unequivocally destroyed by the academic success of immigrant offspring who rose to become approximately 25 percent of Harvard's student population by the mid-1920s. Genes cannot change nor can IQ rise that quickly.

Efron then discounts culture as a driving force, but fails to say why. Instead, he attributes recent Jewish success to circumstance—namely, great opportunities available to Jewish immigrants in the United States from 1900 forward. That is true, but he fails to mention that opportunity existed for almost all immigrant groups that arrived. Why did the Jews move so far so fast? Why not the Italians, Irish, Germans, Scandinavians, and others? We now know it was not a second-generation phenomenon, nor were the Jews simply in the right place at the right time.

Efron said his concern about the nature and nurture theories is that they imply success will continue. He then describes the diminishing number of Jews pursuing science, and it worries him. As noted earlier, the rate of disproportionate Jewish achievement may well be in decline—it is part of the motivation for this book. However, Efron does not appear to understand that if he has misdiagnosed the reasons behind disproportionate Jewish achievement, he is less likely to have useful insights about how to turn things around.

164. Shuffling Genes in Our DNA – Robert Sapolsky

On October 12, 2013, *The Wall Street Journal* ran Sapolsky's column titled "Mind and Matter." It dealt with the frequent shuffling of human DNA. He began with examples of what many would call, "the apple doesn't fall far from the tree"—references to ancestral inheritance. He notes that virtually every cell in the human body is "commanded" by the DNA inherited from two parents.

But Sapolsky tempers that position by noting that we now know that humans also have "jumping genes" known as "transposable genetic elements." (See also item 138 above.) These elements occur when stretches of DNA move around and are copied to some other position along the DNA string. This can even happen with brain cells. The "mistakes" or mutations sometimes result in an unforeseen aspect of our evolution, for good or ill. But more often, they have no consequences. Consequential or not, the lesson of "jumping genes" is that while we have three billion base pairs of DNA in every cell, they aren't nearly as unchanging as was thought just a few years ago.

165. Further Work on Gene Mutations Tied to Cancers

On October 16, 2013, Ron Winslow wrote in *The Wall Street Journal* of further progress in studies of genes common to cancers found in multiple organs. He said the journal *Nature* had just issued an update on the Cancer Genome Atlas research project funded by the National Institutes of Health. The goal of the work was to improve speed and accuracy in the diagnosis of cancers, and assist in the development of treatments.

Researchers analyzed genes from 3,281 cancer tumors in a wide range of organs to come up with a common reference gene panel. They used this and earlier research findings to conclude that 200 to 400 mutations fuel all cancers. Of that number, 127 were identified as a result of the gene panel compilation.

Much work remains to be done to refine and better understand these mutations. The BRAF gene is already implicated in more than half of melanoma cases, and has now been identified in 7 percent of certain lung cancer tumors, 4 percent of colon cancers, and smaller percentages of brain, bladder, head and neck, kidney, and ovarian cancers. One new drug has already been approved for melanoma that exhibits the BRAF mutation. It has promise in treating some lung cancers as well, but appears to have little effect on BRAF-driven colon cancer tumors.

Genetic medical insight continues to make impressive advances while insight to traits is languishing.

166. The Roma: Primitive or Just Poor? – Dan Belefsky

On October 20, 2013, *The New York Times* featured a column by Belefsky titled, "Are the Roma Primitive or Just Poor?"

The contrast of Roma (Gypsies) and Jews has long fascinated me. Both are among the longest surviving tribes in history, and both have survived countless generations of discrimination. Roma and Jews were both gassed and fed to the same ovens in Auschwitz, yet the Roma remain as controversial as ever. Part of what intrigues me is that one tribe includes the highest achievers over at least the last 200 years; the other generally occupies the lower range of human achievement. One tribe is literate and accomplished in sophisticated endeavors; the other generally is not. But Roma accomplishments in petty and not so petty crime are legend.

If Darwinian evolution is about the survival of the fit, how is it that the Roma have survived for so long when perhaps their most notable accomplishment is skill at crime? I recall visiting France's Camargue years ago, where Europe's Roma have an annual celebration. Their apocryphal legend says Christ granted them dispensation for stealing because they saved him the pain of a fourth nail that would have otherwise been hammered through one of his feet. Because they stole that nail, he gave them license to steal on every day except the days of the Camargue celebration.

Theft, child prostitution, stealing from ATM machines, begging, organized criminal activity—it is all there and often organized by parents or other adults for whom use of children provides some insulation from the law. And the idea they are all poor is belied by the lavish homes of some Roma kingpins. To date, most efforts at Roma cultural reform have failed. Occasionally, a self-motivated individual or family will pursue an education and higher goals, but that is rare.

Europe has 11 million Roma, most having arrived from India centuries ago. Many arrived via present-day Bulgaria and Romania, where 2.6 million live today. Turkey has 2.75 million Roma; Russia 825,000; Hungary and Spain 750,000; and Serbia 600,000. There are at least a few Roma in every European country, and an estimated 1 million in the United States. The world has 12 to 14 million Jews, and they too have been dispersed throughout the globe, although much less so over the last 60 years.

The one bright spot may be Spain: half its Roma population is under age 25. Nearly all finish primary school, yet few make it through high school. But where 75 percent lived in substandard housing in 1978, today that number has dropped to 12 percent. Spain's free housing, education and healthcare may atone for Franco-era repression by offering a successful and more widely adopted path to progress.

But why have both Roma and Jews survived for so very long? Perhaps it is simply an instinctive skill independent of a positive culture, but it would be interesting to have a more rigorous analysis of the similarities and differences that may account for both having survived despite their dramatically different cultures.

167. Amsterdam: Literacy, Liberality, and Commercial Success

The Economist's October 23, 2013 issue reviewed the book *Amsterdam: A History of the World's Most Liberal City* by Russell Shorto. In reading the review, I was reminded of Simon Schama's 1987 book, *The Embarrassment of Riches*. Both authors have a great respect for Amsterdam and the Dutch.

The story of the Dutch Golden Age, roughly 1590 to 1700 CE, is testament to the achievements of this tiny country that changed the world with its literacy, liberality, and commercial successes (see item 17 above). Shorto gives great credence to the work of Jonathan Israel, the Princeton historian, who credits the Jew Spinoza as the ultimate champion of logic and facts, and a radical thinker who rebelled against religious dogma and became a prime mover of the Enlightenment.

Dutch liberality was supportive of Jews. In 1654, when Governor Peter Stuyvesant, director-general of New Amsterdam (New York) was reluctant to grant entry to 23 Sephardic Jews fleeing the Inquisition, he petitioned his Dutch West Indies Company superiors in Amsterdam for approval to block their immigration. Instead, he was ordered to grant entry to the first Jews to live in what would become the United States.

168: "Jumper Cables for the Brain" & Smarter: The New Science of Building Brain Power

On November 3, 2013, *The New York Times* Magazine ran an article titled, "Jumper Cables for the Mind" by Dan Hurley, science writer and author of the widely read 2012 article, "Can You Make Yourself Smarter?" (124. above) Hurley unleashed a firestorm with his exploration of whether certain mental exercises and training might improve memory and raise intelligence.

Hurley interviewed more than 200 scientists and also made himself a guinea pig to test the proposition that intelligence could be improved. At Harvard, he underwent "transcranial direct-current stimulation (tDCS), which delivers low-dose electrical stimulation to the brain. As early as 1981, scientific journals had published material saying tDCS could be helpful, and later double blind studies at the National Institute of Neurological Disorders and Stroke in Bethesda, Maryland proved that partially-paralyzed stroke victims could benefit from a single 20-minute session (albeit a modest 5 to 10 percent).

In 2005, research at Harvard University showed that tDCS can enhance working memory. Other research indicated it was helpful with depression, and when used in conjunction with the drug Zoloft, it resulted in benefits greater than the administration of either treatment separately. The U.S. Air Force also discovered it could be helpful in enhancing vigilance.

Hurley was intrigued by the potential of tDCS, which is still controversial and, despite the positive research results, has numerous skeptics. Thus it remains difficult to obtain funding for further and larger studies of this relatively inexpensive and interesting technique.

Hurley concluded with a mental agility flashcard experiment. In his first session, after 20 minutes of iDCS, he got 53 answers correct and seven wrong. Five days later, and after eight iDCS sessions, Hurley had no wrong answers and his average response times dropped from 3.1 seconds to 2.6 seconds. And while he acknowledges that practice helped, he says 200 experiments showing the same results and proving no placebo effect lead him to believe his improvement was genuine.

Hurley's follow-on book, *Smarter: The New Science of Building Brain Power*, was released December 26, 2013. It goes beyond tDCS to explore drugs, exercise, music, meditation, and cognitive training, as well as brain stimulation. Many scientists are skeptical of his conclusions, but he has many believers as well. Hurley's position is best expressed in his own words:

> If intelligence is calculated by what we do, you hold in your hands the single best measure of mine (this book). My days of training were filled with purposeful, challenging tasks of all kinds...the tasks were hard, but they were fun. I got along better with my wife and daughter. I no longer found myself getting into my car and realizing that I'd forgotten my briefcase. I went on nearly a dozen trips to scientific meetings around the country during the same period, booking all my flights and rental cars and hotels but experiencing none of the stress and sense of being overwhelmed that I'd expected. And then I wrote this book. It sounds pat and clichéd, but what can I tell you? I feel smarter.

Though I too am skeptical, I am guided by the idea that it is all worth exploring and I would be very interested in more rigorous tests of efficacy. If we find we can improve our intelligence with cognitive training we will have gained new and remarkably beneficial insight.

169. Nurturing Nature – Robert Plomin and Individualized Education

On November 30, 2013, The Economist reviewed the book, *G Is For Genes: The Impact of Genetics on Education and Achievement* by Robert Plomin and Kathryn Asbury.

Plomin is one of the foremost twin studies experts. He has focused on the proportion of human traits that arise from genes versus the environment. His efforts have mostly compared identical and fraternal twins raised together, not identical twins raised apart. In theory, because the pairs grew up together with their parents as part of a shared community of schools, family, and friends, their "environment can be thought of as controlled." (Namely, it is the same for both twins). Thus, the difference in traits between twins that share all the same genes (identical twins), versus those share half the same genes (fraternal twins), can enlighten us as to how much a trait may be caused by nature versus nurture.

Plomin believes 80 percent of the differences in learning to read and write are genetic, 60 to 70 percent for math, and 50 to 60 percent for science. Nonetheless, a good indicator of success in a particular subject is confidence, and he says that is 50 percent heritable. Plomin and others have long made the point that our talents and confidence cause us to pursue activities in which we excel or think we excel. We commit our time and energy to them, and in that way, our inherited traits help shape our environment.

Nonetheless, because Plomin believes socio-economic status is 40 percent heritable and thus, children from low-status homes are disadvantaged by dint of a lack of resources, he would like to see that inequity addressed by more individualized education.

The book reviewer found this idea interesting and worthwhile, but impractical as to cost. He also chided Plomin for the absence of any data to show that individualized education would work.

Though he is a long time twin studies advocate, Plomin is also a genetic scientist with a heart who wants to encourage changes in the environment he believes could make a positive difference for disadvantaged kids.

170. "Finn-ished"

On December 7, 2013, *The Economist* reported that the lofty academic scores achieved by 15-year-old Finnish students dropped dramatically between 2006, when they were ranked fifth in the world (with

PISA scores averaging ~542), and 2012, when they ranked tenth (with scores averaging ~520). Meanwhile, Asian dominance continued to improve and topped the scores and rankings: China ranked first at ~613, Singapore second at ~574, Hong Kong third at ~561, Taiwan fourth at ~560, South Korea fifth at ~557, and Japan sixth at ~535. All of these average scores were higher than in 2006.

One obvious observation relating to the Jewish achievement debate is that the gains are coming much too quickly to be genetic.

The Economist concludes its coverage by saying: "New education stars can emerge and old ones fade fast. But the broader lesson may be simple, if brutal. Successful countries focus fiercely on the quality of teaching and eschew zigzag changes of direction or philosophy. Teachers and families share a determination to help the young succeed. Vietnam is now in eighth place for math, besting many rich countries that spend far more. Pushy parenting helps too. Half of all Vietnamese parents stay in regular contact with teachers to monitor their children's progress."

171. Illumina

On January 15, 2014, *Business Week* featured a story on Illumina, the leading U.S. manufacturer of gene sequencing machines. The occasion was the company's release of its two newest sequencers, both of which were expected to fulfill the promise of $1,000 whole genome testing. One machine, the high-volume HiSeqX, can process approximately 20,000 human genomes a year and costs about $1 million. It is geared for medical research centers and national entities. The other machine, the NextSeq500, costs approximately $250,000 and it is targeted at hospitals and other testing facilities.

Both machines sequence all three billion base pairs of DNA and analyze them. Both focus on the 1,600 well-researched genes known to be associated with 1,200 medical conditions. An Illumina subsidiary, Verinata Health, also does prenatal testing for a variety of conditions without the need for risky amniocentesis.

Illumina hopes that, through the adoption of its technologies, medical and research professionals can more quickly diagnose problems, particularly in children and the newborn.

It is astonishing how quickly whole genome testing is becoming mainstream and with that likely to yield ever more breakthroughs.

172. Help for Underprivileged Children – David Brooks

A January 23, 2014 David Brooks column in *The New York Times* discussed his opinion of how we might expand opportunities for children, especially the underprivileged. He said school reform had probably received too much attention and not delivered much in the way of returns.

Brooks posited that the right academic approach doesn't matter much if students cannot "control their impulses, can't form attachments, don't possess resilience, and lack social and emotional skills." He decried the 500,000 children born because of unintended pregnancies, mostly to unmarried women who are unlikely to marry the father. These children need a loving, two-parent family, Brooks said, and we do not know how to bring that about.

Failing that, he continued, help can be furnished in the form of parenting skills, "reading to their kids, speaking more, using consistent and encouraging discipline—then millions of children might have more secure attachments, more structure, and a better shot at an upwardly mobile career." And, in addition, "We've got to learn to control disruptive students estimated at 15 percent of the student population, if only to protect the other 85 percent. Today only 57 percent of kids age 19 graduate from high school, carry a 2.5 or better grade point average, don't get pregnant, and are not convicted of a crime. We also have to get much better at helping those teenage kids."

Brooks is plowing the fields of cultural values. He is encouraging the kinds of values Jews have long held. While changing cultures is never easy, he is focused on how that can best be done. He clearly wants these kids to have the best possible shot at a better future.

173. Is It Time To Retire Nature Versus Nurture? – Alison Gopnik

Gopnik used her January 25, 2014 column in *The Wall Street Journal* to describe a question raised by the website *www.Edge.org*. *Edge* had asked, "What scientific concept might best be retired?" She noted that many respondents nominated the distinction between nature and nurture.

Gopnik opined that it no longer seems the dichotomy makes sense. She raised the issue of epigenetics, saying it explores the linkages by which the environment shapes genetic processes—and the notion that whether a gene is expressed or not, the epigenetic regulation can be passed on to from one generation to the next. She also referred to a study that looked at two genetically identical mice strains where one strain is smarter than the other. Researchers swapped the infant mice so that each strain's pups were raised by the mothers from the other strain. The mice from the less intelligent strain got smarter, and then passed that along to their offspring.

Gopnik went on to suggest that new theories contradict the older idea put forth by evolutionary psychology that human genetics are largely calibrated to a stone-age environment. Today, she said, many scientists believe humans have instead adapted to the realities of change. The world is unpredictable and variable. The skills required for survival are not situation-specific; they are fluid. We develop the ability to change from generation to generation to meet whatever we face.

Gopnik concluded by paraphrasing anthropologist Pascal Boyer, who said that while it is tempting to talk about the culture of a group as though it is a mysterious force beyond biology and independent of evolution, culture, he said, is a biological phenomenon. "It is a set of abilities and practices that lets members of one generation learn and change and to pass that along to the next generation. Culture is our nature, and the ability to learn and change is our most important and fundamental instinct."

174. A Gene for Height or Smarts? Don't Bet On It! – Robert Sapolsky

Sapolsky used his February 1, 2014 column in *The Wall Street Journal* to talk about the state of play in nailing down genes for traits. He said that in the eleven years since the human genome was sequenced, as scientists look at all 23,000 genes in relation to traits, this powerful tool has produced some surprising results. "For the most part," he said, "what has emerged...is evidence of the minimal extent to which some trait is 'in your genes' and how relatively unimportant any given gene is."

Sapolsky gave the example of the 2010 study in the journal *Nature*, which looked at the genes for height (see item 148 above). He also cited a study that looked at body-mass index. After looking at 250,000 subjects, the most important gene accounted for just 0.3 percent of body mass.

Sapolsky also looked at the educational attainment (not IQ) of more than 125,000 subjects. The most important gene was responsible for about 2 percent of attainment. The conclusion was that, "educational attainment looks to be very polygenic" (a lot of genes are involved, but it is unclear whether they make a big difference). This underscores how far science still needs to go to understand the genetics of traits such as intelligence and the possible links to human achievement.

175. Me, Myself, and Why – Jennifer Ouellette

On February 3, 2014, Ouellette's book, *Me, Myself, and Why*, was reviewed in *The Wall Street Journal* by Matthew Hutson. The book is something of a survey of the many ways one can respond to the question: Who are you? For example, take a personality test, write your own autobiography, dictate a stream of conscious thoughts, make your medical history available, or offer up a whole genome scan. Ouellette, a science writer, looks at all these and more. She begins with genetics.

Hutson's take on her content is that, "while genes form the ingredients of our creation, they are not one's destiny—except in the case of earwax. Despite talk of a 'warrior' gene or 'gay' gene," he quoted Ouellette in saying, there aren't enough genes in the genome for the one-to-one model to work. In discussing the complexity of the brain in the context of genetics, Ouellette then quotes technologist Emerson Pugh, "If the human brain were so simple that we could understand it, we would be so simple that we couldn't."

176. The Triple Package – Amy Chua and Jed Rubenfeld

On February 4, 2014, Amy Chua and Jed Rubenfeld's book, *The Triple Package*, was released. It received huge coverage in the news and popular media. My phone soon rang—it was a *Miami Herald* book reviewer who told me that *The Golden Age* had been cited frequently in *The Triple Package* index. He wanted my thoughts. Later, a friend told me Chua and Rubenfeld made reference to *Golden Age* data during interviews.

I was intrigued but skeptical, in part because I do not think the critical factors behind the disproportionate achievements of Jews and others can be boiled down to just three elements as *The Triple Package* suggests. I suspected Chua and Rubenfeld would be skewered by a barrage of snarky reviews and media commentary, similar to what happened after the release of Chua's *Battle Hymn of The Tiger Mother*. I anticipated another round of politically correct warfare from those whose battle hymn is "all groups (and cultures) are equal," and who see racism in anyone who distinguishes the achievements of one group from another.

But a long flight from Moscow to San Francisco gave me time to read *The Triple Package* cover to cover. I was very impressed. My skepticism about the three elements remains, if slightly tempered. But like Lawrence Harrison, Thomas Sowell, and others, Chua and Rubenfeld have written a remarkable book describing many groups of high achievers from whom we can learn a great deal.

Other writers had previously made the case for Jews, eighteenth-century Scotts, the Off-shore Chinese, Mormons, post-Mao Chinese, Indo-Americans, Caribbean Blacks, and others as high achievers. To these groups, Chua and Rubenfeld added Nigerians, South Asian/

Indian-Americans, Vietnamese-Americans, Cuban-Americans, Iranian-Americans, and Lebanese-Americans.

At its core—and despite criticisms from some—*The Triple Package* is a powerful argument against race as a driving force behind success or failure. None of the groups Chua, Rubenfeld and others have singled out are thought to be racially, ethnically, or genetically superior or inferior in any way. But the cultural values and attributes of these achievers are compelling. Among the values they treasure are education, deferred gratification, a sense of duty, ethical behavior, family, and hard work. Most high-achieving groups share these or similar values.

Chua and Rubenfeld also made the case that a moderate sense of superiority, plus a modicum of insecurity, and a high level of self-discipline (impulse control) are major reasons why these groups have done so well. And like me, Chua and Rubenfeld have concerns that the era of Jewish and American disproportionate achievements may be coming to an end—but we all feel it may be possible to turn this around and we should try.

177. "The American Precariat" – David Brooks

On February 10, 2014, Brooks wrote a column in *The New York Times* that dealt with what he saw as a recent increase in a sense of "precariousness." Brooks believes this reflects a lack of confidence and a growing fear of risk-taking among some Americans.

In support of his point of view, Brooks cited data on declining mobility. In 1950, one in five Americans moved every year; now it is one in eight. This is a historic low for the United States and is reflected in residential rental trends as well.

Brooks said the highly educated are still moving as much as ever, but it is the less educated that seem stuck in place. He believes their self-confidence has eroded and they don't want the additional hardship of a move. When they do move, more of them move to communities with lower income and housing values to save money, rather than moving "up" to communities where there might be greater opportunity.

Fertility rates are down, and only 46 percent of White Americans believe they have a good chance to improve their standard of living. This is the lowest level since the General Social Surveys began in 1972 (see 157. above for an opposing paradigm).

Brooks sees no easy answers, but is focused on something that is increasingly part of the American dialogue. It is all germane to human achievement.

178. Prodigal Son: A Precariat Follow-up – David Brooks

A week after Brooks wrote his "Precariat" column in *The New York*

Times, he followed up with a column about the biblical prodigal son. His take was interesting; he chose not to side with the hardworking older brother who felt his father was wrong to welcome the wayward younger brother back home. Instead, Brooks supported the father and put the older brother on par with the young prodigal. He called the older brother, "self-righteous, smug, cold and shrewd" and noted he was working for material rewards.

Those who read both columns will likely conclude Brooks wished to clarify his earlier content by suggesting that moral condemnation of the American underclass is the wrong way to go. It is more likely to alienate than inspire. Successful remedies will have to be more oblique; Brooks favors "projects that bring the "older and younger brothers" together to work on shared goals such as national service, "infrastructure-building, strengthening a company, or a congregation. He sees everyone winning with that approach. And we may just be able to stimulate more of us to aspire and achieve more with our lives.

179. Your Ancestors, Your Fate? – Gregory Clark

"The Great Divide," an opinion piece by Gregory Clark, appeared in *The New York Times* on February 23, 2014 as part of its Inequality Series.

Clark, an economics professor at the University of California, Davis, has looked extensively at the incidence, over centuries, of selected family names that are part of the upper and lower reaches of society. His point was that "status" is essentially timeless. He says the same names tend to show up in the same social strata (and perhaps income and net worth levels) over hundreds of years in Sweden, England, the United States, India, Chile, Japan, South Korea, and China, as well as other countries.

Clark also said studies that suggest 10 percent of variation in income can be predicted "based on your parents' earnings" are wrong. He challenged that research, saying he and his colleagues "estimate 50 to 60 percent of variation in overall status is determined by your lineage." For Clark, "genes predict life chances more than culture or money do." Apart from pure IQ, he notes, a "compulsion to strive, talent to prosper, and the ability to overcome failure are strongly inherited." And while he acknowledged the difficulty of knowing "for certain what the mechanisms for that inheritance are, we know that genetics plays a surprisingly strong role." And further, he says, "Alternative explanations that are in vogue—cultural traits, family economic resources, and social networks—don't hold up to scrutiny."

Clark then went on to explain how he and his colleagues poured over the data country by country, accessing records going back as early as 1170 CE to gather names which he placed in five categories: Top

Three Surnames, Selected High-Status Surnames, Middle-Status Surnames, Selected Low Status Surnames, and Bottom Three Surnames.

Clark said, "Culture is a nebulous category and it can't explain the constant regression of family status—from the top and the bottom." He made similarly dismissive arguments about family resources and social networks, saying even the Nordic programs promoting social equity may help individuals with income, but "have not changed their relative social position." Further, he acknowledged that his ideas regarding genetic transmission of drive and ability may unsettle some. But in the adoptive records and twin studies, he said he found outcomes that confirmed his theory—"genetics is the main carrier of social status."

Interestingly, Clark devotes a few paragraphs to Jews, noting a history of discrimination in admittance to "elite schools," but he said, "Starting in the 1970s, Jews began a slow overall decline in social status. He indicates that as measured by the doctor's directory and at the current rate, it will be 300 years before Ashkenazi Jews cease to be overrepresented among American doctors."

I would encourage Clark to talk to my Jewish cardiologist who practices at the University of California, San Francisco where he is also a professor. Over the decades, he has observed precipitous declines in the numbers of Jewish medical students. I see it as well. It seems each time I come for an appointment, I am greeted by a new UCSF fellow or resident who is not Jewish, but rather is Sikh, Chinese or some other nationality. Clark should also read Ron Unz who has chronicled the amazing drop in the disproportionate Jewish academic performance in recent years.

Conversely, the Ashkenazi Jews of the Russian Pale were at the bottom of the social milieu in the late 19th and early 20th Century. Today, their fourth- and fifth-generation offspring have libraries, hospitals, foundations, and colleges named after them and they are 35 to 40 percent of America's most generous philanthropists. Like Gladwell's book *Outliers*, Clark's data do not adequately explain phenomenal Jewish achievement and rapid gains in status.

And if Clark explored the Forbes 400, he might be surprised at the huge numbers of newcomers (Jews and non-Jews) to the list who arose from middle or lower middle class backgrounds (including of course the 31 percent that are Jews, most of whom are descendants of the impoverished and illiterate Jews that immigrated between 1880 and 1924). Then, there is Buffett, Gates, Ellison, Jobs, Dell and so many others who did not arise from nobility nor did a goodly number of them graduate from college. To this we could add the Kennedy's from Ireland and countless more from other places.

180. Predicting IQ at Six Months of Age – Kenneth Chang

On April 7, 2014, Chang's column in *The New York Times* Science section marked the 25th anniversary of a Gina Kolata article about researcher Joseph F. Fagan, III. Fagan, who passed away in 2013, was a Case Western Reserve University psychologist, who wanted to find out which infants would respond well to stimulation. He later came to believe his testing yielded meaningful information about IQ.

Fagan observed the infants reactions to experiments with flashcards that depicted faces. A research colleague says that as the faces were changed on the flashcards, he and Fagan soon realized "babies with below average intelligence did not exhibit the same attraction to the novelty." The reverse was also found to be true, (smarter kids were attracted) and thus arose the notion that the test yielded some level of predictive insight to IQ. (Also see item 144 above.)

At the time, one intention was to provide enrichment programs for infants with the potential to benefit from such programs, particularly for families of limited means. Fagan also wanted to encourage programs to benefit infants at the lower end of the IQ spectrum, fearing they would fall farther behind without help.

Chang said that 25 years later, the test still holds up, and before Fagan passed away he went back to look at those he tested two decades earlier. Fagan said the infant-age predictions of IQ and academic success were manifested in the now 21-year-old adults.

But while the test is still used, it did not become widely adopted. Political correctness may have played a part, but so too did concerns about self-fulfilling prophecies. This is the same reason private New York City schools no longer test 4- and 5-year-olds for IQ.

And while Dr. Scott Barry Kaufman, scientific director of the Imagination Institute at the University of Pennsylvania, and author of *Un-gifted: Intelligence Redefined*, said, "It's really good science," he also later says the Fagan test was only, "moderately predictive of later academic success...not accurate enough to forecast the intellectual trajectory of a particular child."

In his last decade, Fagan was drawn into the nature (genes) versus nurture (environment) debates and noted he had found babies from different cultures performed equally on his tests. He believed the data contradicted the idea of an underlying biological reason for the achievement gaps between different cultures or races. I find something of an "echo" in Fagan's observations with those who have explored the topic of female capabilities in math and science. (See items 114, 140, and 146 above.) Namely latent potential may require the right environment to be expressed.

In a book published by Dr. Kaufman in 2011, Fagan wrote: "A parsimonious explanation for the finding is that later differences in IQ between different racial-ethnic groups may spring from differences in cultural exposure to information past infancy, but not from group differences in their basic ability to process information."

181. Self Theories – Professor Carol Dweck's Stanford Class

The April 18, 2014 Education section of *The New York Times* carried a brief write-up about a course at Stanford University taught by Carol Dweck, a professor and PhD. It is a freshman psychology seminar that receives 100 to 200 applicants for its 16 seats.

Dweck instructs her students to tackle something they "never had the guts to try" as one assignment. One student sang "Phantom of the Opera" on a public bus. Another, who thought of himself as an introvert, ran for co-president of his dorm, gave a speech despite his high level of anxiety, and won the election. A third introduced himself to strangers in San Francisco.

Dweck's research is shaping attitudes about achievement and success. She has found that one's mindset is critical in times of major transitions. If you think your IQ and personality are pre-determined, you are more likely to be incapable of handling a setback. But if you think your abilities are more malleable—if you have what she calls a "growth mindset"—you realize that struggles can often be overcome with strategy, effort and good instruction. This is a vital message for the freshmen she teaches, particularly at a school like Stanford where they will interact with so many gifted colleagues with great potential.

Though not analogous, Dweck's instruction reminded me of an exercise I heard about when I was at Harvard Business School. Students were asked to answer a topical question by framing their response as a percentage. Just prior to the question, an arrow was spun in a circle, randomly landing on a number. Almost invariably, the students' answers correlated in some way to the number on which the arrow landed—the students' minds had been subconsciously conditioned. Or as one professor put it, "Expectations influence outcomes."

Dweck, like Professor Henry Higgins, provides a Pygmalion cultural influence that may trigger heightened levels of aspiration and confidence.

182. A Troublesome Inheritance: Genes, Race, and Human History – Nicholas Wade

It is fitting that we near the end of this Chronology with Charles Murray's review of Nicholas Wade's book, *A Troublesome Inheritance*, from *The Wall Street Journal.* Murray's review appeared on May 3, 2014. I augment Murray's comments with some of my own from having read the book as well.

It is fitting, in part, because so many of Wade's own groundbreaking reports of important research findings are included in this Chronology. And fitting, as well, because Charles Murray, the book's reviewer, provided material and commentary for *The Golden Age of Jewish Achievement.* Finally, it is fitting because the Wade book and the Murray review bring together important arguments from two experts who lean toward genes as the most significant force behind high achievement.

By contrast, this book, *The Debate,* is by an author who respects them both but finds culture to be the stronger force and better explanation. I suspect the difference between my opinion and theirs is closer to 60/40 than 90/10, and any debate between us would be both interesting and mutually respectful.

Wade makes the case for genetics as a very real driver of race and ethnicity in different peoples. He does so knowing full well that he is taking on the politically correct establishment that wants to link any such findings to Nazism and prejudice. These "multiculturalists" are often outspoken advocates for all cultures being equal. To them, race is simply a fabrication of no real usefulness, except as a rationalization for discrimination. Wade's position is that this argument is effectively a Luddite position, reflecting a bias that willfully denies the existence of provable facts.

Wade believes the genetics are indisputable. One of the most obvious evidences is skin color: mutations (or beneficial genetic variations) as natural selection adapted skin to the sun, the seasons, and changes in climate as humans began to migrate out of Africa. What works for Eskimos is not likely to work for people who live in central Africa or the Amazon Basin.

Multiculturalists—many of whom are social scientists or in the mainstream press—disagree. In his 1972 paper, "The Apportionment of Human Diversity," geneticist Richard Lewontin said, "…the races are so close to genetically identical that 'racial classification is now seen to be of virtually no genetic or taxonomic significance." The late paleontologist, Steven Jay Gould expressed the view that except for cosmetic differences, human evolution stopped before humans left Africa. As a result, he said, "human equality is a contingent fact of history." Multiculturalists generally believe that race is a "social construct," racial differences do not exist, and anyone who seriously studies them or espouses them must be academically and publicly ostracized. Nonetheless, Lewontin and Gould's views are disproven by the results of the Human Genome Project and further research which has followed in the years since 2003.

The New England Journal of Medicine acknowledged as much after it ran an article supporting a multiculturalist viewpoint and shortly afterward retracted it. Leading genetic researchers had reminded the Journal that the incidence of diseases such as sickle cell anemia, Tay Sachs, and others, conclusively proved that racial differences are real. (See items 38 and 44 above) Further, the geneticists said that denying the factual data could harm millions of people by hindering research and delaying the development of drugs.

Murray points to Wade's work in describing how a computer directed to categorize genetic sequences across the breadth of humanity based on likeness and differences will tend to group the results by race and ethnicity. He says that cannot be an accident.

At the same time, Murray adds a very important qualification: "Let me emphasize, as Mr. Wade does, how little we yet know about the subject of racial and ethnic differences. Work in the decade since the genome was sequenced has taught us that genetically linked traits, even a comparatively simple one like height, are far more complex than previously imagined, involving dozens or hundreds of genes plus other forms of variation in our DNA, plus interactions between the environment and gene expression. For emotional or cognitive traits, the story is so complicated that we are probably a decade or more away from substantial understanding."

The second half of Wade's book gets into different groups, including Jews, Chinese, Europeans, Indians, Muslims, and others. The Jews, for example are described in complimentary terms for their scientific and artistic contributions. It is here that Murray says Wade may well be factually accurate, but that his "inquisition" is likely to go forward nonetheless. Namely, dealing with the rise of the West over the last 600 years will set off many alarm bells.

True to Murray's prediction, on May 16, 2014, a book review in *The New York Times* by Arthur Allen played to form. While acknowledging Wade's contributions to the *Times*, and bowing to Wade's notable work, Allen found the glass mostly empty. He cited population geneticist Luigi Luca Cavalli-Sforza who said, following the Holocaust, "the very concept of race is a matter of scientific debate." And he noted that political scientist, economist, and socio-economic author Francis Fukuyama has a different explanation for Europe's success. It seems curious that dropping a few prominent names are thought sufficient to trump the data.

Allen makes some interesting points, but pejorative sentences predominate. For example: "Wade's argument starts to go off the rails" and Wade presents "a few scattered genetic studies and attempts to weld them into a grand theory of global history." Allen concludes his review with, "While there is much of interest in Mr. Wade's book, readers will probably see what they are predisposed to see: a confirmation of prejudices, or a rather unconvincing attempt to promote the science of racial differences." Allen seems to be describing himself.

So how do I reconcile Wade's genetic predisposition with my own cultural predisposition? Wade has said mandatory literacy is the most important force that led to genetic selection in Jews. I share that belief with both him and Murray. In fact, after watching Wade give a CNN interview, I told a Jewish friend that Wade must have read my manuscript—or more likely, Botticini and Eckstein's *The Chosen Few*. I believe I get something of a last laugh, however, in pointing out mandatory Jewish literacy was the cultural value that, in turn, had genetic consequences. I make the point only in passing though, since I also believe there is much more than just mandatory education behind the driving force of culture as the major impetus explaining the phenomenal performance of Jews.

183. "New Blood" Can Benefit More Than Organizations

A May 5, 2014 article by Ron Winslow in *The Wall Street Journal* reported on work by scientists at Stanford University, the University of California, San Francisco (UCSF), and Harvard University, published in the journals Nature Medicine and Science.

The Stanford/UCSF study found that transfusions of blood from younger mice had positive benefits for older recipients. It reversed cognitive declines associated with aging and improved memory and learning ability. The Harvard study exposed older mice to proteins present at high levels in the younger ones. They found measurable benefits in brain and exercise capability. Earlier, the same researchers found protein injections helped reverse the adverse effects of aging on the hearts of the mice.

While not performed on humans, both studies were intriguing and pointed to something in blood that affects cognition and aging. Brian Kennedy, chief executive officer of the Buck Institute for Aging Research, who was not involved in the research, said, "These are really exciting papers...we are finding more and more potential strategies to target age-related tissue decline and aging itself."

184. Study Ties Hard Work to Asian Students' High Grades – Ehrenfreund

A May 5, 2014 *Washington Post* column by Max Ehrenfreund described a study published in the Proceedings of the National Academy of Science. The researchers, Yu Xie and Amy Hsin, concluded that hard work is the key to Asian students' remarkable academic successes. Hsin, born in Taiwan, was raised in the United States and Canada. She is now at Queens College, City University of New York. Xie is at the University of Michigan.

Like a number of studies dating back to the late '80s and early '90s, this one said it is hard work that matters most. The subjects were 4,246 Whites and 989 Asians. Xie and Hsin looked at academic grades, teachers' responses to questions about willingness to work, intelligence as measured by standardized tests, family socio-economic status, and "natural thinking ability" before concluding that hard work was predominant. As an example, Xie and Hxin noted that Asians who said math did not come easy to them were more inclined to work harder and not give up, than were Whites.

Their conclusion was a surprise to some who thought natural intelligence might be more significant than hard work. Others opined that Asian cultural values and family support for education were also critical. The Asian values share many elements in common with those of Jews.

185. The 3% Solution?

On May 10, 2014, *The Economist* ran a story based on a recent issue of *Cell Reports*. The subject matter was sufficiently intriguing for *The Economist* to subtitle its account, "A potent source of genetic variation in cognitive ability has just been discovered."

The work, done at University of California and Gladstone Institute, both in San Francisco, looked at the protein klotho, which is encoded by the KL-VS variation of the KL gene. Researchers had determined this variation promotes longevity, and they wanted to find out if it might also affect cognitive decline. Their study involved 220 volunteers age 52 to 85.

The surprise was that while KL-VS did not affect decline, it appeared to raise IQ by an estimated six points no matter what the age of the recipients. (The results were extrapolated to arrive at the estimate because the study had not directly measured IQ.) In addition, the KL gene variation may account for as much as 3 percent of the variation in IQ in the general population.

The Stanford and Gladstone researchers then did additional

research, adding the "murine equivalent of KL-VS" to the genomes of mice. The mice were able to navigate mazes more effectively and their memories were better. The researchers observed some strengthening of connections in the brain synapses, suggesting how the gene variation brought about the improvements in memory.

The researchers then reviewed two counterpart studies done by other groups involving about 500 volunteers. Both had results similar to the UCSF/Gladstone project. And in both studies, the VS version of the VL gene was found in about 20 percent of the human subjects.

If the results are replicated in further research, they might well yield important new insights in the quest to enhance and sustain IQ. That, in turn, could have positive consequences for human achievement.

---

186. The Character Factory – David Brooks

The final entry—for now—in the ongoing chronology of nature, nurture and human achievement arose as this book was being prepared for publication. On July 31, 2014, David Brooks' column in *The New York Times* rather elegantly captured much of the essence of this book's perspective, and particularly my "Further Reflections on Culture" comments at the end of Part 1. With appropriate permissions, I have reproduced the text here:

"Nearly every parent on earth operates on the assumption that character matters a lot to the life outcomes of their children. Nearly every government antipoverty program operates on the assumption that it doesn't.

"Most Democratic antipoverty programs consist of transferring money, providing jobs or otherwise addressing the material deprivation of the poor. Most Republican antipoverty programs likewise consist of adjusting the economic incentives or regulatory barriers faced by the disadvantaged.

"As Richard Reeves of the Brookings Institution pointed out recently in National Affairs, both orthodox progressive and conservative approaches treat individuals as if they were abstractions—as if they were part of a species of 'hollow man' whose destiny is shaped by economic structures alone, and not by character and behavior.

"It's easy to understand why policy makers would skirt the issue of character. Nobody wants to be seen blaming the victim—spreading the calumny that the poor are that way because they don't love their

274   2013 to Date: Medical & Cultural Advances, Traits Slower

children enough, or don't have good values. Furthermore, most sensible people wonder if government can do anything to alter character anyway.

"The problem is that policies that ignore character and behavior have produced disappointing results. Social research over the last decade or so has reinforced the point that would have been self-evident in any other era—that if you can't help people become more resilient, conscientious or prudent, then all the cash transfers in the world will not produce permanent benefits.

"Walter Mischel's famous marshmallow experiment demonstrated that delayed gratification skills learned by age 4 produce important benefits into adulthood. Carol Dweck's work has shown that people who have a growth mind-set—who believe their basic qualities can be developed through hard work—do better than people who believe their basic talents are fixed and innate. Angela Duckworth has shown how important grit and perseverance are to lifetime outcomes. College students who report that they finish whatever they begin have higher grades than their peers, even ones with higher SATs. Spelling bee contestants who scored significantly higher on grit scores were 41 percent more likely to advance to later rounds than less resilient competitors.

"Summarizing the research in this area, Reeves estimates that measures of drive and self-control influence academic achievement roughly as much as cognitive skills. Recent research has also shown that there are very different levels of self-control up and down the income scale. Poorer children grow up with more stress and more disruption, and these disadvantages produce effects on the brain. Researchers often use dull tests to see who can focus attention and stay on task. Children raised in the top income quintile were two-and-a-half times more likely to score well on these tests than students raised in the bottom quintile.

"But these effects are reversible with the proper experiences.

"People who have studied character development through the ages have generally found hectoring lectures don't help. The superficial 'character education' programs implanted into some schools of late haven't done much either. Instead, sages over years have generally found at least four effective avenues to make it easier to climb. Government-supported programs can contribute in all realms.

"First, habits. If you can change behavior you eventually change disposition. People who practice small acts of self-control find it easier to perform big acts in times of crisis. Quality preschools, K.I.P.P.

schools and parenting coaches have produced lasting effects by encouraging young parents and students to observe basic etiquette and practice small but regular acts of self-restraint.

"Second, opportunity. Maybe you can practice self-discipline through iron willpower. But most of us can only deny short-term pleasures because we see a realistic path between self-denial now and something better down the road. Young women who see affordable college prospects ahead are much less likely to become teen moms.

"Third, exemplars. Character is not developed individually. It is instilled by communities and transmitted by elders. The centrist Democratic group Third Way suggests the government create a BoomerCorps. Every day 10,000 baby boomers turn 65, some of them could be recruited into an AmeriCorps-type program to help low-income families move up the mobility ladder.

"Fourth, standards. People can only practice restraint after they have a certain definition of the sort of person they want to be. Research from Martin West of Harvard and others suggests that students at certain charter schools raise their own expectations for themselves, and judge themselves by more demanding criteria.

"Character development is an idiosyncratic, mysterious process. But if families, communities and the government can envelop lives with attachments and institutions, then that might reduce the alienation and distrust that retards mobility and ruins dreams."

Afterword

This is the culmination of my endeavors as an author. What a delight it has been. It is time to move on to some other kind of mischief and I am looking forward to that.

Perhaps many will understand the trepidation I felt when I first considered writing about Jewish achievement in The Golden Age. And even more, the nervousness at the prospect of standing before an audience to talk about Jewish achievement and culture—mostly to audiences whose Jewish existence meant they knew so much more than I ever could about their people, their past, and their culture. How presumptuous of me!

Without exception, they were kind and gracious to me, the interloper, the guy dealing in the kind of topics that automatically raise the question, "Yes, but is it good for the Jews?" I will leave them to be the judge of that, while thanking them for their kindness and their interest in listening, reading, and talking about that book, and now this one.

I am also grateful for the friendships and acquaintances that have come from my experiences as an author. There is Dr. John Stace, the outback Western Australian physician who somehow found parts of what I was doing on the Internet, and encouraged me as I was writing *The Golden Age* and afterward. There is Marilyn Berger Hewitt, whom I met on a Manhattan street corner as we both waited for our two-minute presentations before the Jewish Book Council. Her book, *This Is a Soul*, and her adoption of Danny, an Ethiopian orphan, are both personal inspirations for me. She is a wonderful friend. And it was Natalie Solomon, who hosted me before the Birthright Israel Alumni Association in Manhattan. She was so nervous that evening when Occupy Wall Street decided to interrupt and "occupy" my presentation. What a hoot that was. Lawrence Harrison took a genuine interest in my endeavors and encouraged me, while also allowing me to use elements from his books in this endeavor. He also passed a copy of *The Golden Age* to David Brooks, who kindly mentioned it, with Start-Up Nation, in a January 2010 *New York Times* column. Linda Kaplan somehow nudged the wonderful folks at the Bureau of Jewish Education in Orange County—led by Aviva Forster—to invite me to be part of their "Dinner with a Scholar" program. It was a very enjoyable evening (and a wonderful compliment, though I am certainly not a scholar). There was Brad Pommerance, who invited me to appear on a Jewish Life Television program featuring *The Golden Age*. Later that day I had a fascinating hour or so with Dr. Joshua Holo, Dean of the Los Angeles Campus and Associate Professor of Jewish History at Hebrew Union College – Jewish Institute of Religion, Jack H. Skirball Campus. His perspective on anti-Semitism, and the sensitivities of work like mine has stayed with me for years. Howard Metzenberg not only gave me his time and access to his library for the first book; he also spent considerable time with me and helping me to learn a good deal about genetics. That is something he knows infinitely more about than I ever will.

Deborah Daly helped enormously with this book just as she did with *The Golden Age*. Without her, my efforts would never have looked so professional and she served as my invaluable guide in all matters having to do with contemporary publishing and printing. Lucy Peterson was a godsend. Her global and detailed editing talent is outstanding. She knew exactly what it was I was trying to say and helped me to say it, just as she did with a prior challenging assignment involving my work in Russia. Michael Denneny, like Deborah, helped both with this book and with *The Golden Age*. He is a proven industry professional and a great consultant. Alycia Case was incredibly thorough and helpful in her copy-editing while my step-daughter, Bernadette Calhoun, put in countless hours. She was invaluable in making sure that the summaries I wrote for Part 2 – The Chronology accurately reflected the sources from which they were drawn and did not overstate or wrongly interpret the underlying facts.

Danny Kaplan has long been my sage advisor, willing to look over what I wrote and help me avoid land mines. Same with Larry Harrison, Les Vadasz, and others. Each weighed in with invaluable suggestions. One even "nudged" me from time to time. Thanks to you all.

More than anyone, thanks go to my wife Joyce, who served as "official photographer" for the first book (she made sure to be its first buyer when it became available on Amazon.com). But more, my appreciation for the many nights she sat doing crossword puzzles while I typed away on the computer keyboard. With my days as an author at an end, I am hoping we can spend evenings doing something together that will be more enjoyable for her.

Select Bibliography

American Jewish Historical Society. *American Jewish Desk Reference*, New York, New York: The Philip Lief Group, Inc. Random House, 1999

Ariel, David S. What Do Jews Believe: *The Spiritual Foundation of Judaism*, New York, New York: Schocken Books, 1995

Armstrong, Karen. *A History of God: The 4,000 Year Quest of Judaism, Christianity and Islam*, New York, New York: Ballantine Books, a division of Random House, 1993

Asa-El, Amotz. *The Diaspora and the Lost Tribes of Israel*, Hugh Lauter Levin Associates, Inc. 2004

Barnavi, Eli and Denis Charbit. *A Historical Atlas of the Jewish People*, New York, NY: Schocken Books, 2002

Barone, Michael. *The New Americans: How the Melting Pot Can Work Again*, Washington D.C.: Regnery Publishing, Inc., an Eagle Publishing Company, 2001

Bellow, Saul. *The Adventures of Augie March*, Penguin Books, New York, 1996

Biale, David. *Cultures of the Jews: A New History*, Schocken Books, New York, 2002

Ben Ami, Shlomo. *Scars of War, Wounds of Peace: The Israeli-Arab Tragedy*, Oxford University Press, Oxford, New York, 2006

Benbassa, Esther & Aron Rodrigue. *Sephardi Jewry: A History of the Judeo-Spanish Community, 14th–20th Centuries*, University of California Press, Berkeley and Los Angeles, California 2000

Bergsman, Steve. *Maverick Real Estate Investing*, John Wiley & Sons, Hoboken, New Jersey, 2004

Bickerman, Elias J. *The Jews in the Greek Age*, Harvard University Press, Cambridge Massachusetts, 1988

Birmingham, Stephen. *Our Crowd: The Great Jewish Families of New York*, Syracuse, New York: Syracuse University Press, 1967

Birmingham, Stephen. *The Grandees: The Story of America's Sephardic Elite*, New York, New York: Dell Publishing Company, Inc. 1971

Bloom, Stephen G. *Postville: A Clash of Cultures in Heartland America*, A Harvest Book: Harcourt, Inc. San Diego, New York, London, 2000

Boorstin, Daniel J. *Hidden History: Exploring Our Secret Past*, New York, New York: Vintage Books, a Division of Random House, 1989

Boorstin, Daniel J. *The Daniel J. Boorstin Reader*, New York, New York: The Modern Library, a Division of Random House, 1995

Botticini, Maristella and Zvi Eckstein. "Jewish Occupational Selection: Education, Restrictions, or Minorities?" *The Journal of Economic History*, Volume 65, Issue 04, December 2005, pp 922-948.

Botticini, Maristella and Zvi Eckstein. *The Chosen Few: How Education Shaped Jewish History*, 70-1942, Princeton University Press, Princeton, NJ., 2012

Brawarsky, Sandee and Deborah Mark. *Two Jews, Three Opinions: A Collection of Twentieth-Century American Jewish Quotations*, New York, New York: A Perigee Book, Berkley Publishing Group, a Division of Penguin Putnam, Inc., 1998

Brzezinski, Matthew. *Casino Moscow: A Tale of Greed and Adventure on Capitalism's Wildest Frontier*, The Free Press, Simon & Schuster, New York, 2001

Bullock, Alan. *Hitler and Stalin: Parallel Lives*, New York, New York: Vintage Books, a Division of Random House, Inc. 1993

Cahill, Thomas. *The Gift of the Jews: How a Tribe of Desert Nomads Changed the Way Everyone Thinks and Feels*, New York, New York: Nan A. Talese/Anchor Books, Imprints of Doubleday, a Division of Random House, Inc., 1998

Chernow, Ron. *The Warburgs: The Twentieth-Century Odyssey of a Remarkable Jewish Family*, New York, New York: Random House, 1993

Chetkin, Len, *Guess Who's Jewish (you'll never guess)* Norfolk/Virginia Beach: The Donning Company/ Publishers 1985

Chua, Amy and Jed Rubenfeld, *The Triple Package: How Three Unlikely Traits Explain the Rise and Fall of Cultural Groups in America*, The Penguin Press, New York, 2014

Cohen, Abraham. *Everyman's Talmud: The Major Teachings of the Rabbinic Sages*, New York, New York: Schocken Books, 1995 Reprint of the 1949 edition published by E.P. Dutton

Cohen, Rich. Tough Jews: Fathers, Sons and Gangster Dreams, New York, New York: Vintage Books, A Division of Random House, Inc., 1999

D'Epiro, Peter and Mary Desmond Pinkowish. Sprezzatura: 50 Ways Italian Genius Shaped the World. Anchor Books, Random House, 2001

Dershowitz, Alan. The Case for Israel, John Wiley & Sons, Inc. Hoboken, New Jersey, 2003

Dimont, Max I. *Jews God and History*, New American Library, New York, 1994

Diner, Hasia R. *The Jews of the United States: 1654 to 2000*, University of California Press, Berkeley and Los Angeles, California, 2004

Dinkelspiel, Frances. *Towers of Gold: How One Jewish Immigrant Named Isaias Hellman Created California*, New York, New York: St. Martin's Griffin, 2008

Dobbs, Stephen Mark. *The Koret Foundation: 25 Years as a Catalyst to Positive Change*, Western Jewish History Center, Berkeley, California, 2004

Duke, David. *My Awakening: A Path to Racial Understanding*, Free Speech Press, Mandeville, Louisiana, 1998

Economist. *The Pocket World in Figures: 2002 Edition*, London, England, 2002?

Encyclopedia Britannica. *The New Encyclopedia Britannica: Volume 22* Macropedia, Chicago, Illinois:Encyclopedia Britannica, Inc., University of Chicago: 1988

Etkes, Asher B. and Saul Stadtmauer. *Jewish Contributions to the American Way of Life*, Northside Publishing Inc., Long Island City, NY, 1995

Falcon, Rabbi Ted, Ph.D. and David Blatner. *Judaism for Dummies*, New York, New York: Hungry Minds, Inc., 2001

Felder, Deborah G. and Diana Rosen. *Fifty Jewish Women Who Changed the World*, New York, NY: Citadel Press, Kensington Publishing Company, 2003

Feldman, Burton. *The Nobel Prize: A History of Genius, Controversy and Prestige*, New York, New York: Arcade Publishing, 2000

Fox, John G. and Julian Krainin. *Heritage: Civilization and the Jews*, New York, New York: Thirteen/ WNET, 1994 & 1998, (A DVD video)

Francis, Richard C. *Epigenetics: The Ultimate Mystery of Inheritance*, New York, New York: W. W. Norton, 2011

Gabler, Neal. *An Empire of Their Own: How the Jews Invented Hollywood*, New York, New York: Anchor Books, Random House, 1988

Gilbert, Martin. *The Jews in the Twentieth Century: An Illustrated History*, New York, New York: Schocken Books, a Division of Random House, 2001

Gilbert, Martin. *The Routledge Atlas of Jewish History, Sixth Edition*, Routledge, New York & London: 2003

Gilbert, Martin. *In Ismael's House: A History of the Jews in Muslim Lands*, New Haven, Connecticut: Yale University Press, 2010

Gilder, George. *The Israel Test*, Bloomington, Minnesota: Richard Vigilante Books, 2009

Gladwell, Malcolm. *Outliers: The Story of Success*, New York, New York: Little Brown & Company, 2008

Harris, Leon. *Merchant Princes: An Intimate History of the Jewish Families Who Built Great Department Stores*, New York, New York: Harper & Row 1979 and Kodansha America, 1994.

Harrison, Lawrence E. and Huntington, Samuel P. *Culture Matters: How Values Shape Human Progress*, New York, New York: Basic Books, A Subsidiary of Perseus Books, LLC, 2000

Harrison, Lawrence E. *The Central Liberal Truth: How Politics Can Change a Culture and Save It From Itself*, Oxford University Press, Oxford, New York, 2006

Harrison, Lawrence E. *Jews, Confucians, and Protestants: Cultural Capital and the End of Multiculturalism*, Rowman and Littlefield, Publishers, Inc., New York, 2013

Hart, Michael H. *The 100: A Ranking of the Most Influential Persons in History*, Secaucus, New Jersey: Citadel Press, 1987

Herman, Arthur. How the Scots Invented the Modern World, Random House, New York, 2001?

Hurley, Dan. *Smarter: The New Science of Building Brain Power*, Hudson Street Press, The Penguin Group, New York, 2013

Hyman, Paula E. and Moore, Deborah Dash. *Jewish Women in America: An Historical Encyclopedia, Volumes I & II*, Routledge, New York, 1998

Jacobsen, Howard. *The Finkler Question*, New York, Berlin, London, Sydney: Bloomsbury 2010

Jewish Publication Society. *Tanakh: The Holy Scriptures*, Philadelphia, Pennsylvania: The Jewish Publication Society, 1985

Johnson, Paul. *A History of the Jews*, New York, New York: Harper Perennial, A Division of Harper Collins Publishers, 1988

Kamenetz, Rodger. The Jew in the Lotus, Harper Collins, New York, 1995

Keter Publishing House, Ltd. *Encyclopedia Judaica*, New York, NY: Lambda Publishers, Inc.

Kertzer, Rabbi Morris N. *What Is A Jew?* New York, New York: Collier Books, A Division of Macmillan Publishing Co., Inc. Fourth Edition, 1978

King James Version. *The Holy Bible: Containing the Old and New Testaments*, Nashville, Tenn.: Memorial Bibles International, Inc., 1976

Kleiman, Rabbi Yaakov. *DNA & Tradition: The Genetic Link to the Ancient Hebrews*, Jerusalem, Israel, Devora Publishing Company, 2004

Konner, Melvin. *Unsettled: An Anthropology of the Jews*, Penguin Group, New York, 2003?

Korman, Abraham K. *The Outsiders: Jews and Corporate America*, Lexington, Mass.: D.C Heath and Company, Lexington Books, 1988

Kugel, James L. *How to Read the Bible: A Guide to Scripture Then and Now*, Free Press, New York, London, Toronto, Sydney, 2007

Kushner, Harold S. *When Bad Things Happen To Good People*, New York, New York. Avon Books, Harper Collins, 1981

Kushner, Harold S. *The Lord is My Shepherd: Healing Wisdom of the Twenty-Third Psalm*, New York, New York. Alfred A. Knopf, 2003

Landes, David S. *The Wealth and Poverty of Nations: Why Some Are So Rich and Some So Poor*, New York, New York: W. W. Norton & Company, 1998

Lebrecht, Norman. *The Song of Names*, Anchor Books, New York, Random House, 2002?

Lustiger, Arno. *Stalin and the Jews*, New York, New York: Enigma Books by arrangement with AufbauVerlag GMBH, 2003

Lyman, Darryl. *Jewish Heroes and Heroines*, Middle Village, New York: Jonathan David Publishers, Inc., 1996

Lynn, Richard. *The Chosen People: A Study of Jewish Intelligence and Achievement*, Whitefish, Montanna: Washington Summit Publishers 2011

Marsden, Victor E. (translator). *Protocols of the Learned Elders of Zion*, Briton Publishing Society, London, circa 1923

Michner, James A. *The Source*, New York, New York: Random House, 1965?

Menchin, Robert. *101 Classic Jewish Jokes: Jewish Humor From Groucho Marx to Jerry Seinfeld*, Memphis, Tennessee Mustang Publishing Company, Inc., 1997

Mearsheimer, John J. and Walt, Stephen M. *The Israel Lobby and U.S. Foreign Policy*, Farrar, Straus and Giroux, New York, 2007

Milton, Joyce. *The Road to Malpsychia: Humanistic Psychology and Our Discontents*, San Francisco, California: Encounter Books, 2002

Moorehead, Alan. *The Russian Revolution*, New York, New York: Bantam Books, Time, Inc., 1959

Morton, Frederic. *The Rothschilds*, Greenwich, Connecticut: Fawcett Crest Publications, Inc., 1961

Murray, Charles. *The Bell Curve: Intelligence and Class Structure in American Life*, New York, New York: Free Press, 1994 and Free Press Paperbacks, 1996

Murray, Charles. *Human Accomplishment: The Pursuit of Excellence in the Arts and Sciences; 800 B.C. to 1950*. New York, New York: HarperCollins, 2003

Murray, Charles. *Coming Apart: The State of White America, 1960–2010*, New York, New York: Crown Forum, and imprint of Crown Publishing, a division of Random House, 2012

Nasar, Sylvia. *A Beautiful Mind: The Life of Mathematical Genius and Nobel Laureate John Nash*, New York, New York: Touchstone Books, Simon & Schuster, 1998

Nusseibeh, Sari with David, Anthony. *Once Upon a Country: A Palestinian Life*, Farrar, Straus and Giroux, New York, 2007

Olson, Steve. *Mapping Human History: Discovering the Past Through Our Genes*, Houghton Mifflin Company, Boston, Massachusetts, 2002

Oren, Michael B. *Six Days of War: June 1967 and the Making of the Modern Middle East*, New York, New York: Oxford University Press, 2002

Patai, Raphael. *The Jewish Mind*, Detroit, Michigan, Wayne State University Press, 1977

Phaidon. *The Art Book*, London, England: Phaidon Press, Ltd., 2001?Pilkington, C. M. Judaism, Lincolnwood (Chicago), Illinois: NTC Publishing Group, 1995

Podhoretz, Norman. *Why Are Jews Liberal?* New York, Doubleday, 2009

Potok, Chaim. *The Chosen*, New York, New York: Fawcett World Library, 1968

Prager, Dennis and Rabbi Joseph Telushkin. *Why The Jews? The Reason for Anti-Semitism*, New York, New York: Touchstone, Simon & Schuster, Inc., 1983, 2003.

Rhodes, Richard. *Dark Sun: The Making of the Hydrogen Bomb*, New York, New York: Touchstone, Simon & Schuster, 1995

Rivkin, Ellis. *The Unity Principle: The Shaping of Jewish History*, Behrman House, Springfield, New Jersey, 2003

Rosten, Leo. *The Joys of Yiddish*, New York, New York: Pocket Books, a Division of Simon & Schuster, 1970

Ruderman, David B. *Jewish Intellectual History: 16th to 20th Century*, (transcript and DVD video), The Teaching Company, Chantilly, VA, 2002

Salfati. *Talmud, the Video, Arte France Development*, Paris 2007?

Shapiro, Michael. *The Jewish 100: A Ranking of the Most Influential Jews of All Times*, New York, New York: Citadel Press, Published by Kensington Publishing Corp., 1994

Schmemann, Serge. *Echoes of a Native Land: Two Centuries of a Russian Village*, Vintage Books, Random House, New York, 1997

Segal, Nancy L. *Born Together—Reared Apart: The Landmark Minnesota Twin Study*, Cambridge, Massachusetts: Harvard University Press, 2012

Senor, Dan and Singer, Saul. *Start-up Nation: The Story of Israel's Economic Miracle*, New York, New York: Twelve, Hachette Book Group 2009

Silber, Dr. Mendel. *Jewish Achievement*, St. Louis, Missouri: The Modern View Publishing Co., 1910

Silbiger, Steven. *The Jewish Phenomenon: Seven Keys to the Enduring Wealth of a People*, Marietta Georgia: Longstreet Press, 2000, and Lanham, Maryland: Rowman & Littlefield Publishing Group, 2009

Singer, Isaac Bashevis. *The Slave*, Farrar, Straus, Giroux, New York, 1962

Slater, Robert, *Great Jews in Sports*, Middle Village, New York: Jonathan David Publishers, Inc., 2000 edition

Slezkine, Yuri. *The Jewish Century*, Princeton, New Jersey: Princeton University Press, 2004

Sowell, Thomas. *A Conflict of Visions: Ideological Origins of Political Struggles*, New York, New York: Quill, William Morrow and Company, 1987

Sowell, Thomas. *Conquest and Cultures: An International History*, New York, New York: Basic Books, A Subsidiary of Perseus Books, LLC, 1998

Sowell, Thomas. *Ethnic America*, New York, New York: Basic Books, A subsidiary of Perseus Books, LLC, 1981

Sowell, Thomas. *Migrations and Cultures: A World View*, New York, New York: Basic Books, A subsidiary of Perseus Books, LLC, 1996

Sowell, Thomas. Race and Culture, New York, New York: Basic Books, A subsidiary of Perseus Books, LLC, 1994

Steinsaltz, Adin. The Essential Talmud, Basic Books, 1976

Stern, David H. (translator). *Complete Jewish Bible: An English Version of the Tanakh (Old Testament) and B'rit Hadashah (New Testament)*, Clarksville, Maryland: Jewish New Testament Publications, Inc. 1998

Stewart, James B. *Den of Thieves*, Touchstone, Simon & Schuster, New York, 1992?Symons, Alan. The Jewish Contribution to the 20th Century, Hampton, Middlesex, England, Polo Publishing, 1997

Symons, Alan. *Nobel Laureates: 1901–2000*, Hampton, Middlesex, England: Polo Publishing, 2000

Teller, Edward with Judith Shoolery. *Memoirs: A Twentieth Century Journey in Science and Politics,* Cambridge, Massachusetts: Perseus Publishing, 2001

Telushkin, Rabbi Joseph. *Jewish Humor: What the Best Jewish Jokes Say About the Jews*, New York, New York: William Morrow, 1992 and HarperCollins Perennial 2002

Telushkin, Rabbi Joseph. *Jewish Literacy: The Most Important Things To Know About the Jewish Religion, Its People, and Its History*, New York, New York. William Morrow & Company, 1991, reissued 2001

Thomas, Baylis. *How Israel Was Won: A Concise History of the Arab-Israeli Conflict*, Lanham, Maryland: Lexington Books, 1999.

Uris, Leon. *Exodus*, New York, New York: Bantam Books, 1958

Van Den Haag, Ernest. *The Jewish Mystique*. New York, New York: Stein & Day, 1969

Wade, Nicholas. *A Troublesome Inheritance: Genes, Race and Human History*, Penguin Press HC, New York, May 6, 2014Wechsberg, Joseph. *The Merchant Bankers*, New York, New York: Pocket Books, a Simon & Schuster Division of Gulf & Western, 1966

Yalom, Irvin D. *The Spinoza Problem*, New York, New York: Basic Books, The Perseus Group, 2012

Zavatto, Amy. *Judaism: The Pocket Idiot's Guide to*, Indianapolis, Indiana: Alpha Books, a Pearson Publishing Company, 2003

Index

About the Author

A CEO specializing in turnarounds, a venture capitalist, and a community activist, Steve Pease has traveled much of the world in the course of heading up not-for-profit organizations as well as public and private companies. Earlier, he was author of *The Golden Age of Jewish Achievement*.

Born and raised Presbyterian in Spokane, Washington, he is a Phi Beta Kappa graduate of the University of Washington with a master's degree from Harvard Business School. He currently serves as co-chairman of the U.S. Russia Foundation for Economic Advancement and the Rule of Law, and was Chairman of The U.S. Russia Investment Fund. Both are nonprofit entities, organized by the United States government to work with Russians, encourage entrepreneurship, civil society, and the rule of law, while also improving the U.S.–Russia relationship.

He is also active in the community affairs of the small wine-country town of Sonoma, California, where he lives with his wife, Joyce.

www.ingramcontent.com/pod-product-compliance
Lightning Source LLC
Chambersburg PA
CBHW031501270326
41930CB00006B/195